Jasmine and Arnica

Also By Nicola Naylor:
Healing with Essential Oils

Jasmine and Arnica

Nicola Naylor

Foreword by Kate Adie

Published by TravellersEye

Jasmine and Arnica
1st Edition
Published by TravellersEye Ltd 2001

Head Office:
Colemore Farm
Colemore Green
Bridgnorth
Shropshire
WV16 4ST
United Kingdom

tel: (0044) 1746 766447   fax: (0044) 1746 766665
email: books@travellerseye.com   website: www.travellerseye.com

Set in Times
ISBN: 1903070104
Copyright © 2001 Nicola Naylor

Printed and bound in Great Britain by Creative Print & Design

To Philip Tata and Yvette Parker without whom I may not have given life a chance

16 Feb 2017

Molly —

This book was written
by a friend of my
cousin. They went to
college together in England.
The writer lost her eyesight,
and in the book, she
records her visit to India.
Enjoy! rj

32 Great Plains Rd., Emerald Park, SK Canada S4L 1B6
Office: (306) 525-5300 • Fax: (306) 525-5320
gm@ramadaemeraldpark.com • www.ramada.com

P.S. I mentioned the book to Katya. She might be interested in reading it when she gets home.

You can keep it!

ACKNOWLEDGEMENTS

Rupert, my partner, for his support and encouragement, for having the patience to read various drafts to me and for his invaluable advice, and his intelligent contributions.

My friend Elizabeth Buchan, the novelist, without whose steadfast belief and practical advice this book would not have been written or published.

My friend and publisher of Barefoot Books, Tessa Strickland for her creative remarks and suggestions.

Hazel Orme, my editor, whose polish has made my story gleam.

Laura Morris and Peta Nightingale whose skills and efforts supported me through various stages in the writing of this book.

To those people whose names appear in the following pages for their part in making my journey the wonderful and happy experience it was.

To those organisations mentioned in the introduction who sponsored my trip.

To my clients who patiently awaited my return from what must have seemed like a foolhardy adventure.

To the many good friends who understood my need to go and sent me away with gifts, contacts and good wishes.

I want to thank the numerous other people who played a part in the success of my journey or in the writing of this book but whose names do not appear in it. This book is a tribute to those hundreds of helping hands.

And finally thanks to my publisher Dan Hiscocks for his passion to publish.

FOREWORD

So many of us travel without really looking. Taking the famous sights for granted, and day-dreaming or dozing or chatting while the countryside flashes by. Sometimes a scent lingers, or a sound pricks up the ears, but much disappears into a blurred memory. And the very business of travelling, the tickets, unreliable timetables, rapacious taxi-drivers and the question of whether queuing is regarded a quaint foreign custom, have all to be taken in one's stride.

So, consider travelling in India for many months, with all these usual elements unseen.

Nicola Naylor has a rare insight into these matters, which was not chosen. Her formidable determination to travel and to participate – and to notice and observe – is a *tour de force*. And her unsparing analysis of her own behaviour when confronted with both the awkward details and the wider implications of travelling – mostly alone – is a remarkable example of self-knowledge.

I write as someone who's got lost, been baffled by language, mislaid luggage, taken the wrong bus, got off trains at the wrong stop, been accosted by numerous dodgy strangers, forgotten my hotel room number, collided with rickshaws and bicycling vegetable vendors, taken a taxi-ride during which two of the wheels came off, and certainly wouldn't dream of eating anything, never mind foreign, without taking a very good look at it – so Nicola's *Jasmine and Arnica* strikes me as an object lesson in courage, yet without any self-pity.

And India comes alive as well – in descriptions that challenge all the usual notions of what someone who has lost their sight might be expected (by the rest of us) to experience.

I cannot imagine putting myself into the situations, on a daily basis, that Nicola deals with. And I can only recommend that you read and discover that there are many ways to travel – and to see.

Kate Adie
Spring 2001

CONTENTS

INTRODUCTION: SETTING OFF

Beyond the doors of the terminal building a mass of people heaved against metal barriers. Men shouted, 'Hotel, very good hotel?' or 'You are wanting a taxi?' The heady smell of curry, perfumes and incense rose above the crowd as they jostled and shoved. Entangled in this mêlée of hot damp bodies scrummaging for space, I tried to fold away my cane. Then Goutam's voice said, 'Nicola?'

Instantly I saw the figure I remembered: small, agile, with masses of bouncy brown curly hair, glasses, a fine moustache, slim except for his paunch. I thought he returned my smile. 'Let's go,' he said. He was concerned to get me out of the clamouring crowd. I placed my hand next to his on the handle of the trolley and followed as he steered. We snaked through the milling people and I snuck my cane into my shoulder bag.

I have always been enthralled by India, even as a child. Images of goddesses and temples with monkeys, elephants and colourfully dressed people crowded my imagination well before I saw pictures of these things or learnt to which part of the world they belonged. As soon as I was able to locate them in

India I wanted to go there. But my travel fantasies dissolved when a congenital problem led to the total loss of my sight as I was finishing my degree at university.

It shattered my life at a time when my peers were progressing with their careers and planning their weddings. I broke down and found myself confined to hospital for a year unable to come to terms with what had happened to me. When I came out, I continued my treatment as an outpatient. Living seemed worse than dying but I could not commit myself to either. I continued in a shell-shocked stupor of indecision and hopeless rage. Well-intentioned consolation, comparison, cajolement and encouragement from professionals, friends and family increased my pain, fury and loneliness. I escaped into a world of madness, full of vivid phantasmagoric hallucinations which, however frightening, were less terrible than the dark blind reality they displaced.

From the devastation I discovered some people and small ways that led me back to life. In the following years I busied myself with home-making, professional retraining as an aromatherapist and business building. But I had not forgotten the temples and goddesses and monkeys of my childhood. By autumn 1992, I had become comfortable but stuck in my home, my success at work and the reassurance of a few good friends. I seldom ventured beyond the safety of my daily life, having a morning swim, working from home, walking my dog with a friend, and going to bed by seven in time for *The Archers,* my favourite radio soap. I had constructed these routines to support me through hard times but they slowly became more limiting than liberating. I wanted to shake up my rigidity, open up my boundaries, test my capabilities and challenge my concepts of how the world is or isn't. India was suitably radical and provocative as it stands so climatically and culturally in contrast to my life in Britain, and I wanted the external travel to be significant enough to take me further on my internal journey in self-confidence, crossing borders which I would otherwise not cross, and experiencing new dimensions of myself by exposure to different aspects of life, and ways to live that life. My journey also had a professional motive. As a practising aromatherapist, I wanted to learn about massage and oil techniques in traditional Indian medicine.

I threw myself into three months of energetic planning – endless letters and telephone calls, networking to set up all the connections for touring the ayurvedic hospitals, which used traditional Indian herbal and healing techniques, aromatherapy centres, massage centres and private practitioners. To start with, I didn't have any professional contacts but one address led to another. I also raised about £1,000 in sponsorship from the Paul Vander-Molen Foundation, the Guide Dogs for the Blind Association and the Metropolitan Society for the Blind, who seek to enable and enhance the quality of disabled people's lives.

My friends were astonished when I told them my plans, which challenged their ideas of what a blind person can do. I too am often dumbfounded by the way non-sighted sight, my 'third eye' perception or a sixth sense can enrich my experiences of the world.

In India I survived, indeed thrived, on people's fellowship and generosity, and gained an insight and involvement in the family and working lives of people from all parts of India. Over the ten months that I was away I stayed with Sikhs, Parsis, Syrian Christians, Hindus and Muslims, some anglicised Indians, some indianised Britons, some very 'British' ex-colonials and some very Indian Rajput (warrior class) Indians. This richness and diversity of cultural exchange came my way as a result of the close contact necessitated by my blindness. Each family I stayed with wanted to make arrangements with any relatives or friends to befriend and help me in other places I intended to visit. My eyes were opened to India by the privilege of this intimacy.

This account is an attempt to share an experience and an appreciation of life which most travellers cannot see to enjoy. I say 'see' because I am celebrating the non-sighted sight that sighted people struggle to comprehend. They find it hard to believe that I do what I do without physical sight, especially since I 'look so sighted'. I see the world through a 'third eye': it includes mental mapping, memorising, calculating probabilities, and intuition. We all have these skills but since I lost my sight I have developed them – in a similar way, one of my friends, John, has built up his shoulder muscles so that he can propel himself on his crutches because he has no legs.

Despite the ways in which I have learnt to adapt, I am still dominated by sight. When I hear a tennis ball thud I turn my head, like most sighted people, and assume my eyes tell me where the ball has hit the ground. But, of course, it is my ears. Sighted people believe they are informed first and foremost by sight. My third eye is uncannily accurate and I trust my survival to it. 'How did you know the dog was standing behind you? How did you know I just looked at my watch? How did you reach for that cup without fumbling?' I am often asked these questions – and, indeed, my prospective publishers requested justification of the visual descriptions I have given in this book. I have endeavoured to share my experience as lucidly as possible but when someone tells me that an object is yellow, I do not ask, 'How do you know it is yellow? Are you sure your eyes see yellow?'

In India, I learnt how to let go of some of my solitude and privacy. I stopped retiring early to bed and found myself in more than one-to-one company. I was able at last to bring the fantasies of my childhood into reality. At last, the visual pictures I created in my mind's eye came from this outer reality. My English teacher at school said, 'William Blake sees angels in trees.' We all tittered and sniggered. I am older and wiser now.

It was with the unblinkered perception of my third eye that I set off for India: it makes sense of the inner as well as the outer world, and I kept it wide open.

I did not go to India in search of my soul or to 'find' myself. I had done that in the early years after I lost my sight. When I realised that I could carry on in a world I would never see again, I emerged with a powerful inner confidence and knew that I had found a new way of seeing the world.

On the plane to Bombay I itched to take the in-flight magazine from the pocket on the back of the seat in front of me. It was not because I wanted to pretend I could read it, but because I find it reassuring to flick through pages.

As a child with little sight and as an adult with none, I have behaved naturally in a sighted way. I put lights on when I don't need them in the dark, I read hardback books before I go to sleep, and I look in mirrors to check my appearance.

My fingers plucked the textured fabric covering my seat as I worried about what my fellow passengers would assume if I picked up the magazine. No doubt they would draw the obvious conclusion based on the evidence of their eyes: I was seeing and reading. It would make explanations complicated if I needed a helping hand later to find the loo.

The air hostess came down the aisle distributing embarkation forms to be filled in by the non-national arrivals. She passed me one and disappeared, returning a little later to hand out menu cards. I wondered what was for lunch. When I had boarded not so long ago she had helped me to my seat. Soon she returned to collect the completed cards. I sensed her hovering over me expectantly. I passed her my card and asked, 'Would you mind filling this in for me?'

She hesitated, momentarily confused. Then, disconcerted, she said quickly, 'I'll do it later. Have you got your passport?'

I found it deftly and caught her eye again when I handed it over. I sensed her wriggle inside, even though her movements were stiff. I felt mean – at least I hadn't been reading the magazine as well.

Suddenly I was frightened of the honesty I would need to judge each encounter and to guide me on my travels. I would have to find the courage to be different from how blind people are expected to be. For the first time I felt a foreboding about the journey ahead.

When I first announced my plans to travel alone round India, people asked, 'Aren't you afraid?' I had become almost ashamed that I wasn't. Friends wondered why I was not daunted by potential physical dangers: the unpredictable assaults and risks to someone single, female, blonde and blind.

In the aeroplane I realised that my fear was not how to negotiate my way around a strange country, but how to be neither too blind nor too unblind in my response to unfamiliar situations and people. I did not want to lose sight of myself and my hard-won acceptance of my disability.

My fingers slid over the magazine. I pulled them away and thought about getting a book out of my hand luggage instead. I was bored. I had several titles with me, regrettably all paperbacks because of the airline's weight restrictions. I preferred hardbacks and have always liked to sit on the loo in the mornings with one held close to my face. This posture was force of habit from when I was a child and could snail my way through a book if I peered closely enough. No one would noticed me squinting and straining if I did it in the bathroom.

Instead I let my mind drift to my old friend Goutam Bhattacharya, whom I had not seen for eleven or twelve years. After I lost my sight my friends had become strangers to me. I had rejected them, pushed them aside: it was too painful to see them getting on with life which seemed so worthwhile compared to mine. Goutam knew I had lost my sight but he had not heard from me directly until I had written to say I was intending to travel in India, and could I come to stay for a few days before I set off?

His response had been prompt and positive. Of course I could come, and what did I want to do?

My friendship with Goutam had begun in Ludwigshafen while I was a student on a work placement and he was a young manager in a chemical company. We had spent evenings in many a *Weinstube* in the Pfalzwald, drinking sweet local wine, eating *bratwurst* and cabbage. Once we drove to Monte Carlo with another friend. We lost money in the casino, headed for the Côte d'Azur, ate fish on a French beach, and slept three in a dingy, noisy room because we couldn't find anything better. On the way back we were refused entry into Italy and nearly arrested because of some irregularity in Goutam's papers. We had to detour through Switzerland to get back into Germany, crumpled, sleepy and broke.

I had changed considerably since those days in Germany. Shock had torn me apart and I had put myself back together in a less higgledy-piggledy fashion. Still, I was nervous about incorporating my new self into our old friendships. On the one hand I wanted the difference in me to be recognised; on the other I didn't want it to get in the way. I wondered whether Goutam was apprehensive too.

I thought of all the positive things I would tell him about the years he had missed. I had a thriving aromatherapy and manipulative massage practice in which I treated up to thirty people a week. I worked from home and had moved only two years before my departure for India to a larger house where I could set aside two rooms for my work. My trip was also to be a sabbatical, an opportunity to compare the therapeutic use of Indian herbal oils with the ones I was using. I was interested in the way they applied their oils through massage in ayurveda (*ayu* meaning knowledge, *veda*, life) and was the first aromatherapist to tour ayurvedic centres in India and observe their methods. Sadly, however, there was no research grant forthcoming from my professional organisation.

One of my clients, who ran his own business, said before I left, 'What I find most admirable is not you going to India without sight and on your own on some wild research project, but the courage it takes to shut up shop and risk everything. You have built your practice up from nothing, and it provides you with your only source of income. What if you lose it all? I don't think I could do it.'

I certainly felt nervous about jeopardising my financial and professional security, but it was important not to feel restricted or tied by commitments to work, family or friends. I had to trust my professional acumen and would have to rely on my personal strength in the event that my clients did not return. As it turned out, numerous clients telephoned my secretary in my absence to find out how I was, and I came back months later to a fully booked diary.

Thinking about my business reminded me of the further shock I had delivered to my friends before I left. I was amazed by how many people asked, 'Had your jabs?', assuming that I had. However, I have a liver condition associated with my eyesight, which means that I cannot tolerate alcohol, oily foods and certain drugs. The anti-malarials and vaccinations on offer would not have agreed with me.

In any case, in keeping with natural health practice, I had decided to use primary health-care measures and herbal or homeopathic remedies to deal with medical problems if they arose. I met with horrified reactions and a few sparks flew in the heated debates that followed. I was generally considered foolhardy; now I was both stubborn and mad. But I lived to tell the tale, without even an instance of 'Delhi belly'.

The secret of this success lay in precaution and common sense. I copied the Indians who befriended me in never taking food from street-sellers and being fastidious about washing my hands before and after eating. I stayed informed about and avoided areas with reported epidemics or malaria outbreaks. I took an excellent water filter, sought homeopathic first-aid advice and kept a list of emergency numbers of homeopaths to call in the event of sickness.

Of all the homeopathic remedies, the one I used most was arnica in its cream and tablet form, a cure-all for bruising. From my range of essential oils jasmine's heady luxurious scent relieved the prick of anxiety, which sometimes needled my resolve.

Towards the end of the flight the woman sitting next to me asked whether I had heard of Sai Baba. I told her that I knew he was a famous guru with an ashram outside Bangalore and a large number of devotees in England. She translated this for her companion occupying the window seat on her other side.

'Where are you from?' I asked, intrigued because I did not recognise the language.

'We are a party from Norway. It is our first time to see India. We are to do the Golden Triangle with the great palaces and the Taj Mahal. Then we go to this Bangalore to sit at the feet of Sai Baba. He is a man of many miracles, I believe. Do you think so? I hope he will be there.'

'I have no idea. Have you booked him? I didn t know that tour operators included gurus in their itineraries,' I said, amused that spirituality could be so conveniently packaged.

'We are very fortunate.' She pulled out what must have been her tour brochure and pushed it into my hands saying, 'Here is his picture.'

I passed over the photograph noncommittally, and handed it back. 'I m not good on gurus and miracles,' I said apologetically. We fell silent.

As I obeyed the request to fasten my seat-belt for landing, I tensed. Old anxieties surfaced as we bumped and bounced down the Bombay runway. At that moment, the prospect of walking through the airport with a white cane and on the arm of an Indian ground stewardess provoked more horror in me than anything that India could ever throw at me.

I had never been able to bring myself to use a cane at home because of the stark associations with blindness that it stirred up. When I first lost my sight a guide dog was the only acceptable solution. I did not imagine that I would be able to use a cane in India to guide me around: the skill and technique of doing so required training, which I had resisted. However, I had reluctantly accepted that I needed some symbol to identify my disability for those times when I needed help. But when the moment approached to take out my cane, I realised I had underestimated my anxiety.

The engines were switched off. The captain made a curt announcement blaming our uncomfortable landing on the atrocious condition of the runway. The stewardess asked me to remain seated while all the other passengers got off. My Norwegian flight companions looked askance. Maybe they thought I was a VIP, or undeservedly getting special treatment. I moved obligingly to one side to let them climb past, and they left, mystified.

By the time the aircraft had emptied I was truly agitated. Finally the stewardess returned with my embarkation card and a member of the ground staff to accompany me through the airport. I got up, unfolded my collapsible cane, placed a tight grip on my unease and the lightest touch on the chubby elbow of the Indian stewardess (the softer I touch, the more accurately I can sense someone's movements) and followed her.

I sensed the suspicious stares of security guards as we passed through the airport building, feeling exposed by their scrutiny and disbelief. I twiddled the mala beads around my neck for distraction and thought back to a pre-departure conversation I had had with the friend who had given them to me. She forced me to look carefully at the way I always want to play down, even conceal that I am blind. She said, 'It depends on how you see yourself. Disabled? Or enabled to have a greater and more unique experience of life?'

When I arrived at the airport I felt very disabled as I was marched through passport control carrying my cane. I wanted to be less self-conscious, less self-deprecating. My one consolation was the knowledge that there had been a time when I would have exploded in rage and terror at the indignity of my helplessness. I would have wrenched my hand free of the sweaty palm pulling me along to stride off and brain myself on the next inanimate object in my path. At least I had improved since those days.

With the stewardess I slipped my hand free of hers and placed my fingers gently but firmly on her elbow. They slid under the end of the cotton sari draped over her shoulder, and the soft fabric fluttered around my wrist as we moved on. All at once, I felt myself back in control, and the fear subsided. I began to experience the answer I would have given my friend had it been clearer at the time. I accepted that I was disabled because I was blind, but I started to learn that my lack of sight had given me the advantages of insight and heightened awareness.

So it was, in those early hours of the morning of my arrival, that India dawned through my third eye – the eye that senses the size and shape of movement and sees faces in the sound of blank space. I outlined a picture of the stewardess: her formality announced by her stiffness, her nervousness portrayed by her anxious clutching at me every time we took a step or rounded a bend. I saw the cleaners: the smooth sweep of their soft brooms followed by the trip-tripping of their thonged shoes and the drag of plastic buckets along the floor. I imagined the guards with barrel chests, their breath restricted by tight belts that paunched their bellies. The nuances of sound and smell were brushstrokes on the canvas that my visual cortex cannot leave blank for long.

I felt alert with excitement as we reached the conveyor belts and waited for my bag. I wondered whether it would still be dark outside, and then whether Goutam would recognise me after all this time Sadly, the cane would mark me out now.

We waited a long time for my bag, probably because the zealous baggage handlers at Heathrow had labelled it with a 'Diplomatic Baggage' sticker to make it easily identifiable. At last it arrived with its stickers and frayed straps, and I was glad to have it back. I carried the lightness of being loved by my friends in this small bag filled with their goodwill gifts.

BOMBAY: GOUTAM, A GATEWAY TO INDIA

The night was steamy but not oppressive. A faint, quivering coolness thinned the air. A little beggar girl approached silently as we reached Goutam's car. She tugged at my free side. I put my hand on her shawled head, felt the coarse cloth, and guessed she was Muslim from her covered head but could not gauge how old she was. Her shoulder brushed my hip, and I knew that she was not emaciated. Goutam paid her off and waved her away. He was embarrassed.

Goutam's new Sierra was squeaky and sterile. This was India's answer to the Range Rover, with the same high status, high fashion appeal. I was introduced to John, the driver, who took my bags and helped me into the front seat. Goutam climbed into the back.

As we swept smoothly down empty highways, skirted Bombay and headed for the north-eastern suburb where Goutam lived with his mother, the first taste I'd had of India disappeared outside the air-conditioned vehicle. Now there was nothing to convince me that I had travelled thousands of miles across the world. Neither sound nor smell penetrated, and all impressions of Bombay passed me by.

Goutam and I began to talk about the years in which we had not seen each other. I asked about his wife, Ratna, and his daughter, Rimi. 'They are away at Ratna's mother's place in Calcutta just now. She is a widow and quite old. Of course, Ratna wants to be with her.'

'How long have they been gone?' I asked.

'Six months.'

'You must miss them both,' I said, 'especially Rimi. How old is she now?'

'Two and a half,' he said. 'You should see her. She is really cute and very bright.' His whole body came to life as he spoke of his daughter. Then he became introverted and quiet once more.

In the silence that followed, I asked John to open the window. Goutam raised a hand but let it fall back into his lap when he heard the purr of the glass descending.

Everything was still outside and the unexpected peace made me think of the last-minute warnings I had received of troubles in Bombay and other Indian cities. They had almost made me cancel my trip. I recalled a letter from a friend of a friend, Samantak Das. He was a university lecturer who had found some student guides to accompany me on my trip. He wrote:

I really do not know how to start this letter since it stands in such contrast to previous ones. I can no longer sanction your coming to India. Hans and Biju, your guides, were all set. And then on Sunday, 6th December all hell broke loose at Ayodhya. This incredible mess leaves no one knowing what state India will be in, in six months, or even six days from now. I always believed that Calcutta, being the most secular of India's cities, would not fall prey to this collective madness. But as I sit here in the bucolic calm of Santiniketan typing this missive, perfectly normal people are trying to kill each other because of the way they cut their beards or wear their saris. The death toll all over India already exceeds a thousand, of which about 50 are in Bombay and some dozen odd in Calcutta. Reading over my letter, it does not seem coherent, but coherence is perhaps the first victim of such chaos. Despite my failure to live up to my earlier promises, I hope to hear from you again.

Now that I had arrived the drama of Samantak's letter, radio and television news items, and travel agents' reports of disruption seemed no more substantial than a play without a theatre. There was no sign of trouble in the Bombay through which we were driving.

When I asked Goutam where the street fires, mobs and barricades were to be found, he was nonchalant about the recent violence. I assumed it had been exaggerated. I was to learn otherwise before my trip ended.

Samantak's letter had arrived less than eight weeks before my scheduled January departure, and I had bought my ticket. But the loss of my guides actually relieved me of one anxiety. I had been worried about the cost of feeding, transporting and accommodating them for five or six months, but now I did not know how I would manage alone. It was not until just after Christmas, with four weeks to go and with Goutam as my only contact, that I had a telephone call from a friend. She said, 'I have a guide for you. He wants to go to India too.'

Tony came round one evening and in the course of our discussion I heard myself saying that I intended to go without a guide. I had realised that an English escort would dilute my experience because I would see through English eyes. I wanted my own impressions with a little local translation of the unfamiliar environment. Tony offered his help in return for a free trip, but I had found that I neither needed nor wanted it. I was liberated by this discovery and was recast in the role of the helper. I knew that I could go without him, but he could not go without me for he had neither the money nor the inclination to go by himself. I decided to use whatever help I could find through Goutam, or whoever I might meet while travelling. I gathered four other contact names and addresses from friends as a support base, and figured that if I were in extreme need, I could use some of my sponsorship money to pay for a private tour guide.

Both the riots and the absence of travel companions meant that uncertain times lay ahead but I was strangely unperturbed. Having got myself to Bombay, though, it was reassuring to be with Goutam and not under siege and alone in the airport.

Goutam's mother welcomed us in from the porch. 'Call me Aunty. I am Aunty to all Goutam's friends. And this is Dolly.' She indicated a small dog darting around our legs.

She was smaller and less bent than I had expected, and I assessed her compact shape and size. The survival instinct had taught me to form impressions quickly. I operate like an animal picking up a predator's vibrations from the ground. Aunty moved inside. She was not slow and I could not guess her age.

I was invited to sit and politeness prevailed, although I longed to roam around the room where my eyes could not take a wander to satisfy my curiosity. Central ceiling fans whirred briskly. Goutam and Aunty sat either side of me and asked about my journey. 'Have some water. Drinking is very important,' Goutam said suddenly. He sounded upset by his oversight, but I hesitated. He encouraged me: 'The water at home is boiled and filtered.' I accepted, not just because I was reassured but because I wanted to locate the kitchen.

Aunty moved to a room to my left off the sitting room and I heard the trickle of water filling a glass.

'You won't be knowing our bathroom,' said Aunty, coming back with the water on a plastic tray, 'but we are having a commode downstairs.'

Goutam explained that there was a western-style bathroom with toilet and shower downstairs, while upstairs it was Indian-style for squatting at ground level. 'Is there paper downstairs, Ma?' I was relieved by the nod she gave as I did not feel ready to use my hand, which I had heard all about.

Aunty went on, 'We are not having servants here staying all the time. That is most unnecessary. But I am having one girl coming every day to prepare everything. Of course, there is a sweeper and washer too.' Her body broadened with satisfaction and she wished me good night.

Goutam led the way upstairs to my bedroom and checked that I had everything I needed. 'Tomorrow you can rest here and relax,' he told me. 'It is wise not to go too quickly. I shall see you briefly before I go into the office. Aunty will be here all day. Good night.'

Unwittingly he had cancelled Christmas: I was feeling as impatient as a child on Christmas Eve about what excitements the next day would bring. I was itching to get out and unwrap all the mysteries of Bombay, and now it was decreed a day of rest. Did Goutam think he was God?

I was to discover that being impetuous and energetic was not compatible with the Indian approach to life. My desire to be on the move all the time was to rush and exhaust many of my Indian companions. By the end of the trip I had wrestled frequently with the frustration of plans thwarted or delayed because I was dependent on the willingness of naturally inactive people to act.

But I also came to respect their ability to be bored. Everywhere I went I found people who did not need entertainment the way we do in the West. They could sit and wait for something for hours without needing distraction, accepting the peace of emptiness.

I flicked the Bakelite light switch by the bed. It was in a cluster of round knobs mounted on hardboard against a wall. The wires were not sunk, the bulbs were bare. My bed had one bottom sheet over a thin mattress. It was simple and hammer-hard. I stretched out because I was warm and did not need to curl up against the cold as I often did during winter at home.

In the morning I was awakened by a cacophony of dogs barking, engines revving, clothes being slapped clean, birds and monkeys raucously beginning their day before the heat set in. We all had breakfast downstairs before Goutam left for the office. Aunty sat in her housecoat and I in my sarong, which kept slipping. There was porridge, which seemed out of place, and fruit that the servant girl had peeled and sliced for me, but the apple and sweet lime had been sucked dry by the heat.

After my bucket bath, swilling myself down with jugs of cool water taken from a pail in the centre of an oblong room with a cement floor, I let my hair dry in the sun on the upstairs veranda. I thought about my friend Laura, who had arrived here six years ago on her way south to an orphanage where she did a year's voluntary work. Although I had not then been in contact personally with Goutam – I was still too raw and despondent to wish to be in touch with anyone – he had been happy to receive a friend of mine with only my letter of introduction. Laura had spent a few days here with the Bhattacharyas. I pictured her poring over street plans of Bombay, with a day bag on her shoulder, then heading off to pick up a rickshaw or bus into town.

I could not follow Laura's lead in any of this and envied her independence. I longed to be free, able to explore where I pleased, and I felt cast down by my disability. The herons, wrens, hummingbirds, hoopoes and Paradise kingfishers who, I had thought, had woken me that morning dropped away as I realised that the strident noises all around came from crows, as commonplace and abundant as the pigeons that overpopulate London.

The morning took its slow course. I sat while Aunty proselytised on health, manners, dress, contraception, marriage, art and religion. A servant girl was squatting on her haunches to sweep the floor with wide circular movements as if she was churning milk in a pail.

'Do you go out much, Aunty?' I asked hopefully.

'Oh, yes, to the park, to the market and to my friends. We are always gallivanting.' She settled back in her chair. 'Goutam says, "Mummy, you will be getting so tired, always out and about." I am the chairman of the Ladies' Club. Everything is just here in Chembur. If I am needing to go to Bombay, Goutam is sending John to drive me. He is a very good son.'

I felt encouraged. 'Are you going to the market today?'

'No, there is no needing. It is a very dirty place. We would have to take the rickshaw. There is no John here right now and Goutam doesn't like me going like that.'

'I thought you only needed John to go to Bombay. Anyway, it would be fun to go in a rickshaw. I've never done that.'

She wriggled her way around my pushiness. 'Goutam would not be wanting me to take you in these three-wheelers. You are his guest. I am very independent-minded, very liberal, but even I am not going out much in these things now. You should not be traipsing through the dirty bazaar. My son is very careful of his mother.'

I was crestfallen. Goutam was a cautious man, but I wondered if Aunty was exaggerating his protectiveness because she was not as gregarious or as confident as she made out.

After lunch she suggested a nap. I took the cue and went obediently to my room. I could not settle so tidied my few belongings into heaps and bundles according to size and use. I took some arnica for bruising and jet-lag; its subtle homeopathic action relieved my aching head.

I began to wonder what I would find in the coming weeks as I observed ayurvedic practices. Would Indian herbalism include essential oils, which are the volatile extracts of plants produced through distillation and used in aromatherapy? An understanding of massage techniques and the use of plant oils in ayurvedic medicine would benefit my work in aromatherapy at home. I knew only that, like aromatherapy, ayurvedic medicine was closely associated with a tradition of massage in which the oils are rubbed into the skin to be absorbed into the bloodstream, where they take effect. The professional motivation behind my trip had given me a purpose and an itinerary, which promised deeper insights into Indian life than the cursory overview that journeying as a backpacker or as a member of a an organised tour would have offered. My special interest would give me an entrée into the workaday world: meetings with purveyors of herbal and aromatic oils and visits to massage centres.

But cooped up on that first day, I was only as able as the help available to me was willing. I was grounded and frustrated by kindness. Then I heard Aunty downstairs on the telephone to Goutam for the umpteenth time and felt cross with myself: I would have to learn how to manipulate the help on offer so that it would be useful rather than restricting.

Late that afternoon Aunty summoned a neighbour, Shobha, to walk me round the colony. Goutam and Aunty had lived for fifteen years in a modern private housing estate of thirty homes. There were three private roads lined with different styles of houses, each with a perfumed garden and thick, broad, strap-leaved foliage at the front. The two play areas echoed with creaking swings and high-pitched children's chatter. A watchman restricted entry at the gates of the complex to authorised persons only.

Shobha was on study leave from Madras where she was due to take her medical exams. She glided along in her sari, tall and beautifully composed, and not half so impatient as I. The pace of life seemed to be measured in our stroll up and down the safe streets.

We took tea at 8.00 p.m. when Goutam returned from the office. There was a choice of sweet or salty biscuits. I was surprised to discover that salty meant a Ritz cracker. 'You will be hungry,' Aunty insisted, despite my protests. 'You people eat so early in your country. We are having dinner only at nine thirty. Goutam is always coming so very late home.'

I was pleased to find a traditional stainless-steel platter in front of me at dinner, because at lunchtime I had been honoured with a china plate which felt less authentic. By me were placed two round stainless-steel bowls like laboratory specimen dishes, but deeper. One contained dhal and the other wet cabbage curry. Aunty dolloped white rice on our plates and served fish to Goutam. I was the only vegetarian. Tonight, I wasn't going to be the only person not using their hand to eat. I discarded the spoon and fork placed by my plate and experimented with my right hand as masher, mixer and shovel. It was glorious. Eating took on a new dimension, with touch and texture adding an interest far greater than that produced by sight and smell. To feel, squeeze and mix the rice with the gravy-like dhal, then scoop it into my mouth without it dropping unexpectedly from a fork, made it taste like ambrosia.

I kneaded and blended the food, anticipating the explosion of flavours. For once I knew what I was going to eat before I put it into my mouth – there were no scalding shocks. I was careful to use only my fingers, not my whole hand, and kept my left hand free, and away from the food: in India it is delegated to lavatorial purposes.

Goutam and I spent the rest of the evening telephoning, discussing and organising. I went to bed feeling optimistic because finally I had some appointments to see doctors with whom I had so far only exchanged letters – people seemed willing to see me at a moment's notice. In particular, I had arranged to visit a Dr Renade and stay overnight in Pune, a hill station about half a day's drive east of Bombay.

The next morning Aunty, my guide for the day, announced breezily at midday that she was ready to leave for Bombay. We had planned to depart at around ten that morning... I had spent the time listening to John squeaking a cloth over the car.

Another half-hour and we were on our way. Once again, the intriguing whirl and bother outside was muted by the drone of the air-conditioning and the sealed windows. I supposed that living in the midst of such commotion would tarnish its appeal quickly, but I was fascinated. At every crossroads the vendors of oranges, balloons and newspapers tapped on the closed glass along with mendicants. We were cocooned, protected from grabbing hands and the poisonous exhaust fumes of cheap grade diesel. I longed to tear down the glass barrier and absorb the life beyond.

We swerved, braked and horn-blasted our way through cars, people, beasts and bicycles for almost two hours towards Marine Drive down past Chowpatty Beach. We had planned to meet Goutam for lunch at his office in Nariman Point, but called first at the Bombay Ayurvedic Hospital where I hoped to observe some of their massage work. It seemed fatuous to worry that we were late for both engagements: no one else in India clung to western concepts of time management and punctuality.

We drew into the hospital drive and at last I could lower the window while Aunty went to find the right entrance. Some road labourers' children splashed in the mud-filled trenches that ribboned the roads outside. Their mothers mixed concrete and dug the baked slippery earth over which they had first poured drums of water. The sacking over their corrugated iron shelters flapped back each time someone crawled into their home.

The hospital foyer was airy and cool. Our names were scribbled down on a notepad and carried through heavy closed doors to the doctor-sahib. Audience was granted. Nothing was said about our latecoming, but we had to sit and wait.

People passed us barefoot. Starched Florence Nightingale uniforms, a relic of colonialism, crackled by. Saris floated while the long skirts of domestics trailed in the dust they were sweeping. A one-legged man hopped past.

In that first meeting with an ayurvedic doctor I discovered a difficulty that I had not predicted: I could not fall back on sign language. Not seeing became a real impediment when explanations were given in language so garbled that it was as indecipherable as bad handwriting. The heavily accented English of the doctor-sahib, and all the other doctors around him, left me dumbfounded.

Aunty interpreted as best she could, but I did not glean much about the type of massage and oil treatments given at the hospital. I would have to learn by being present at a treatment, but was too late to see anything that day. I agreed to return the next morning when the sessions were to take place.

During our brief discussion, the doctor-sahib had been curious about my blindness. He swivelled in his chair for a while and spoke with a cluster of attentive juniors, then offered treatment in a noncommittal way. He told Aunty that he was convinced of a successful outcome. Politely but firmly I chose to ignore his comments. I had not asked for a consultation about my own health and was annoyed that he should interfere.

When I was young, and later when my sight was failing altogether, there had been an inevitable chasing after cures. Now I had settled on living life as it was, and had no intention of beginning another search that would probably cause as much upheaval to me as it had to lose my sight in the first place.

The next day I returned to the massage rooms with Goutam. A young doctor greeted us and gave us an explanation of *pancha karma*, the five-fold purification procedures – *pancha* means five and *karma* means actions – of ayurveda for eliminating the excessive *doshas*, or biological humours, from the body. Enemas and purgatives made of herbal decoctions and fatty oils provoke vomiting, excreting, urinating, bleeding and nose-blowing.

'It is written in the *Vedas*, our ancient Hindu scriptures,' said the enthusiastic young doctor, 'that a dirty cloth cannot be dyed even though the best colouring material is available. We are therefore first removing the toxins and excess *doshas*. Only then can the patient benefit from further treatment to enrich and heal the tissues.'

After that I was glad to hear that we were not going to witness *pancha karma*. Instead we moved to the massage rooms, where 'oleation' and 'sudation' were in progress, two preparatory processes for the *pancha karma*. Oleation makes the *pancha karma* less exhausting for the patient, while sudation widens the natural channels, openings and pores of the body so that the *doshas* in the form of secretions localised in the tissues and skin can be brought from them and into the gastro-intestinal tract for easier elimination.

The general greasing and opening of every possible orifice through steam, hot oil and poultices were grouped under the generic heading of massage, which was what I had come to find out about. A drainage massage, to cleanse and improve the circulation using oils to detoxify, was familiar to me, but what went on here was a long way from the rhythmic, relaxing experience I offered my clients. I had to interpret the meaning behind the slithering, slapping and pounding as well as the explanations given by the doctor in his Indian English.

Suddenly it was my turn and, thank goodness, Goutam was naturally adroit in assessing what guidance I needed. First I was given hot rice poultices soaked in a solution of herbs and milk, then women encouraged me to pummel them up and down the stringy body of a three-year-old girl with polio. She wailed and whimpered while the assistants pinned her down and cried, 'Harder, harder.'

'Don't you think the poultices are rather hot?' I objected feebly, and immediately another was squashed into my hands.

'Come, look here.' The doctor beckoned us to where a man with arthritis was lying on a table. His contorted limb was awash in oil; he slid about like a bar of soap in the bath and squirmed under the pressure of the oiling.

We were propelled further into the room where I could hear hissing and spitting. 'This is a steam spray for sinus disorders,' said the doctor. Goutam described the jet of steam spraying the head of a man sitting on a low stool. Another man lay under a funnel that dripped oil between his eyes. 'This is good for insomnia as he has a brown-sugar addiction.' I imagined that the doctor meant diabetes, until Goutam mentioned drugs and their increased availability on the streets. I felt foolish at my ignorance.

At every corner of this treatment hall a stool or bench was occupied by a naked male body – this was a men's session. Gaggles of assistants worked on each patient. Their willingness to demonstrate and involve me was gratifying, but the absence of consultation with and disregard for the modesty of the patients disturbed me. They were not asked whether they minded that Goutam and I were there.

I have had clients at home who were embarrassed by their nakedness, and who even confessed that they felt less reticent about stripping off in front of me because I could not see them. These men did not even have that comfort: they did not know I could not see.

Later, back in Chembur, Goutam suggested we should go to his local golf club for snacks, savoury morsels eaten with a drink in the early evening. I had had *pakoras* and *samosas* as starters in Indian restaurants at home and thought that this was what he meant. He laughed gently and said, 'You people are taking what we have with an afternoon cup of tea as your starter to a dinner, whereas we do not have a first course as such.' The club had the colonial calm of the Bombay Gymkhana Club where we had lunched that day.

While we munched our baked and spiced chick-peas on the lawn beyond the terrace, we discussed the next day's departure for Pune. I was distracted by a vast family, partying noisily at the table next to us. The American accents, the clink of glasses and bottles, the pop of corks, the clatter of knives and forks, the splash from the swimming-pool, the smack of a club on a golf ball: all the sounds here were distinct and vibrated untrammelled by the clean air. It was so unlike the streets outside where the hustling for space, the din and the grime muddied the atmosphere. Surrounded by clipped, solid hedges, I felt hemmed in here, but I also enjoyed the fine tailoring, the swift, silken bodies, the patina.

Eventually the metallic sound of crickets drowned every other sound and we moved inside. We padded across cropped lawns and on to the polished, slippery marble floors of the vaulted veranda. We sat for a while in cane chairs and listened to the random flip and snap of playing-cards.

I sat in the calm and mulled over the experience of my first few days. I was tired from the mounting frustrations but I knew I had to negotiate a precarious path on what felt like a mountain ascent with some breath-taking views into Indian life. I had to learn to manoeuvre through the intimate and intricate customs of the people whose help I needed, but who I did not yet understand.

My intention was not to plunder the lives of my Indian friends: I wanted only to make a few cultural forays. I was bowled over by the willingness of mother and son to help me on my way, but bowled out by their caution and zealous care. I also realised that already they had given me more to contemplate than I would have found in all the palaces and forts visited on the most extensive guided tour. They had let me into their lives and helped me embark on my explorations. I was glad to be with my Bengali Brahmin family in Bombay.

PUNE: PLANTS WITH DRS PARANJAPE AND RENADE

On the first Sunday after my arrival in India Goutam, Aunty and I, with John driving, made a delayed start for Pune. This is a hill station lying on the Deccan plateau on the far side of the Western Ghats from Bombay. After leaving the industrial suburbs, which reeked of ammonia, John drove through dusty plains, which tasted hot and dry. There were no signs of houses or villages yet people streamed along the edges of the road. They babbled, spat and spluttered in the wake of exhaust fumes from the torrent of lorries that roared by.

One minute we were on the flat, the next we were travelling almost vertically as we started the steep climb, swinging in and out of hairpin bends, to reach the plateau. Half-way up we turned off the road into rolling hills and deep countryside. The air was already thinner and somehow purer. I wondered whether variations in air quality could change how people saw things, like looking through different thicknesses of glass. For me atmosphere and heat alter how things smell and sound.

Goutam dreamed the dream of pressurised business people the world

36

over, the one that colours their snatched moments of reverie: he longed for a piece of land to which he could retreat and in time retire. Eventually we stopped by an old farmhouse where a mass of children spilled over the wooden porch and into the road. A couple of older men approached the car, and Goutam asked about the market garden that he knew was for sale further up the hill. They nodded and smiled but Goutam didn't seem to learn much more from them.

Meanwhile the children surrounded the car, flattened their fingers against its shiny surface and pressed their lips inside-out against the windows. Tongues flicked like lizards against the glass. I felt their unashamed stares and stared back.

As we drove away towards the market garden, Goutam observed, 'The woman standing back in the porch was young and very beautiful. Did you see, Ma?' I had been aware of a presence hovering in the background, cuing her children without a murmur.

Goutam left us in the car at the gate to the market garden, which was an area of planted scrub fenced from the road. I heard water spurting steadily, men's voices and distant children. I was intrigued. I clambered out of the back seat into the glare of the sun, shrugging off cries from John and Aunty, 'Where are you going?'

I made it look as if I was ambling aimlessly in circles around the car, kicking my heels in the dirt, but I was edging towards the sounds by increasing the loops and dragging my feet heavily to warn off snakes and test for what might be underfoot.

Aunty decided to join me. She enthused, 'So very wonderful, all these beautiful flowers.' I was confused to have pictures of dahlias, daisies, lupins and marigolds painted in my mind as she listed the varieties in the beds. I had imagined I was surrounded by orchids, arum lilies and gerbera while behind these I had conjured rows of fat tomatoes, cauliflower and smooth, shiny peppers.

Goutam returned quickly. He said the garden was too neglected to be profitable and the manager too drunk to make sense. The air was saturated with alcohol and I realised that the man was tottering by our car, waiting to wave us off.

On arriving in Pune we lunched late in the Hotel Amir's restaurant, whose splendidly studded door swooshed with a surprising smoothness given its great weight. We sat in an empty dining room with tables already laid for the evening. The intermittent sounds coming from the kitchens were muffled by the padded seats and heavily upholstered furnishings. I ran my fingers over the painted-wood wall panelling, the Mogul latticework and the large figures of musicians and elephants behind me. We were surrounded by the mascots and designs reminiscent of Cotswold curry houses. Which came first? I wondered. The Indian restaurant in India or in Britain? Traditionally, Indians have cooked and served their meals at home, and ideally the food was touched only by freshly bathed Brahmins. The best food I ate in India was prepared in private homes. Time-consuming, laborious grinding, pounding and mixing were part of the daily domestic routine in most of the households where I stayed. The most modestly affluent families had at least one servant to help.

I experimented with *roti*, Indian flat bread: only *chapattis*, or variations of this basic flour and water bread made on the *tava*, a slightly concave cast-iron griddle, were prepared in the home. I decided that when I ate out, I would sample the breads that had to be baked in a *tandoor*, a hot brick oven found in eating-houses. Goutam ordered both a *tandoori roti* and a *naan* bread to accompany some fish dishes for himself and Aunty, and a vegetable dish for me.

When the food arrived my fingers delved into the *naan*'s soft folds. They sank into the sponginess where it was slightly undercooked and scratched over the burnt edges. The surface of the *tandoori roti* was harder, and every so often my wandering fingertips dropped into unexpected craters. I worked one-handed, of course, and noticed that the *naan* was more glutinous, and therefore harder to tear – more likely to betray my lack of dexterity.

We decided to check our accommodation before contacting Dr Renade. That evening Goutam had to return to Bombay with John for work the next day. He had insisted that Aunty chaperone my overnight stay, and that we should take seats in the ladies' carriage of the Deccan Express back to Bombay the following evening. We were to stay at the West Indian Automobile Association, which he, as a member, had been able to book.

At first I had protested: what would Aunty do in a day on her own while I attended my meetings? But I was excited, too, by the prospect of my first Indian train ride. However, a ladies' carriage was not quite what I had in mind. I had read about carriages full of families having picnics, piled high with trunks, crammed with hens, and with scores of legs and arms hanging out of open windows, but I didn't think that could be true of an air-conditioned ladies' carriage. I had thought I might go third class. If only Aunty would return with Goutam.

Back in the car on the way to our rooms, I considered making one last attempt to persuade Goutam that I would not need Aunty once I had made contact with Dr Renade, who would undoubtedly show me round and put me on the train back to Bombay. I remained silent: all previous endeavours of a similar nature had been fruitless, and I did not want Goutam to feel I was rejecting his generosity and kindness. If I stuck clumsily to the western model of independence and self-sufficiency I knew I risked offending my Indian friends. My behaviour would appear both selfish and brutal to their way of thinking. They would assume that I did not care about their anxiety. I was beginning to see that giving and receiving help altruistically, according to need and opportunity, was an integral part of Indian culture, a vital interdependence in a country with so many people and so much poverty. People seemed more able to receive and even ask for what was given without shame or expectation, and give what they had to give without compulsion or calculation of reward. A thought slid round in my mind about how the ties of dependence might have a strengthening as well as a restricting pull, while independence could be an isolating strait-jacket. I decided I needed to discover a little more about this approach and for a while be a less intrepid, less selfish explorer.

John drove into a multi-storey car-park in the centre of Pune, above which were tall blocks of flats and offices. Goutam got out to look over the Automobile Association flat. I was determined not to miss out on any inspection, especially if it involved my sleeping quarters.

Goutam suggested, 'Why don't you stay here with John and Ma and I will go up?' I remembered the earlier visit to the market garden when Goutam had left us in the car. This time I felt that as the purpose of the visit directly concerned me I was not going to be left in the car like a child. People have often just 'nipped' to do this or that and left me to wait because they thought it easier and quicker than asking me to come. It makes me feel like an inconvenient appendage or, worse still, a nuisance invalid or child.

Aunty also assumed that the inspection was her domain as it was a domestic matter. We got out of the car simultaneously, one at each side, and stood square, facing Goutam, unequivocally ready to accompany him.

The flat smelt noisome. I ran my hand discreetly over the bed. The sheets, although straightened, still had the crumpled, faintly greasy creases left by the last occupant. The bedroom adjoined an office area with an adjacent wash-room. Goutam was guided by our disapproving silence and did the honourable thing. He paid the hundred rupees for the room because we had reserved it, even though its dinginess meant we were not going to take it. We returned to the Hotel Amir and were shown to a double room with air-conditioning, a television and a bathroom *en suite* for 550 rupees, which Goutam also insisted on paying.

Alone with Aunty in the evening, I tried to persuade her to take a stroll in the street outside the hotel. 'No no,' she objected, 'it is so very dirty, oh, so very busy, and what to do? Best stay here.' She was getting irate with the unfamiliar operating panel on the television as well as with my persistence. Exasperated, twiddling the knobs to no avail, she summoned Room Service to switch it on.

Two men knocked and entered. They listened silently to her complaints. One pressed a button on the set and it came on loud and clear. They left repeating urbanely, 'No problem, madam, no problem.'

'Aunty, please let us take some fresh air.' I tried to capitalise on how clearly hot and bothered she was.

Instead she flicked the switches on the air-conditioning system and enquired indulgently, 'Are you too hot?' The motor choked and coughed up recycled air. 'It is so noisy! What do they be thinking of? Far too noisy for sleeping. Now I am not hearing the programmes.' She turned up the volume on the television and started to tamper with the air-conditioning unit. Amid the rattling and shouting, she marched towards the telephone.

'You're not going to call them again?' asked, embarrassed by the prospect of another visit from the room boys within five minutes of the last.

'And why so very not?' she asked sweetly, picking up the receiver. They arrived just as quickly as last time and obligingly adjusted the air-conditioning without a hint of a snigger.

When they went, I lay on my bed fermenting in frustration while Aunty settled to watch television. The volume was still turned high and the voices sounded distorted above the drone of the air conditioning. Despite myself I found I was having to grapple with the familiar molten rage inside me: an intense fury of self-pity, fed and sustained by those many occasions in my life when I have not been able to enjoy the simplest freedoms without taking extreme risks or co-opting someone else. Again I was thwarted by dull, commonplace obstacles. I felt like a creature from *Doctor Who* who, however powerful, intrepid and cunning, can be melted or rendered inert by a splash of water. My internal furnace, however familiar, still scared me: I feared its corrosive power and was shocked that it should still be so intense. Perhaps it was so strong because there were so many memories of times when I had felt stampeded by difficulties, corralled and crushed. I hated the way the bitterness took hold so inexorably, but at least I was less likely now than when I was younger to erupt and destroy everything in my path. Still I brooded, sinking into the usual black despondency. Everyone else can go where they please, when they please. I can't.

The loss of this freedom has been the true agony of blindness. As a child with limited sight in only one eye, it was an unnamed fear aching in my side. I rode my bicycle, hunted ponies and went Saturday shopping alone on the bus. Crashing my bike, falling off my pony and getting lost in town were the ineluctable consequences of being a partially sighted child. With adolescence, everything was harder, seemed more unfair; the pain was more acute. There was no way around intolerable injustices like not being able to drive. The exquisite taste of freedom that comes with being a teenager, and in which my friends revelled, was never to be mine. I was grounded at a time when I wanted to fly.

My remaining sight began to fail in my early twenties, and becoming mistress of my own destiny seemed an attainable ambition for everyone but me. It was excruciating for me in my youthful arrogance to have to contend with basics like how to walk down a street. I remember once not wanting to ask or wait for a friend to accompany me to the supermarket. 'Do it anyway' had always been my motto. And I got there, only to knock several pints of milk on to the floor. The staff thought I was drunk. Things got worse: I became totally blind and desperate to hold on to any scrap of freedom or dignity. I made many more journeys alone, which eventually led me once too often to Accident and Emergency. I could bear the injuries to body and mind no longer and collapsed in hospital.

When I left hospital and began to rebuild my life I tried to use mobility aids and guide dogs to regain some independence. At first I was violently resistant to all such forms of help: I saw them as imperfect and emasculating compromises. Relying on help in any form, especially these conventional aids used by blind people, seemed the ultimate failure to me: I had grown up struggling proudly to manage without aid – and mostly denying a problem existed that might require special assistance. On those few occasions when my sight problems were acknowledged, my bravery and determination 'to boldly go where no blind person had gone unaided before' were acclaimed so fervently that it became even harder for me to find a sense of personal worth and achievement in the acceptance of help. Redefining my values and my identity had been and still was a struggle.

That night I knew that if I tried to go out without Aunty and risked the dangers, worry would force her to join me. It would be kinder to stay put and try to be cheerful. However, obstinacy and determination ungraciously took over. I jumped up, resolved to go alone if necessary. Aunty came with me. Out on the street I self-consciously took out my white cane: the throng was so thick that we needed to clear enough ground for two to walk abreast. I didn't have the impression that anyone attributed any meaning to this symbol of international significance. No one moved out of the way.

I was aghast at the sudden rush of white noise. The sounds were too numerous and strange to distinguish. The situation was so unfamiliar and overwhelming that I lost all ability to fathom, predict and judge my surroundings. I jumped at every unexpected bang. This was my first proper experience of Asian streets.

My abrupt reflex jerking to all the sudden sounds reminded me of how I had convulsed and trembled in the same way when I first started going out after losing my sight. Now I was attending a firework display of horns, cries, banging, tinkling, scuffling and roaring. Slowly I began to discern the shriek of horns or the whir of an engine become higher-pitched as it came up closer behind me. But I could not tell how close the source of the sound was.

Because there were no pavements, we walked hazardously in and out of the traffic. A man ran over to me and said, 'Please don't be taking this the wrong way, but may I be helping?' I was surprised: my cane did register with some small percentage of the population. He walked us back to the hotel and disappeared without a word.

Back in our room I was exhilarated and vibrant. Aunty was depleted. She didn't get out and about as much as she thought she did and certainly not with an energetic blind woman on her arm. In the morning I heard her slip out to fetch the fruit we had agreed we would prefer for breakfast. I let her go alone, pretending that I was still asleep.

At 9.30 a.m. Dr Renade arrived with a colleague, Dr Paranjape, to take me to Dr Paranjape's clinic in the centre of town where I would meet the latter's wife. Both he and she were ayurvedics, as well as gynaecologists with allopathic training. There were more than ten generations of ayurvedics in their family.

The building we arrived at stood sandwiched between others in a congested central part of town. It was the Paranjapes' home as well as their hospital. We squeezed down a narrow passageway and clattered up a metal fire escape for several storeys. We reached an empty outpatient clinic and met Lady Doctor Satie, Dr Paranjape's wife.

The Paranjapes were a Maharashtrian family rooted in that state's heartland, and they cultivated its traditions in the way that they lived and worked. Their English was heavily accented with Marati. They were small and stocky, like most central and southern Indians, while Dr Renade was tall and lean, more like a northerner. He spoke in a clear, almost academic English.

Dr Renade was the Professor of Ayurveda at Pune University, travelling extensively, lecturing and writing on his subject, and both men wanted to promote ayurveda within India and export its benefits and uses to other countries. They gave a formal perspective of ayurveda to those whose knowledge and skills stemmed from tradition they had already been taught.

I was left alone when the two men went to receive another visitor, a naturalised German doctor, Herr Dr Dandekar. Soon Dr Satie would come for me. I walked around the waiting room. It was small, square and bare. I run my practice from home and have set aside a large room for consultations and a smaller one for massage treatments. My clients have always enjoyed the privacy and personal comfort that a home practice can offer. This was on a larger scale but the homely atmosphere made for an easy bedside manner.

Eventually Dr Satie appeared and ushered me into her consulting room. She sat me down with some milky coffee, served by her daughter who was training to be an ayurvedic doctor. They both had a warm presence, both elegant in their saris, although the mother was more authoritative. Perhaps she just seemed so because she carried more weight.

For a time Dr Satie and I discussed massage techniques. Then she summoned a cleaner to act as a demonstration model. Our subject obediently loosened yards of material from the rolls of fat around her middle and clambered on to a table that was too high and too narrow for her. The doctor pushed and pressed the muscles away from the base of her spine while maintaining a series of firm strokes flowing away from the heart.

I placed my hands on top of Dr Satie's and followed her movements. The girl seemed askew, tilted on her side. I would have had her lying prone and straight. Her thick waist explained the lower back pain she said came when she was carrying and bending at work. I thought there was neither enough precision nor force in the massage to loosen the shortened muscles, but it was impossible to give a deeper massage or any manipulation because the couch was at a fixed height, wedged against the wall. Dr Satie had to ask the girl to turn whenever she wanted to work on her other side.

I realised that the elementary massage was all that an ayurvedic doctor needed to give because the herbal oils achieved the desired results after they had penetrated the skin and been transported in the blood to the organs and other parts of the body. Ayurvedic massage aims to introduce as much of the selected plant substance as possible into the patient's bloodstream. Which is also the intention of aromatherapy massage. However, aromatherapists attach great significance to massage techniques to achieve relaxation in the patient and to work the muscles and joints.

Massage is not the only way to give an aromatherapy treatment: the essential oils can be absorbed through steam inhalations, baths, pessaries and suppositories. And in ayurveda, I discovered there were many more ways of applying plant oils. The word 'oiling' seemed to cover all treatment forms including massage. I picked up a rubber skull cap, like a highlighting cap used in hairdressing. The doctor explained that oil would drip through the perforations on to the skull of the wearer without going into the eyes. While we talked our model disappeared so silently that I hardly heard her go.

Dr Satie explained that in massage sesame or coconut oil was used as the medium for the essential oils or other herbal extracts. The 'carrying oils' were more than a simple means of transport: they were base oils with therapeutic properties of their own. The actions of the herbal oils were enhanced by the quality of the base product. It was only in the late eighties that aromatherapists began to recognise the value and potential of vegetable base oils beyond that of lubrication.

All the ayurvedic oils were prescribed according to the patient's dominant *dosha* or biological humour. The classical theory of the four cardinal humours – phlegm, blood, choler and melancholy or black choler – that determined the temper of the body and the mind was familiar to me. In ayurveda I found there were only the three *doshas*: *vate*, *pitta* and *kapha*. The permutations and combinations of the three generated seven types of human constitution. A predominance of one *dosha* or a combination to the exclusion of another would result in a state of imbalance and lead to disease.

Dr Satie gave me a bottle of oil. I sniffed. It was not aromatic. She was mysterious about its contents but assured me that it would be good for me because it cooled and reduced excess *pitta*. I remembered the car journey that morning with Dr Renade. After looking me up and down, he had informed me that I was a *pitta* type. I had to keep cool and drink a lot. I made up my mind to find out more about these *doshas*, especially *pitta* types.

While I was buying some *naran* oil from Dr Satie, recommended as a cure-all for pain and inflammation, a woman entered and heaved herself up on to the table. I was confused: was this our model returning or a genuine patient? There were no introductions, no words spoken.

Dr Satie invited me to drip oil into each of the woman's nostrils. She pushed my hand firmly against her own chin to demonstrate how to tilt the head right back. I wondered whether my clients at home would suffer in silence while I performed this 'massage' to cure their migraines, allergic rhinitis or congested sinuses. It didn't bear thinking about. More relevant, perhaps, was how the unsuspecting patient might have reacted if she had known I was blind. Would she have remained silent? I decided to forgo this learning experience for all our sakes. I would probably miss her nose altogether. I was practised at pouring warm oil into the ears to melt wax and relieve blockage, but ears are more convenient receptacles than nostrils. They are shaped like trumpets rather than piccolos. (An earful of oil, I was to learn, also had its place in ayurveda: incredibly, it was a calming treatment for stinging, itching or running *eyes*!)

Dr Satie lifted the oil dropper and said, 'Just be watching then.' She was so keen to show off her treatments that it didn't seem to matter to her that I couldn't see what she was doing.

After ten minutes the woman hopped off the couch and left as

46

wordlessly as she had come. She had submitted to treatment with unquestioning acceptance while the doctor had proceeded without any explanation or reassurance. I was uncomfortable with the lack of patient participation.

Dr Satie and I moved to the floor below, where their in-patients stayed, and I accompanied her on her ward round. We toured three or four rooms with the same number of beds in each, which made rectangular blocks of sound in each corner. There were no serried ranks of high hospital beds standing in crisp conformity, just a frowsty, homely atmosphere and a hot breeze lingering around the metal-latticed windows.

Some of the women were languishing listlessly on the beds. Dr Satie said, 'Here they are having no families, no work, they are very happy. Indulging in the bed rest.' Others were occupied in nursing new-born babies. In the delivery room an incubator was propped on the sideboard. It felt like a huge old-fashioned fish tank. 'We are having both the allopathic and ayurvedic medicaments here,' said Dr Satie. Since no babies were on their way, we made our way up two floors to the family home for lunch.

We slipped off our shoes in the outside balcony corridor that led to the kitchen. Some sons, daughters and cousins had already lunched and were leaving. Arun, Dr Satie's sixteen-year-old son, stayed to talk to me. 'What are you most liking about India?' he asked shyly.

'The hard beds, the people, and getting up in the morning without feeling cold,' I answered, as the food arrived. There were stainless steel bowls overflowing with potato and cabbage curry, and freshly made *pooris*. These deep-fried breads were puffed up with oil like balloons. They made wonderful crisp-soft sponges to mop up the curry. When I thought I was full, a bowl of *khir* arrived. This sweet vermicelli milk pudding was as smooth and thick as pure cream.

Luckily I had learnt from Goutam that delighting in food depended on moderation, or the oil and sweetness would become cloying. I appreciated the novelty, the culinary effort and expertise that had gone into creating it, and savoured the textures and tastes but ate little.

Arun continued to chat. I was impressed by his knowledge of British history, and remonstrated with myself about my poor knowledge of Indian history pre-Empire. My education exhibited cultural élitism: this vast sub-continent had not been deemed worthy of a place in my school curriculum.

After I had washed my eating hand, Dr Satie introduced me to her eighty-six-year-old mother. She spoke tenderly, with a cherishing reverence, to the old lady. There was none of the sing-song diction in her voice that so many people reserve for the very old, the very young, invalids and pets. I sat quietly by her bed, thankful that the slatted shutters were drawn against the intensity of the heat. The back room was a large and airy inner chamber in the hospital house. People buzzed in and out. I felt as if I was in the presence of the queen bee.

The old lady was propped against a pile of pillows, which were tumbled and strewn around her. She seemed serene and unscathed by life's blows. I knew she had led a life as a busy mother and an ayurvedic doctor seeing to the needs of others, but there must have been hardships. I sensed a frail child fading under my clasp as I took her hand. She was disappearing into the delicate shape of a tiny china doll. But her power was not shrunken.

Dr Renade arrived to collect me and we drove through the streets, which swirled with the usual medley of vehicles, people and animals, to the university campus to pick up Dr Dandekar and Dr Paranjape. Entering the campus was like stepping from a noisy, crowded beer bar into a comfortable smart saloon. An abundance of hibiscus and bougainvillaea filled the lawns around the wide approach avenue and fragranced the hot air. I could hear only bicycle pedals, soft voices and birds.

We picked up the others and headed for a government-funded medicinal-plant cultivation centre. Dr Dandekar and I soon established that we had a common cause concerning our approach to the precision with which we used plant products. For his research and practice, carried out in Germany, he required a guarantee of the genus and species of each plant. The properties of *Lavendula spica* would have a different therapeutic action from those of *Lavendula vera*, yet both products were commonly available under the all-embracing label of lavender. Ayurvedic doctors, it seemed, applied the same discretion as an increasing number of aromatherapists in selecting the exact plant variety. Dr Dandekar could produce valid research material only if it was based on a certainty about the correct horticultural classification.

I was pleased to find a comrade-in-arms in what had been a quest among the more discerning aromatherapists in England to encourage producers to define their plant material more accurately. The need to specify which properties were integral to which type of sage or juniper or cypress, for example, and produced which physiological changes when used to treat human disease was hardly recognised in aromatherapy back home.

As we pulled up by a gateway opening to a grass track leading to the centre, our theorising stopped. I hoped that one of the three men would offer me his arm to guide me to the reception building, but I had to call after them: they had wandered off, forgetful and unobservant of my need.

In the director's office we were given water in preparation for the thirst that would sneak up on us as we walked in the grounds. Dr Dandekar warned me sharply in German that it was bound to be tap water and not to take it, so we sat dry-lipped while everyone else slurped and swallowed noisily.

Since I had studied German at university and had lived in Germany for almost a year, I chatted easily with Dr Dandekar in his language. Unlike me, he had no difficulty in following the Indian-English conversation with our hosts that ensued for he had once lived and worked in India. I wished I could understand more of the heavily accented English that most of the doctors and specialists spoke: usually I find languages a source of freedom and can learn them easily. I was relieved to move into the gardens where I could smell and feel rather than plough through a mire of unintelligible gesticulations and words. Until my ear accustomed itself to Indian speech patterns I often found myself deaf-blind.

Around the veranda were clay pots containing various herbs. The director stroked, snapped and pulled off bits of plants. He passed them to me to identify. I felt nervous, like a witness attending an identification parade. I was expected to get it right. Worse, I had not come across some of the plants before. However, it seemed to my companions that since I lacked sight I would therefore be able to perform great olfactory feats. I had met with similar misconceptions before – 'All blind people are musical' is probably the most common fallacy. I didn't like to disillusion my audience but their crass assumptions and unreasonable expectation made me hostile. I didn't even raise the plant samples to my nose. Instead I stared down, turned and rotated the leaves and stalks like someone trying to place a piece in a jigsaw picture. I studied marjoram, basil and mint. The scents passed me by because I had unplugged my nose. The men grouped around me were attentive throughout. Eventually they dispersed, perplexed and disappointed.

I can be stubbornly contrary when a suggestion has arisen that I should be a certain way because I am blind. Some clients have assumed I have a miraculously healing touch. If I had any such gift it would have little to do with whether I could see or not. For the record, I can't sing or play a musical instrument. I can't recognise certain smells and tastes. My fingers lack the sensitivity to read Braille fast enough to make it worth the effort to learn. Yet I have an eye for interior decorating and a love of books and am an artistic flower arranger.

A heightened emotional response to odours, rather than a superior olfactory sensitivity, is the most plausible explanation I have encountered for why some people become very aware of smell. It is known as hyperosmia and has been seen in hysterical patients owing to their extreme emotional state. When I was in the throes of the initial trauma and shock of losing my sight, I felt invaded by the onslaught of both unexpected odour and noise. I found myself vulnerable and exposed, and would recoil from the slightest sudden sound and smell. It was my emotions, not my other physical senses, that had become more acute.

Dr Renade passed me a large gnarled root, solid with twists of coarse twine-like hair hanging at irregular angles. There was no mistaking the smokiness in the depths of the aroma. 'It is a *Vetiveria zizanoides*, vetiver root, from which grows a lemon-scented grass,' he volunteered. 'It is a close cousin of this *Cymbopogon nardus*, citronella.'

I took the long lissome leaves he held out, crushed them in my fingers and released their tangy notes. 'We use both these plants in aromatherapy,' I said, 'but I think the sharper lemon scent of the grass without the acridity of vetiver is also used as an insect-repellent and in household disinfectants.'

'We are doing the same,' said Dr Renade.

Once we started walking and I was no longer the focus of expectation I felt happier to join in with everyone else's appreciation of smell and textures. There was so much variety and abundance that I almost missed another member of the *Cymbopogon* family, *palmarosa*, because its aroma was so gentle and soapy. Further into the gardens, we crossed patches of dry brittle ground and came across the sweet silage-like stench of *Acorus calamus*, calamus, and the more fetid *Valerian officinalis*, valerian. An avenue of eucalyptus trees decongested the hot, stuffy air, while a climbing hedge of jasmine screened the sun with a narcotic haze. Myrrh and frankincense appeared as dried desert trees, hiding their balsamic, resinous perfume a deep within their trunks.

The centre was striving to improve the availability and purity of plant material for ayurvedic medicine. The director said proudly, 'An out-of-tune sitar is not producing melodious music, and a hybridised herb is not giving harmonious health.' They had succeeded here in acclimatising plants from tropical Sri Lanka and from the mountainous heights of Nepal, while maintaining the integrity of each plant's character.

I might have been at an Indian feast rather than in a horticultural centre because the air was so heavily flavoured with combinations of spices, seasonings and fragrances. By the end of the tour my nose was saturated.

Dr Dandekar and I agreed to share a taxi back to Bombay as Dr Renade had not been able to reserve any train seats. We returned to the Hotel Amir where Aunty had spent the day waiting. We haggled with a recalcitrant taxi driver, who tried to charge extra for our bags. The fare to Bombay was fixed but not in the mind of our driver.

I calculated that the journey was about the same distance as it is between London and Oxford, and marvelled that it would take an hour and a half down the motorway in England, while here I was in for a five-hour bone-shaking ride.

Aunty seethed in the sun streaming through the back windscreen. The hot wind blasted through the open side windows and dust coated our clothes, our hair and our skin. She pulled up her sari into a hood around her head and veiled her face. She was tired and crotchety. Nothing would soothe her except a speedier return than was either possible or safe.

The driver certainly did not need any encouragement to hurry or take risks. He was already horning his way along the centre of the road, swerving round bullock carts, people and bicycles to both right and left. We rattled round hairpin bends to the plains below in a do-or-die descent.

We stopped for *chai* in Khopoli, the town at the foot of the hills, because Dr Dandekar was thirsty. Aunty stayed in the car in sullen protest at this further delay. I was torn between the two of them, but curiosity got the better of me and I joined the doctor. Aunty snorted loudly at my betrayal.

Beggars swarmed around the car, pestering, following us to the tin-roofed canteen. It was a primitive shack with a mud floor, wooden bench tables and seats. Dr Dandekar swilled the glasses with water from our own bottled supply before he let the boy pour the steaming *chai*.

I extracted the bill from a plastic tray of fennel seeds. I did not know what lay between me and the counter. Dr Dandekar offered and paid it in the space of my hesitation.

As the heat of the day became less ferocious so did Aunty. She smouldered in her fatigue and discomfort. I felt she had been kept away too long from her home and the surroundings where she rested, confident, in her routines.

Our drive through the barren wastelands of Bombay's industrial suburbs was a brutal contrast to our wanderings through the fecundity of Pune's plant-research centre. Ammonia hung in the air from factory waste pipes and open untreated sewers, while gases puffed into the atmosphere from chimneys turned it caustic.

I was squeezed dry by the detritus of this industrial belt. I scraped the accumulating grime from my skin and flailed at the foggy pollutants in horror as they wafted over my face. This concrete jungle was as bleak and as poisonous as the most devastated city landscape depicted in films of the nuclear aftermath. I looked out of the windows and saw skeletons, not people, dressed in rags, wasted figures crouching in corners, and scurrying down streets. Of course, I told myself sternly, I was imagining things, but I shuddered all the same.

Aunty's imperious tones rose above the hullabaloo of the more vibrant and noisy part of town we had just reached. We stopped, and Aunty chastised the driver for the final ignominy of her day: he would not detour from his regular route to the centre of Bombay to drop us at home in Chembur. Dr Dandekar explained, politely and quietly, that the driver would forfeit his licence if he was seen with passengers out of the area in which he was permitted to work. Aunty was outraged by what she saw as impudence, and got out to summon a rickshaw-wallah to take us the remaining short stretch home. I said a hurried farewell to the doctor as Aunty marched me away.

When we got home Goutam was waiting. He was agitated. Aunty complained to him vociferously in Bengali. I was glad I couldn't understand what she was saying. Dolly yapped nervously, skipped and scooted under our feet. Goutam and I were both embarrassed, so we changed the subject and began to talk of the success of my visit. Then I described how shocked and depressed I had felt by the grime and pollution encircling Bombay. To see how people's lives are blighted by permanent and bleak industrial winters had upset me.

'It is like so, Nicola,' Goutam rationalised. 'Take the people I work for, they have more houses and Rolls-Royce cars than they can count on the fingers of two hands. Now they might be thinking, this poor Goutam living with his one house, driver and servant, doesn't he have a bad time of it? But for me it is very comfortable. And so it plays all the way down the scale. Take John, who earns two thousand rupees a month and lives in a house with no electric or water. He will pity the guy who sleeps on the street by night and begs by day. It depends on what you are used to.'

I lay awake in bed that night, feeling the impact of our drive through the suburbs and slums of Bombay. For the first time I had seen the consequences of importing industrialisation from first-world nations into a third-world country. Slowly my eyes stopped streaming tears of irritation from the clouds of thick black smoke that had belched out of the exhaust of every vehicle and every factory chimney we had passed during the day, but I could still smell the chemicals that coated my skin and taste the dirt lining my tongue even though I had had a bath.

Before I had come here, previous travellers had warned me that it might be hard to cope with the poverty. They had described the shanty dwellings made from sheets of hardboard, tin or sacking. I had now met the maimed and bedraggled beggar-children who scraped at car windows crying, 'Ma, Ma,' or thrust an amputated limb-stump at me. They were the ones paying the price of third-world industrialisation and I had never seen the cost so clearly before.

MADRAS: A PARSEE CALLED PEEROOZE

After only a week the dust and fumes of Bombay had given me a quirky, ambushing sneeze. I had heard that my next stop, Madras, India's fourth largest city, was more like a large village, so I was hoping for some clean air.

I had not wanted to be on another aeroplane, but there I was. Goutam's anxiety about how I would manage once I left him had increased towards the end of my stay. We risked colliding as we approached the obstacles obstructing my onward journey. 'You see, it is like this, Nicola, you will fly to Madras on Tuesday. I will confirm the ticket.' He could not understand that I did not want to fly over great tracts of India in the most modern and convenient manner. I just wanted to gather dust. I wanted to kick my heels all the way down the south-eastern coast from Madras to Madurai, visit all the places in between, trek up into the southernmost Palani hills to the Kodaikanal hill station, and back down the western side to Trivandrum. I wanted my journey to be as pedestrian and as indirect as I could make it.

'How do you think you will get from Madras to this ashram in

Pondicherry?' Goutam had continued. 'And after that why go to Madurai? You can fly straight down to Trivandrum where your next meetings are. There is no need for Madurai.'

'Okay, I can go by train or bus so long as someone puts me on the right one.'

'And who will meet you in Madurai? We are not knowing anyone there. And where will you stay?'

'Things will sort themselves out.'

'It would be dangerous to take a car alone from Pondicherry to Madurai. Is that what you're planning? If there was a breakdown, you would be left alone in the middle of nowhere in the heat. It would be difficult to find a trustworthy driver. You are a young and pretty blonde white woman.'

'Goutam is right thinking,' Aunty had interjected.

I had realised suddenly how overwhelming this was for Goutam. He felt responsible for my safety, because I was a woman travelling alone. I preferred his worrying about the vulnerability of my sex than about my disability.

The experience of travel was as necessary to me as my professional programme. The contacts it gave me with everyday life in different parts of India and the process of getting from meeting to meeting were as important as what I was going to learn about the links between aromatherapy and ayurvedic plant oils in massage treatments. Goutam's fears for my comfort and safety made him meticulous. He behaved like a picture-framer, fastidiously mitring corners and smoothing edges without stopping to consider the painting that the frame was meant to show to its best advantage.

However, I wanted my picture framed, and I was relieved to know that my stay in Madras would be secure. Peerooze, a business friend of Goutam, had agreed to give me a bed and help me follow up my appointments. His cousin, Mehernosh, would meet me at the airport. The arrangement promised another fascinating picture of Indian family life.

I was not used to such solicitude for my welfare: my parents had seldom expressed any concern about my various exploits and this had sometimes felt like a lack of interest, even neglect. I was beginning to enjoy Goutam's attentions, in spite of his attempts to control my movements. His care was reassuring, and I liked the male protectiveness, which made me feel loved rather than patronised. I just wished I could lessen his worry while maintaining his involvement.

Before I boarded the plane for Madras, he said, 'I haven't known Peerooze all that long. He is, shall we say, special.' He chuckled and added, 'You know, it is a question of getting the right people. You can't ask just anyone.'

I squeezed his hand warmly.

The food on the flight was disgusting, and I slopped about with a steaming curry in a silver foil plate. My tongue twisted around something strange: snake, rabbit or rat sprang to mind. Surely, I reasoned, in India of all places, where vegetarianism is respected because of the large Hindu population, my request for a vegetarian meal cannot be misunderstood. Now there was something rubbery in my mouth and I could not bring myself either to swallow or spit.

The stewardess had even asked before serving me, 'Vegetarian or non-vegetarian?' But maybe she had assumed from the colour of my skin that I ate meat. Sight blinds people, I thought angrily. They only use their eyes to confirm their convictions. I swallowed hard, gulping down panic.

Something in my tray felt squashy and squelched when I prodded it. I peered down to see what it was – I still react uselessly in this reflex way. Then I looked to compare my meal with the non-vegetarian one I had heard my neighbour order. Frustrated, I put my fork down and tried to stem my increasingly nauseous imaginings.

'Don't you like Indian cheese?' my neighbour enquired.

My discomfort evaporated. 'No, I am a pure vegetarian and don't eat dairy products.'

He shrugged. 'I am Muslim. My wife is Spanish and is cooking

57

very good paella with lots of shellfishes. We are living in Sri Lanka. Where are you going? Where is your husband? What is that?' he asked, poking my folded white cane stuffed into the magazine net on the back of the seat in front of me.

'That is a stick I use because I can't see.' I amazed myself by how directly I answered.

He did not question me further. Instead, he told me about his family from Sind province and how they split up after Partition in 1947, when many Muslims went west to what became Pakistan or east to Bangladesh, and many Hindus migrated to what is now India. He was returning from Dubai where he had been visiting his brother. I liked how incurious he was about me. Then I was only just brave enough to tell people straight that I could not see, and was tense about the variety of responses it might provoke. In Bombay and Pune I had left Goutam and Aunty to tell those we met that I was blind. When they did so they lowered their voices and spoke in Hindi, Bengali or Marati. After a while I could identify the words for 'She can't see' by the hushed tones in which they were voiced. People everywhere seem to whisper about loss and bereavement because there is awkwardness and fear in the face of pain. It took me a long time to be open about my loss.

I often rely on other people to communicate that I am blind. Most introductions are made by a friend or colleague who, I always assume, has prepared the way. I have no compunction about avoiding the responsibility of telling people that I cannot see: the burden feels halved when it is shared. However, there have been times when I have found myself in the middle of a conversation, getting to know someone, and realised that no one has mentioned my disability in advance: the new acquaintance will say something like 'Isn't the view from here extraordinary?' If I can 'see', in the sense of 'understand', it seems unnecessary to interrupt the flow of conversation. If I did, it would force a change of subject or induce another lengthy discussion about my blindness, which I often don't feel like having. The trouble with not revealing it is that people feel stunned or stupid when they find out.

They feel – unreasonably – that they should have noticed. They may even feel misled and indignant, as they rush back through their memory checking for any indiscretion or insensitivity that might have slipped out in their ignorance.

One of the advantages of having a guide dog in England is that all this confusion and embarrassment is bypassed. The disadvantage is that dog-lovers want to launch into a conversation about the 'lovely *blind* dog'.

In my work I often receive new clients, who will have been referred to me by their friends or my colleagues. In spite of this, some people arrive unaware that I am blind. In our first meeting, I type their case history and reasons for seeking treatment into my computer, which has a speech programme that reads back the information sentence by sentence or word by word as I type. I can usually tell which clients know I am blind from their reaction to the hollow, robotic voice. Those who don't know are mostly too reticent to seek an explanation so I volunteer one. I think some of my more troubled clients are put at greater ease to know that having 'something wrong' is not unique to them.

Increasingly I have come to accept that the need of others to know that I am blind is greater than my need not to tell them so. For a long time I avoided letting people know because it was a way of silencing the loss that surfaced every time I acknowledged it. Yet saying nothing denied a part of me, and the more hidden I kept that part, the more ashamed I was of it. Uninformed people thought my behaviour odd, drunk, mad or bad, and reacted to me with anger. I felt victimised, misunderstood and ostracised until I realised that honest self-disclosure, however painful, would gain me more acceptance. I still catch myself trying to avoid the subject or soften the declaration by letting my dog, computer or friends do the talking.

I did not have symbols like my dog or the computer to signal my blindness to the people I met on my Indian travels. I experimented a little with dark glasses and the cane, but this meant I had to explain myself more, and be open to the varied responses I received while travelling unaccompanied. I was still unskilled and fairly unwilling.

My flight companion pressed a business card into my hand. I stuffed it into the part of my wallet I had allocated to this collection. It was already bulging as hardly anyone did not have one to flourish. It seemed a matter of status and pride. 'I don't have a card. We don't carry them as much as you do,' I apologised, feeling stripped of credentials like a student at a graduation party without a degree. I made a mental note to inform the collators of *The Lonely Planet Guide to India* to mention the importance attached to calling cards in their next edition.

At the airport Mehernosh padded up to greet me. He was a great bulky man, who took up a lot of space in front of me. His huge soft body seemed to smile as he greeted me. His good nature was so genuine that I was not offended when, after ten minutes in Peerooze's flat in central Madras, I heard him telephone Peerooze and gush, 'She is really knowing her way around already!' There was nothing patronising in his admiration. He had just walked me around the flat, where he was also staying, anxiously convinced that I would collide with every piece of furniture and lose my sense of direction in going from one room to the next.

It is difficult for sighted people to conceive of mental-mapping as they rely on seeing rather than storing configurations of data and information. Once I have filed an environment, my mind can extrapolate all sorts of eventualities. Not only can I remember the layout of a new place, but I can also draw conclusions about where certain things may be. Rather like a computer program appearing to be intelligent when merely making connections based on saved data, I may appear to be sighted when mental-mapping.

While I was listening to Mehernosh I was putting my clothes away. From his conversation with Peerooze I knew where the telephone was. When I heard him make tea I located the kitchen and made my way to the table in the central room when he plonked down the cups. I moved with a precision that Mehernosh found disconcerting and I wondered if I should stumble a bit to help him out. I have a well-exercised memory, which is strongly visual: it instantly converts what I sense into visual images. I can still shut my eyes and see the flat today. It had appeared to me almost as quickly as it *felt* to me. It was a disorderly male enclave.

'Do you want to take a walk?' Mehernosh asked, as we finished our tea. I was delighted. I had yearned for more movement and more opportunities to explore since my arrival in India and could not believe my luck. We delayed only long enough for Mehernosh to introduce me to his colourful birds, which he kept in cages on the balcony.

Out in the street below the apartment block, I was struck by how easily I had drawn false conclusions. I had assumed that all houses in India would be in sealed colonies like Goutam's. Now I was walking down the middle of an unmade road with a block of flats followed by large residential bungalows with sprinklers raining on the front gardens. As we approached the end of the road, the houses became taller, double-storey, with noises coming from the upper levels. There were no front gardens here to distance the convivial sounds from the road.

After circumnavigating a cow and a cow-pat we stepped through a gate. Mehernosh had all but waltzed me around these hazards: he could not quite trust my ability to follow him by the light touch I maintained on his elbow. Once through the gate, we arrived on a front-door step. 'This is my friend's house. We will just call and say hello.' As Mehernosh was saying this a tall man materialised and waved us in with offers of tea.

Just inside the house the main room was huge, cool, echoing and dark. It reminded me of a snooker room in a town pub. The television, mounted up on a far wall, boomed and the central fan whirred. Rows of canvas garden chairs lined two sides of the room. Mehernosh and I sat next to each other on one side while his friend, a surgeon, sat smoking on the other. He felt so far away that I got little sense of him, and I could not follow the intermittent, casual exchanges because the noise from the television and the fan obliterated the words. I sensed people milling in the gloom and guessed that servants were waiting for instructions. One brought me tea, which I put on the simple screeded floor.

'My friend here is just back from the United Arab Emirates and may be returning, isn't that right?' Mehernosh must have received a nod in confirmation from his friend as I heard no reply.

I sipped my syrup-sweet tea while catching enough of the general drift of chat to know that the surgeon had gathered, from the way Mehernosh had led me to my seat, that something was odd. Mehernosh was now explaining the situation, proudly stirring up amazement and admiration in his friend, wanting to show me off.

After twenty minutes we left and decided to head for Marina Beach, which stretches from one end of Madras to the other. I realised that Mehernosh, who had come from Bombay to work with Peerooze, was often at a loose end when Peerooze was busy elsewhere.

We jumped into a rickshaw, which scooted in and out of the cars, cows, bicycles, pigs, and people making their way, higgledy-piggledy, through the wide, packed avenues leading to the sea-front. We swung and swerved, slowed and speeded, squeezed through gaps so narrow I thought someone's chicken or child would be toppled on to my knee. Stuck in a jam and crammed so close to the scooter next to us, I heard the rider talk to the woman behind him. Squashed between them was a young child who was shouting a question over the squeal and throb of engines. As the scooter spluttered and stalled in an attempt to move off, another child in front of the rider called on them all to look at something.

Four on a scooter, Mehernosh assured me, was quite normal, with the woman side-saddle behind the rider. It all made sense that, in a place where there were lots of poor people and few affordable luxuries, four should fit on a vehicle made for two. Their saris meant that the women rode side-saddle: it was the only way to remain elegant. Given the gyrations and gymnastics performed on the roads, though, I squirmed at how precarious the seating arrangements were.

'Someone has expired,' Mehernosh said, as I turned to focus my ear on the patter of bare feet amid ringing bells and singing. A flower petal from those strewn by the small family procession following behind the hearse fell on to my lap.

Once at the beach we walked and talked, and enjoyed the evening activity of beach life as the working day ended. The waves folded into the shore, making a scalloped frothy edge that I traced with my foot. A large group of young men applauded one another as they practised acrobatics in the sand. A young girl nudged me with her basket and a waft of fresh jasmine tempted me to buy some from her. Fisherfolk gathered up nets and sat in the setting sun, their boats lying where they had been dragged up on to the sand. These *Swiss Family Robinson* vessels consisted of three long solid slices of a tree, bowed in shape, bound together with strong rope. We sat in the curved middle of one until it became dark, then made our way back to find Peerooze.

As we left the beach I smelt the hurricane lamps that lit the barrows and stalls. A hollow tap, a swish of liquid like milk shaken in a churn, a loud crack and a final split rent the air. 'Do you want to try tender coconut?' Mehernosh asked. As he haggled with the seller, I knew that I would never fail to locate nourishment in India: I would hear coconuts being split. Mehernosh removed the drinking straw in case it was dirty and passed me half a green coconut to savour its rich liquid. Next the coconut man loosened the white flesh with a knife and passed it back to us with a shovel made from some of the shell. I ate nervously - an odd acidity tainted the flavour.

When we arrived Peerooze greeted me warmly. He was separated from his wife, but his two sons visited each evening. Sarosh and Varun, aged twelve and nine, jumped on Mehernosh and clowned around. Peerooze talked a little with me while he blended home-made soup. There were no other indications of effort in the domestic domain: piles of unwashed dishes, empty bottles and half-empty paper packets of all shapes and sizes filled every bit of work surface I touched.

'Hey, Mehernosh,' he called, 'still no maid to clean up this place. We'll have to find someone else. Susan has someone, I think.' He turned to me and continued, 'You will be meeting Susan so she can take you around a bit. She is a very special woman.'

Susan was a charity worker who ran a crèche to finance some of her aid work in two tribal villages outside Madras. She also promoted and sold the handicrafts the villagers made. To do this, she had given up her role as a partner in a firm of solicitors.

Later that evening we swept into the drive of the Taj Hotel to pick up one of Peerooze's clients. The car door was opened by a doorman, stiff in his formal, ornate uniform. The burst of brightness coming from within the foyer made my pupils contract. It was the first evidence I had had of the opulence and shimmer for which these great Indian hotels were so famous. Peerooze's guest, Rajiv, climbed into the car.

We ate a green pea curry and a *bindi* – okra – curry with *tandoori rotis* in the gardens of the Madras Club. It was the first really hot food I had sampled in India. Until then, I had tasted only home cooking, which was less pungent and spicy. I suspected that more westerners than Indians enjoy the eye-streaming, sweat-pouring blast of chilli-invested dishes.

Rajiv was cool and clipped: he was full of distrust and cynicism, which had been absent in the Asians I had come to know. His business travels and fraught endeavours to set up factories in Leicester and Brighton seemed to have diluted his natural candour. He sounded disingenuous about his dealings and distrustful in his opinions, and I wondered what subtle forms of racism he had endured. At eleven thirty we dropped him back at the hotel, and Peerooze announced that we were on our way now to see Susan, who had been expecting us all evening.

She opened the door in her nightdress, and we three piled into her one room. Peerooze apologised for the lateness of the hour. I guessed that Susan was not surprised by Peerooze's chaotic time-keeping, because she had been his friend since their college days. Although

Susan was expecting to meet and help me, I was not sure how much time she could spare to be my chaperone, but she was unhesitating and agreed straight away to go with me the next day to the Indian Medical Practitioners' Co-operative, Pharmacy and Stores (IMPCOPS), a siddha medical centre. Siddha is a variation on the theme of ayurveda, but uses substances other than plant materials, which ayurveda uses exclusively.

Sleep was scarce in the company of Peerooze, and I no longer rued the inactivity and immobility of my first few days in India. The next morning I joined him for his dawn constitutional, a brisk walk around the block at six a.m. Between greeting fellow early-morning exercisers, he told me that that he, a Parsi, had wed a Hindu for love rather than undergoing an arranged marriage. Despite their culturally different backgrounds, they had tried to live together harmoniously, but they had had to compromise constantly over food, dress, the rituals of daily life to such an extent that he had become in favour of arranged marriages, which aimed to match attitudes and ways of life. Love, in a society so clearly defined by cultural and family parameters, had not been enough to keep him and his wife together.

When we got back to the flat it was already seven thirty, the time we had planned to leave. Peerooze was unflustered, so I decided to telephone A.V. Balasubramanian of the Sree Chakra Foundation. Dr Renade of Pune had told me he was an authority on the alternative medical traditions of the Madras area. We arranged to meet on the following day. Making things happen in India seemed unusually easy, provided I did not expect them to happen on time.

First I went with Peerooze to his office to collect my train ticket for Trivandrum. Although I would not be making the journey that week, I needed to reserve my ticket well in advance. This had been done for me the previous day by one of Peerooze's office boys. I was horrified that I was fifth in line on a waiting list. Five people would have to cancel their tickets before I could be guaranteed a seat! Everyone reassured me that being fifth was promising. The odds were apparently in favour of five people cancelling their travel plans. However, I would be in Pondicherry over the weekend and not in Madras to get confirmation for my ticket, so we decided that I should return to the station and buy a tourist quota ticket. These were reserved for foreigners and were issued with immediate travel confirmation. The office boy was scolded for not getting one of these tickets in the first place. His ignorance of the foreigner's privileged status was no excuse.

'I will send someone with you and Palani, the driver, not this boy, someone who can speak English and is knowing what to do,' Peerooze said.

'Why two people? Can't the driver help me?'

'He has to stay with the car.'

Convention was such that a driver did not run errands and an office boy did not drive. I was introduced to P. S. Natyasangham. Peerooze told him that I would take his arm and he should let me follow. Once in the car, Palani and P. S. Natyasangham chatted in Tamil, which sounded more sing-song and happier than the Hindi or Marati I had heard so far. They conducted their conversation like an orchestral piece with vigorous gesticulations. Their heads danced in energetic half-nods and half-shakes and their fingers tap-tapped their speech rhythm on handy surfaces like the dashboard or steering-wheel.

I suspected that the nonchalance these two men had shown me belied how perplexed by me they felt. I thought it would be better to try to use my cane and not rely simply on P. S. Natyasangham to assist me through the railway station. This was my first visit to an Indian station, and if the elbowing crowds and bulldozing were as bad as they were reputed to be, I would need all the help I could get.

The crowd was so dense that my cane rebounded off ankles, bags, children, prostrate bodies and rubbish. My guide tried to direct it by lurching for the end of it and pointing it in another direction to avoid whatever it was about to hit. Due to the vast number of obstacles, he was swooping down every ten seconds. When we reached a flight of stairs he bent to scoop up the cane lest it knocked against the edge of each step. Consequently the cane hovered in mid-air above each step so I had no idea of where or how high each one was. He treated it as though it was a lazy limb that he had to protect along with the rest of me

We queued for ages but not as long as other westerners because my Indian guide knew how to queue-jump, one of the imperatives of Indian life. The right word in the right ear was like having the right change for a drinks machine. A few English youths bleated in the background as I slipped my cane in front and made my way to the desk. The Indian official cooed in wonderment when P. S. Natyasangham explained why he had to fill in my forms for me, 'She is travelling alone?'

I booked a second-class air-conditioned sleeper for the seventeen-hour journey to Trivandrum. I had relinquished my hope of hiring a car and driver to go south, which had meant forfeiting the chance to visit Madurai and the south-eastern corner of Tamil Nadu. I had succumbed to the combined objections of Goutam and Peerooze, and noticed again that my drive for independence was weakening. To satisfy my lust for adventure on the road to Madurai would have left my friends in constant anxiety.

When I had my ticket, we picked up Susan from the crèche and left Mr Natyasangham to his next job. She was slight and swift in movement and her diaphanous sari enhanced my impression of fluidity and weightlessness. She was concerned that I had missed breakfast and lunch and insisted that we stop to stock up on oranges, biscuits and water.

We did not have an appointment to see Professor Dr P. Jeyaprakash Narayanan of IMPCOPS but this did not seem to bother anyone. Susan said, 'We will wait,' and we did, outside the doctor's room. After a while a man came out and left the building. We waited. Clearly Susan was determined – and reconciled – to wait in a way I never could, apparently unperturbed by the coming and going around us while I lived in hope that every movement and sound might signal a summons for us to enter the room.

I fidgeted, flitted my head about and got hot and exasperated. Eventually I persuaded Susan to ask again if the doctor was likely to be available soon. I heard the receptionist repeat the answer she had given when we arrived, 'So very soon, very soon, please just sit, be comfortable.'

Susan preferred to endure the wait rather than travel back through heat, crowds and dust to return at another time. She understood that an 'appointment' in India was merely an agreement to meet; the agreed timing, however exact at the point of arrangement, would always be down to fate. People were sidetracked, delayed or taken up with the unpredictable and chaotic distractions of an overpopulated and under-resourced country. Everyone was always unhurriedly engaged by the call of the moment, whether it be lunch, a visit or a sick friend, rather than commitment to any prearranged agreement. As a stressed westener, accustomed to being managed by a clock, I found this initially charming but was soon maddened by the unpredictability.

My meeting with Dr Narayanan was brief and unremarkable. Once again I was baffled by an accent and came away with a vague notion that siddha medicine, his speciality, was a variation on the theme of ayurveda. There was an additional communication difficulty in south India: Tamils respond rhythmically to questions with silent nods and headshaking. Although I can distinguish the movement of a nod from a shake, it was impossible to tell what was meant when answers came in the form of frantic head-waggling.

However, Dr Narayanan was proud to present himself and his hospital for our inspection. He talked most about the siddha cure for Aids. I was surprised that I had not heard of such a breakthrough, but tried to reserve judgement until somebody could read aloud the report he handed me. He also suggested I would benefit from a two-to three-month stay in the hospital to start restoring my sight. He made it all seem so simple, like dropping in at the lost-and-found desk in a public building. My scepticism was founded in an unwillingness to revisit the disappointment and exhaustion of the fruitless search for a cure to my condition. Lost sight is rarely returned.

The doctor prescribed two oils for me to be applied in a massage to be given the following day. I accepted because I wanted to experience the masssage techniques by feeling what was done to me. Susan asked for a prescription to treat her spondylosis, a degenerative condition of the spine, which caused pain in her upper back. We headed for the pharmacy, which was a long wooden counter behind which men rushed between metal shelves stacked with brown bottles. The pharmacist tried to induce me to buy concoctions that had supposedly made the blind see, but I collected only the oils for my massage. I was given one oil for use on the body and one for the head massage, which, the pharmacist insisted, would stimulate my optic nerves.

As we walked through the extensive grounds to the main gates where we would find a rickshaw, an American woman approached us.

'Hi, are you guys staying here too? I'm just on my walk. Want to join me?'

'Actually we're just leaving.' But I stopped. I was curious to know what had attracted a foreigner to become an inmate here.

'Oh, it's just fine. I come for a couple of months every winter to see to the joints. It's the joints, you know. They know about joints here. Still I'm kinda ready to go now. I'll miss the massage but the oils are kinda stinky.'

We flagged down a rickshaw to take us to Susan's office. When she instructed him to turn his meter on, he became sulky. Suddenly Susan shouted, 'Stop!' pulled me out and thrust money into his hand. He was taking us for a ride about town to increase the fare. Susan was not from Madras, and he had mistaken her accent as an invitation to profit from a passenger who did not know the town's geography. We stood in the road, which was swarming with other rickshaws pap-papping incessantly, zipping in and out of cars and cows. It was as if we had suddenly found ourselves standing among dodgems in a fairground where collision is part of the fun.

It was already late afternoon and I was concerned about being late for my four-thirty appointment with Sri Balasubramanian of the Sree Chakra Foundation. Peerooze was to collect me from Susan's office. When we got back there was no sign of him.

There was still no Peerooze by five o'clock. To pass the time, Susan began to read the opening to the introduction of Dr Narayanan's report on Aids, 'The dreadful disease Aids, a clinical manifestation of unbridled sexual activity, is now threatening the entire nook and corner of the planet earth.' It was worthy of a Hindi movie.

Eventually Mehernosh turned up, breathless and full of apologies, in Peerooze's place, and we hurried out. Our rickshaw-wallah failed to locate the right building and happily drove round in ever-increasing circles. I suggested getting out and searching on foot, so we wandered along quiet residential roads asking for directions every few minutes. Each person we stopped advised us with great confidence, pointing with conviction and a well-wishing smile, and we were guided to a large variety of locations. The only thing that all these places had in common was that they were not the Foundation. We returned home.

That evening Peerooze, Mehernosh, the children and I had dinner with Peerooze's aunt, an imposing lady afflicted with diabetes, glaucoma, deafness and arthritis. She kept a large, beautiful house, which she had built herself and ran with the help of retainers who had been in her service for twenty years. She must have been formidable when she worked as a district medical adviser. During the meal she supervised the ribaldry of the male quartet, while encouraging Varun to eat his egg dish – 'A good Parsi loves his eggs.' He ate his eggs, the black gram dal, drumsticks – a tubular, bitter vegetable – spinach *bhaji*, green beans and *paneer* with a gusto that had more to do with the promise of *shrikhrand* for dessert than out of any religious loyalty. Later he spooned down the sweet thick curd flavoured with cardamon and saffron as his reward.

We made another midnight visit to Susan to enlist her help in the next day's plans. Peerooze had to be at work so she agreed to wait at IMPCOPS while I had the massage, although this meant she would

70

have to delay her departure for one of the tribal villages north of Madras where she ran a project. Peerooze promised to bring me over to her early in the morning so that her journey would not be pushed back even further into the heat of the day. The following morning, despite his good intentions, we were – predictably – late yet I did not discern a flicker of irritation in Susan. Peerooze drove us to the hospital, and decided to stay anyway and consult a doctor about his back problems. Susan's day had been needlessly hijacked, but Peerooze seemed as heedless of this as I was embarrassed. Susan remained unconcerned.

The massage took place in a side building behind the office and the pharmacy. The waiting room in which we sat had a concrete floor and bare walls. Peerooze chatted to a couple sitting next to him and was impressed to learn that the wife, who had been coming every day following a stroke, had noticed a vast improvement in her mobility. I clutched my bottles of oil and grinned nervously at my companions. Then I heard Peerooze telling someone, 'She can't see, you will have to show her the way.' No one came to me and offered their arm for guidance, and I had no intention of blundering in the direction of the voice. There was a paralysing moment of embarrassment, broken by Susan, who manoeuvred the masseuse and me on our way through a ragged curtain.

My masseuse was small and chubby and pulled me to the end of a long room where her colleague was waiting. They laughed in a general badinage from which I felt excluded. As if in afterthought one said, 'Clothes off.' I heard her arms rub up against her plastic apron as she swept them up in a gesture to indicate instructions to undress.

I could not work out whether she was indicating yes or no when I asked, 'Shall I take my knickers off?' so I left them on, hanging my clothes on a solid wooden screen that separated my massage area from the next.

I slipped around eel-like on a wide wooden table with an inch-high lip to stop the oil running on to the concrete floor. It was crude compared to my padded couch at home, which has an electric bar-switch control to alter the working height. I heard a burner and realised that my oils were being warmed. Then one of the women ladled about half a pint over my body. I felt warm and slippery, like a piece of soap ready to slide through the masseuses' hands every time they squeezed and wrung my limbs. I could not imagine oiling any of my clients so lavishly at home unless I moved my equipment into the bathroom. The dessertspoon of oil I use is about as greasy as most of my clients would care to be made.

The women working on me thought my appendectomy scar was from a Caesarean section: 'How many children?' they asked. They assumed I was a mother because producing babies was what most Indian women did once they reached maturity. As they chatted across me, they synchronised long, one-handed, flowing strokes. They included a few basic manipulations of my shoulder and knee joints, bending, flexing and extending. The massage was unsystematic by comparison with the routine common to massage in the West of moving muscles in specific directions.

I wanted to rub oil out of my eyes but my hands were dripping and likely to make them worse. Basted like a Christmas turkey, I was motioned to sit up and swivelled round so that my legs dangled over the side of the couch. The back massage was done in a sitting position, which I did not find very relaxing. I pointed out a particular stiffness in the upper area of my back, which the masseuse obligingly rubbed; but she did not know how to ease and tease the muscle free. The curative nature of the treatment was clearly the oiling, not the expertise in bodywork. Once I had accepted this, I enjoyed a glorious head massage with a musty-smelling oil and felt revived, like lettuce being transformed into a salad with ample amounts of well-fermented French dressing.

The last stage was a series of warm poultices soaked in oil, which were gently thumped over my entire body. Finally the excess oil was scraped off with sharp-edged banana leaves. 'Bathroom, come, come, where is your towel?' I had no towel but was delighted to hear there was a bathroom where I could clean up before dressing. 'Sit, sit.' The masseuse pushed me down on a wooden stool, which was only ankle height. The time had come to part with my knickers. With my knees reaching my neck I sat with a huge bucket in front of me while the woman fetched a small grubby towel. She filled the bucket with hot water and poured jug after jug of water over me. I was scrubbed with gritty chickpea soap. She was alarmingly thorough, missing not an inch of my anatomy, but I was left to dry myself. My knickers lay in a pool of water on the floor, wet and greasy. I dressed and left knickerless, feeling like a horse, strapped and power-hosed after a training session. I was loose and limber, if still a little slippery – and I would remove my knickers for future Indian massages.

I made a plan to be massaged around India. It promised to be enjoyable and the best way for me to learn. I intended to volunteer for every treatment as I had to feel what I could not see. I had no notion of what I would discover in the way of aromatic and sensual delights, but I wanted to experience as much as possible as I felt my way through the months ahead.

Susan had relinquished all hope of keeping to her arrangements that day, so Peerooze took us both to the Sree Chakra Foundation. He had rearranged the appointment I had missed the previous day and was delighted by how easily we found the Sree Chakra, gloating that Mehernosh was a 'hopeless buffoon'. We slipped off our shoes and kicked them into a pile of *chapples* – sandals – by the narrow stairs. A large open-plan attic was full of people busying themselves.

The director, Sri Balasubramanian, greeted us warmly: 'Call me Balu. I will send out for some cold drinks.' He continued, 'This is Dr Shyam Sundar of the Lok Swasthya Parampara Samvardhan Samithi [LSPSS] who is working with us. The *samithi* is an organisation working to reconstruct local health traditions. He is an ayurvedic doctor so can be most helpful to you.' Balu stepped back and I sensed a slight downward sweep as Shyam bent forward and greeted me traditionally with his hands in a prayer position. I was struck by the contrast between the two men: Balu was small and agile while Shyam was large and lumbering.

The Sree Chakra was an institution devoted to higher education and research on Indian heritage, science and technology. Shyam was there from the LSPSS, which was an all-Indian network of individuals and groups, committed to reviving the indigenous systems of health care and the widespread folk health traditions that had existed for centuries throughout Indian society but had lost their popularity in more recent times.

'After lunch Shyam will go with you to some of our traditional healers. He is from central southern India where you say you will be continuing your researches, so he can give you some contacts, eh, Shyam? We can get you something from outside for lunch because we have all brought food from home.' Balu's invitation was so spontaneous and considerate that I felt inspired and optimistic. He was one of the few professionals whose accent I had no difficulty in understanding.

Before everyone gathered to eat Peerooze and Susan left. I was introduced to a series of people as they came to sit with their tiffin carriers dangling from their arms. There were the sounds of stainless-steel mugs, flasks and metal dishes clanging gently as water was poured, and rice and vegetable dishes doled out. A rustle indicated that my lunch had arrived. The unwrapped newspaper, in which it was packed, served as a tablecloth, while the banana leaves folded around my *dosa* flattened out to make a disposable plate. The *dosa* tasted nothing like the pancakes sold as *dosas* in England. It was stuffed with a blend of potatoes and onions, crispy on one side, softer and more doughy on the other. There was a coconut chutney, which I discovered dolloped at the top of my banana leaf, and which I wished I had left undiscovered because it was so hot. I was told that the batter used to make *dosas* is a parboiled ground rice and *urad dal* – split peas – left to ferment overnight. Breads made of fermented rice are nourishing and highly digestible. They are the breads of the south, whose staple is rice, rather than the north, which is wheat-based. This was my first meal without wheat *chapattis*.

Shyam sat by me and talked about his work while I nimble-fingered my food into mouth-size balls. 'I am the technical adviser on a publishing project partly funded by central government. We are producing monographs, small books to inform people about Indian plant science or various types of traditional medicine like ayurveda, siddha or unani. We have also run workshops for orthodox medics to teach them about alternative health traditions and how they work. If they see they are viable, they may stop trying to replace traditional methods with modern ones. Even the World Health Organisation sends midwives to tribal villages to retrain traditional birth attendants to use modern primary-health-care techniques. They never stop to think that these people have the tried and tested knowledge of aeons. Their methods should be extended and adjusted, not obliterated as worthless.'

'Can we get to see any of the village healers at work?'

'I will ask Dr Dharmalingam, who we are going to see now. He is the fourteenth generation of varma specialist in his family and comes from the deep south. But it will be difficult as even I have not been to these remote places.'

Dr Dharmalingam ran his own clinic called Dharma in Madras. As we sat in the waiting area a man hopped past on one leg and a crutch. Dr Dharmalingam was a siddha doctor and specialised in varma, which is similar to marma therapy, as practised in ayurveda. Varma and marma techniques are like acupressure whereby pressure is exerted on specific points, 'marma points', as it is believed that blockages are released and healing processes stimulated.

Dr Dharmalingam was young and enthusiastic. He expressed vibrancy and verve through a stream of gestures. He communicated with his hands, gesticulating energetically with each finger. I was transfixed by the vibrations he made, clawing and patterning the air as he spoke, and Shyam translated. His dancing fingers gyrated and emphasised his explanations with dexterity and precision.

I was enchanted by his exuberance, although I ignored his inevitable offer of treatment for my eyes: twenty-one sittings would apparently be enough to get some improvement. Proudly he showed me the centuries-old Sanskrit manuscripts recording the knowledge of his art, which had been passed down to him. They were written on parchment and tied with palm leaves. He seemed to forget that I could not see them until Shyam reminded him. He said it was written in the manuscripts that a terrible disease spread by sexual promiscuity would emasculate and eventually annihilate mankind, and he claimed that varma therapy had the potential to cure Aids. I was more excited by his research work into yoga *asanas,* or postures, and how they altered the energy that passed through varma points.

That evening, Peerooze and I planned to travel down the coast south to Pondicherry, where I was to visit the Aurobindo ashram. Peerooze had organised some business visits *en route* for the next day. I was glad that he had decided to accompany me, and spare me a bus journey at the end of which there would have been no one to meet me, for now I was stepping into less charted territory. I had arranged my stay at the ashram by letter from England, but now I had experienced Indian attitudes to seemingly firm commitments. I was nervous, anticipating the difficulties I might encounter, alone and with no personal contacts, if the ashram had forgotten about me.

PONDICHERRY: MANOB AND THE AUROBINDIANS

'Pull over.' Peerooze's tone was imperative and I was shocked. There was an urgency in it that I could not explain.

We were entering Pondicherry, approaching through the shade of banyan trees that lined a long, straight road. I was relaxing to the sound of tinkling bells and the soft whooshing of bicycle wheels. The breadth and straightness of the town's boulevards were strikingly different from any other Indian road I had yet encountered. Pondicherry is a former French colony and is now one of India's union territories directly answerable to Delhi, and independent from the Tamil Nadu administration, but it had clearly retained some individual character from its conception and history.

'Well, my friend, you've done it this time. Wind down the glass.' Peerooze's reproof to Palani was gentle but ominous. He wound down his own window and spoke in Tamil to a policeman. They fell into English every so often and I worked out that Palani had driven straight through a red light.

'Tambi, he is foolish, what can I do? What do you want?' Peerooze was placatory, protesting his driver's guilt rather than pretending any innocence or extenuating circumstance. To mollify the stonily silent policeman he held a wad of money low in his lap. I heard him peel back the notes. The policeman told his fellow officer to signal the traffic to skirt round where we were stopped. This was unnecessary, given the width of the road and free flow of vehicles: it was simply a means of keeping a look-out lest they were caught taking a bribe. He moved to my side of the car, which was away from the street. Peerooze talked and peeled back notes until the policeman reached across and took them. Peerooze had set about this process as if he was bargaining in a bazaar. It was nothing unusual. The police were enthusiastic about spotting minor traffic offences.

I wanted to learn the 'going rate' and was annoyed that I could not see what denominations Peerooze was counting out. He did not answer my impertinent question about how much it had cost him, just said, 'It is worth it because it would cost me more by the time I would be in and out of the police station, waiting for hours and filling forms. If I objected, they would have seen to it that I paid for it anyway. But now *you* will pay for it, my friend Palani.' I did not know whether he was serious or not.

The ashram and its community dominated Pondicherry; the buildings and facilities sprawled across the town, rather like an English university extending beyond its campus boundaries. We located the registration office where Peerooze intended to leave me, only to find that the booking clerk had not been informed of the special nature of my visit. I had exchanged letters with Harikant, a guardian of the ashram, to arrange to see their physiotherapy and massage work and the use they made of oils in their 'cottage industry' or workshops. Harikant had confirmed that he could accommodate me, my interests and my need for assistance. I was worried that they did not seem to be expecting me.

The girl at the desk took my passport and checked me in as a foreign visitor – many came to take part in ashram life, to attend lectures and meetings. She seemed indifferent to my circumstances, and my anxiety mounted but I fell into gloom instead of erupting in anger. I noted that her English was good, and Indians were also speaking French just outside the office.

Eventually the girl found my booking but insisted that no arrangements had been made for my stay other than the normal room reservation and meal-ticket provision, for which she asked me to pay. I could not listen to the instructions about mealtimes and the whereabouts of the dining hall: I was too horrified by the prospect of making my way unassisted across town to some crowded refectory. I pictured myself blundering through the diners with plates crashing and people shouting. Dal would splash and splatter on the walls. People would skate and slide on a sea of slopped curry and I would be crumpled among the commotion and carnage. My anxiety made me petty and I refused her meal-tickets, insisting she should deduct their cost from the bill, which was less than a pound a day anyway.

For the first time I felt utterly forlorn and in need of a companion. I had been on enough hectic, disorderly streets without pavements and full of potholes to feel unequal to the challenge of managing alone. I knew Pondicherry was laid out in a uniform grid plan and would be easier than other Indian towns, but even so, a few more pavements and a few straight lines were not going to quell the turmoil of life on the streets.

Peerooze was far more presumptuous and brash than I, determined to tease out the girl's better nature: 'Can't you find someone to help her around?'

'We have things of our own to be doing.' She left the room with a stack of papers.

When she returned Peerooze persisted, 'For a just a little help, someone could be earning pocket money, a few rupees.'

I doubted that an Aurobindo devotee would take kindly to his swashbuckling behaviour. This was a self-sufficient community in which everything was provided. The girl was peremptory and dismissive.

I girded myself to keep to my plans. My fall-back position had always been surrender. If my journey became too difficult or unpleasant, I would take the next aeroplane home. There had never been a set number of destinations or a time frame that would decide the success or failure of my trip. I felt that I could return home at any time still having benefited from the act of going.

Now that I had reaffirmed in my mind that there was an easily available escape route and no shame involved in taking it, my resolve was galvanised enough to continue. I was just about to start reassuring Peerooze when the girl said absentmindedly, 'There is a young man assigned to take you around, to show you what you have come to see. He is coming now. He is Manob.' Had she known this all along or just been told? Was she so insensitive to my vulnerability? By then I was too furious to feel any sense of relief.

I was still learning that in India anything was possible. At home, surviving as a blind person had made me resourceful in combating problems and not accepting the sighted person's definition of 'impossible'. To me 'impossible' was a dare, and 'inadvisable' positive encouragement; the words 'brave' and 'foolish' are often interchangeable before an outcome is known. I avoided and denied the difficulties I couldn't fight, and I had acquired some skills in the art of circumnavigation. In India, though, there was a new, less active but equally fruitful tactic to be learned, which was to wait persistently until the solution appeared. Insistent passivity and a belief that there are 'No full stops in India' is how most Indians arrive at what they want. Indians wait. They accept their situation while stubbornly waiting for it to change. Even young children are imbued with an attitude to life that cultivates patience and tolerance. They put up with the discomfort of heat or hunger without any murmur of complaint.

We were directed to the top floor of the building from which the cottage industry operated. As we climbed the stairs I smelt incense and sandalwood from the workshops. My room was clean and simple, with a bed, chair and table. Doors opened on to a long balcony that ran round the top of the building. The attached bathroom had an Indian squat toilet and a cold-water shower. Peerooze came out of the bathroom and said, 'You must drink more water. Your urine smells acidic.' He was so unashamedly direct that I could not find the words to protest that I *was* drinking a lot but when travelling I had to balance my water consumption with the lack of loos. I knew I would miss Peerooze, and I hoped to see him again in Coimbatore later on my travels. His parents lived there and he had already arranged for me to stay with them while I was visiting the area. He frequently went home to work with his father.

It was mid-afternoon and Peerooze still had customers to see before he returned to Madras that evening, yet he insisted on taking me over to the café for some tea before he left. Back at my room, we casually exchanged cheerios, and I was alone. I wandered out to the balcony, leant on the rough concrete ledge and took a deep breath. I had passed out of the hands of friends into those of strangers. From the square below, the rhythmic hop and jump of children playing hopscotch rebounded up to me on the thick evening air. Like a maudlin Rapunzel I wanted to unfurl my hair down to the street for my knight to climb up. My imprisonment, though, was not about locked doors and towers, but an unnavigable world.

The lightest of taps on the door pulled me back to reality and Manob came into the room. My anxieties subsided. He was tall and slim – this was particularly noticeable as I had grown accustomed to the smaller, stockier build of the south Indians, whose voices came directly at me rather than travelling down from above. At only five feet two (and a half!), I had relished the opportunity to feel as tall as, if not taller than, those around me. Manob had a gentle, reassuring voice, which calmed me after the heat and tension of my arrival. He did not stay long but confirmed that he would return over the weekend to show me the workshops where the ashram packaged their oils and herbs for sale, and to introduce me to their physiotherapist. He said that a boy called Ranjan would come to take me to the nearby café for meals. If I wanted to visit the town or the beach, Ranjan would see to that too. I busied myself with unpacking and showering.

The night before, Peerooze and I had sat in the back of his Ambassador, while Palani drove south along the coast. Ambassadors dominate Indian roads and their dated bulk, despite the new models that come on to the market periodically, creates an ambience of the forties or fifties. Everyone travels at thirty-five or forty miles per hour: swerving around goats, people and buffalo carts means there is never a clear stretch on which to accelerate even if the car is up to it, which it usually isn't. Drivers indicate their intention to overtake by bleeping their horns. Peerooze told me that 'Horn, please' signs are pinned to the back of lorries so that the drivers know when someone is coming up behind and wants to overtake. Mirrors are strictly decorative. However, no driver ever pulls over, because they have become inured to the incessant horn blasts.

Peerooze had known that I wanted to visit the coast and Mahabalipuram, a seaside town famous for its stone-carvings. He had made sure that this touristic foray dovetailed with both of our itineraries. First, that evening, we dined in the beach restaurant belonging to the Taj group's five-star hotel in Covelong. It was a secluded fish restaurant where my hands rested on a starched white tablecloth, and I slipped off my shoes to sift the cool sand through my toes. We had meandered our way through palm trees and down the terraces around the hotel's swimming-pool until the clink of cutlery and ring of laughter from the poolside diners were replaced by the rush of waves on the shore. The cooking fires crackled, and the evening was glorious: it was warm yet full of the wind that made the palm fronds sway and rustle. The fresh sea breeze fanned us as we ate. Afterwards we scuffed along the beach, letting the sea swill our feet. I waded in far enough to convince myself that this was the warmest sea I had ever experienced under moonlight.

When we returned to the car, Palani was sprawled out asleep on the back seat with the doors wide open. Peerooze gave him the doggy bag he had asked the waiter to make up from the remains of our dinner. I was concerned that Palani would be insulted, but Peerooze knew he would enjoy the good food.

Further along the Covelong road we stopped at Silver Sands, a resort of bungalows with a central restaurant, bar and dance area on the beach. Peerooze wheedled a cottage for us for the night. Amazingly, he happened to know the proprietor, which clinched the deal – and the discount. He had already asked me if I minded sharing a cottage for the night. I didn't know what that might mean in terms of sleeping arrangements but I agreed. I wondered whether there would be two bedrooms and if there was a subtext in Peerooze's question. He asked Palani if he wanted to sleep on the veranda, but Palani seemed embarrassed and went off to where the hotel staff and visiting drivers ate and slept.

The cottage turned out to be a large, simple single room with a sitting area, bathroom, kitchenette and a large double bed with a mosquito net hanging over it. In the sitting area a large, double-seated south Indian swing hung from the ceiling.

I undressed in the bathroom, put on my thin sarong and darted to the bed, where I lay with the sheet wrapped firmly around me. Water splashed in the bathroom where Peerooze was taking his turn in the shower. I wondered what Palani thought the arrangement between Peerooze and me might be. Then I wondered what an Indian woman would have done in such a situation, and concluded that she would probably not have been travelling alone with a man anyway. Finally, I dared to wonder about Peerooze's intentions. I had not contemplated, let alone experienced, romance since before I lost my sight. I had lost so much self-esteem that I had not entertained the possibility that a man might find me feminine and attractive, rather than asexual and blind. But however awkward and unskilled I felt, I knew I didn't desire Peerooze.

He slipped into bed beside me, a soapy smell and a warm weight. He leant over and kissed me good night. 'What is it like sleeping next to a strange man?' I was uncertain whether this was an attempt to gauge my interest. A provocative reply seemed unwise. Peerooze went on to compliment my long blonde hair covering the pillow and shifted his weight about in the small bed. I turned over and shrank to the edge, half expecting to have to leap out if I felt a tentative hand rest on me. There was a silence, which I broke with a cheerful yet affirmative 'Good night.' I fell asleep reassured in the status quo of our friendship.

The previous night seemed a long way from the approaching one as I sat tired and alone in my room. Then from the open balcony door I heard someone call, 'Hello there, can I enter?' A small-framed woman stood close to me and said, 'You can write. You write beautifully, but you don't see what you write?'

She had been looking at the letters I had begun before I had drifted off in thought about the last twenty-four hours with Peerooze. I bristled at both her observation and that I had been observed. Blindness tends to evoke fascination and moves people more often to curiosity than to pity, and they watch, often thinking that they cannot be seen to be watching. I don't like being studied and I often sense when it is happening.

'I am a nun from South Korea and I thought you might need some help. Would you like to go to dinner? I have been here and in other ashrams because I have a sabbatical year.'

I warmed to her. I liked her robes, which were full and soft compared with the light, silky slither of the saris to which I had become accustomed. She talked more about her sabbatical year and then left, accepting that I had made other plans for dinner.

That morning Peerooze and I had been in the still warm sea at sunrise. I had run wildly along the empty beach, confident that there was nothing to bump into. I am always exhilarated by a spurt of energy when I can move unattached to someone's arm, a dog or a cane.

Then Peerooze had shown me round the shore temples carved out of rock. The carvings were well defined to the touch, but touching objects is not the way I assimilate information best. Just being within the ancient site, absorbing the atmosphere and visualising the descriptions I was given, allowed me to appreciate and enjoy it.

The site was full of groups of schoolchildren, who were more interested in me than in the ancient remains of their Pallavan heritage. The girls and boys grouped themselves according to sex with the boys' voices dominating the foreground of what felt like a monument of children. I offered to photograph them, which caused high excitement and a lot of pushing and shuffling until suddenly silence reigned to signal their readiness. Then there was only the motionless pose of hundreds of children, until the camera click released them into scurrying, giggling particles of energy scattering in all directions.

We were sold moonstones by one of the many stall-wallahs who had a trestle table laid with trinkets. The moonstones were fake, but it did not matter because Peerooze had knocked the price down to a negligible amount anyway. The vendor was delighted to think we believed his stones were the real thing. Peerooze knew how to bargain: if the price stuck too high he would stroll off with a dismissive wave and pricked ears, but he had calculated precisely the desired effect. A cry would haul him back only if it was followed by the price he had originally offered.

There were monkey-handlers, food-sellers and beggars. 'You have two arms and two legs. You should not be begging,' Peerooze told children, kindly but firmly, who approached for money. They would stick to him limpet-like until he repeated his admonishment four or five times, and in almost as many languages to ensure that they understood. As we left he dropped some coins into the hand of an elderly cripple propped by a telegraph pole.

Our final stop that morning was in Chingleput, a dusty town with a factory on the outskirts where Peerooze had a meeting. I waited in the car. A siren howled and a stream of workers poured past me. I heard each man being frisked as he passed through the clanging metal gate. My attention was caught by the sound of a skateboard rolling by on the gravel and scraping to a halt. A match was struck at ground level, there was a sudden whiff of spiralling smoke, and the skateboard rattled away. I realised that a man with no legs was paddling his way home for lunch.

Ranjan came to escort me to the café. I decided to be assertive about how he should guide me to avoid any embarrassment he might feel about what to do. 'Let me take your arm and you lead the way.'

No sooner had we locked the door behind us than we heard, 'Hi there, it's me again.' Peerooze had returned although he should have been half-way back to Madras. He said casually, 'I just thought I'd check that someone was coming to take you for something to eat.' He glanced at Ranjan and continued, 'That's good, but I fancy a bite. I'll go with her now.'

In the café I sipped fresh mango juice and poked at a *poori*, a deep-fried puffy bread that deflated to my touch. It was soft rather than crisp and I licked my finger, surprised at how unoily it was. Peerooze was using his pile of *pooris* to mop up curry.

'I was thinking about your trip back to Madras on Monday,' he said between mouthfuls. 'I won't be there as I am going to my parents in Coimbatore. Has this boy Ranjan got your bus ticket yet?'

'I don't know, but he has been asked to make a reservation.'

'Then he must make two,' Peerooze said. 'There is some work outstanding which can be finished by one of my men on Monday morning. I will send someone down on Sunday night and he can accompany you back on Monday morning after he has done the work.'

'But I don't need anyone to travel with me on the bus. The people here know to get me on the right one. Once I am in Madras you said Palani would meet me and take me to Susan's, and then on to catch my train to Trivandrum. It is really kind of you to concern yourself but I am fine. Please don't put yourself to any more trouble.' I was flabbergasted by the extent of Peerooze's kindness and did not know how to receive it. I was filled with qualms about inconveniencing him and reticent lest he felt I was a burden.

'It is all done now anyway. Mr Supremanium has to come and collect some money. I will tell him to report to you on Sunday night and come back again on Monday morning to go to the bus with you.'

The next morning Manob and I travelled the short distance from the guest reception building to the ashram proper on his motorbike. I rode Indian style, side-saddle on the back, feeling I might slip at the slightest swerve. We arrived at a building with a heap of bicycles parked higgledy-piggledy outside. 'This is the nerve centre of the ashram,' Manob informed me. 'Do you have your pass?' He checked it before ushering me through a crowd by a door into a tiled, perfumed courtyard. 'You have to take your shoes off here. This is the main building where Sri Aurobindo and the Mother lived.'

Pots of flowers were banked up to the right and left of us making a passageway that channelled hushed ashram devotees towards the sound of trickling water. It was impossible to push our way through the throng without brushing against blooms or crushing leaves and releasing more scent.

'The Mother loved flowers and gave them all names,' Manob explained. 'There are flowers of love, trust, patience, conscience and so on.' I recognised geraniums, marigolds and chrysanthemums from the petals I handled.

The interconnecting buildings making up this heart of the ashram throbbed with members and visitors coming to pay their daily respects. In the centre, in a tree-shaded square, we visited the Samadhi, a white marble shrine that held the remains of Sri Aurobindo and the Mother in two separate chambers. Sri Aurobindo was the ashram's founder and the Mother was his disciple and successor until her death in 1973. Every morning fresh flowers were placed on it, and all day long people made a silent vigil and offered more flowers. The reverence and silence were awesome, but made me feel mutinous because I don't like conforming to a crowd, especially when the crowd consists of votaries contemplating the presence (or absence) of one who has supposedly reached 'the divine state'. I did not believe that this was the way to self-realisation.

The rooms leading from the courtyard were used as offices and for administration. Manob took me into one to meet Harikant, one of the five trustees who governed the ashram. The room was cool, dim and tranquil with the sound of papers fluttering under a fan. Harikant and one other trustee present appeared as distant, softly spoken figures in the shadowy chamber. They welcomed me and gently reminded Manob to take me to visit the chambers of Aurobindo and the Mother before we visited the physiotherapy and naturopathy centre.

'We are too early to go the rooms of the Mother and Sri Aurobindo – it is only nine thirty – so let us go across the road to our school. It is recess time so we can take soup with them,' Manob suggested.

The play area was shady and green with a central open-air stage and buildings all the way round the perimeter. Soup instead of morning milk seemed novel to me. I heard the chatter of French all around me as children mingled and merged in various groupings. The first language taught was

French, then English, and Hindi was introduced only after nursery school. Most children spoke a fourth language, either an Indian one or a European one depending on where they came from. A tall, elegant woman sat by us while we sipped our mugs of soup. She twirled a parasol, spoke English with an unmistakable French lilt and oozed French sophistication. In fact, she was Indian. Born in Calcutta, she and her sister had become refugees following the bombing during the Second World War. The Mother, a Frenchwoman, had brought them to Pondicherry.

Manob had spent all his life in Pondicherry after his parents gained him entrance to the ashram as a child. At twenty-eight he was an ashram member, which meant he was committed to surrender to the inner spiritual force and to reject all that opposed its workings. In practical terms, this meant no drink or drugs, no smoking, no sex and no politics. He was quiet and thoughtful in his dealings with the people we greeted in passing.

'You don't seem like a *sannyasin* – I suppose I mean an ascetic. But you devote your whole life to the ashram's inner world – inner thinking,' I said, provocatively: much of what I have discovered about myself has come through experiencing the world at large.

Manob did not seem to feel confronted and replied, 'I do not retreat from outward life. I have my work running the cottage industries. We sell our products all over the world. *Moksha*, liberation from worldly existence, is not the teaching of Sri Aurobindo. He says it is inner freedom and not outward renunciation that is required. My work is an opening into the Divine. The Mother calls it, 'To work for the Divine is to pray with the body.'

'What is the Divine?' I persisted.

'It is the Divinity within us, an awareness of the true self. We aim to enlighten the ignorance of the mind, the body and life by bringing this knowledge of Divine consciousness to them. We want to create the Divine in the material world, not just in some out-of-reach higher level.' I was humbled by the simplicity and equanimity of Manob's words.

Someone jangled the recess bell in the gardens. When the wrist action of the bell-ringer was vigorous, the brassy sound rose to become shrill and urgent, clearing each corner of children. Then it died back to a hollow tinkle as the hand tired, the wrist fell limp and the children filed inside.

'Come, we will go to make our visit,' Manob said. We crossed back into the main building and entered the former rooms of the Mother and Sri Aurobindo. The rooms were preserved as if the former occupants were still in residence. A glassy silence acted like a window on the world into which I was entering, and I wanted to smash it rather than look through it. The hush, the reverence, the beatification of a dead place and its dead inhabitants made me feel cross, not at peace like the devotees in attendance.

We sat in the Mother's room facing her chair, which was positioned on a dais with her sari draped across it. The iconoclast in me railed against it. I sat and struggled with this incipient rebellion until Manob tapped my shoulder to beckon me to pass through Sri Aurobindo's room as a final mark of respect on our way out. A grumpy old man scolded him for whispering a description of this room, which was roped off like a period setting in a museum. He was a little more forgiving when Manob signalled an explanation. I was given a flower to place as an offering to the long-dead man.

Kaluda, the physiotherapist, did not seem very busy and chatted about his naturopathic and diverse approach to treating illness. His practice was more than manipulative: he amalgamated the best from homeopathy, ayurveda and yoga in his treatments. Whereas Dr Renade in Pune read the three *nadi*, pulse or energy points, on the wrist, Kaluda located them on the abdomen to make diagnostic decisions. After he had examined me, he concluded, like Dr Renade, that I had a *pitta* excess and needed to drink more water and avoid constipation.

This brief overview was followed by a return visit to the school. Kaluda was keen to introduce me to as many children as possible. He seemed to know all four hundred by name, and stopped frequently to greet pairs and groups: 'This is Nicola Naylor,' he would say. 'She is a very good physiotherapist. She is blind and has come all the way from England.' He repeated this introduction as we proceeded inside, going from classroom to classroom. I was embarrassed by his desire for the children to admire me:

it was as difficult to be revered as to revere. The children were dutifully astounded, and Kaluda encouraged their awe and interest. He asked me to talk to a group of the older ones, which I agreed to do mainly because it seemed churlish not to. I realised that I challenged the normal, narrow concept of what it was to be blind, yet to find myself so obviously perceived as extraordinary was as sweet-and-sour tasting as a tamarind chutney.

Manob and I ended our day sitting on the grandstand steps overlooking an enormous sports stadium. People were running on the track, which encircled hockey and football pitches. Behind us was a thirty-three-metre swimming-pool, and I was aware of the sound of water lapping up against flapping filters. 'Manob, these facilities are marvellous, so well kept and so extensive. Can anyone use them?' I asked.

'We all do. They are here for members only. We have built a community with a spiritual centre in which to live, work and play. When the Mother settled here in 1926, the ashram began to develop. Originally there were only twenty-six members, but as more and more people came, arrangements had to be made for housing, food, a decent living and health care. This was all a spontaneous growth, not a planned creation of the Mother and Sri Aurobindo. Now there are twelve hundred members and many non-members who join in. We have not renounced life but have created another sort of life.' His voice was full of conviction and pride.

I found the sports ground more expressive of the intentions of the Aurobindian community than the contrived and self-conscious other-worldliness in the chambers and tomb of Sri Aurobindo and the Mother.

Manob and I exchanged information about plant products. He managed the cottage-industry production of incense sticks, perfumed bags, pot-pourri and terracotta oil burners. I advised him on the blending of essential oils to make massage oils and bath drops for general relaxation and stimulation, so that he could extend his range. In return he was a valuable source of information about the availability of oils in India. He explained why it was hard to get genuine sandalwood. The trees were generally kept in government conservation areas and the wood was seldom sold. He had sourced eucalyptus, geranium, lemon-grass, pine and jasmine oils, and was refreshingly open about giving me contact names and addresses in Kodaikanal and Ootacamund, the hill stations of the south where most growing and cultivating took place.

I had known the hill stations were an area worth exploring for oils but until then I had had no contacts. I was particularly pleased with this information as I had relinquished my plan to go to Kodaikanal via Madurai, one of southern India's oldest cities and a centre of learning and pilgrimage for centuries, in the face of objections from both Goutam and Peerooze. Now, although I had lost the chance to see Madurai, I was armed with the wonderful 'necessity' of work to justify a trip to Kodaikanal. All considerations about how I would manage the journey alone belonged to a less triumphant moment. I told Manob that, without a doubt, I would include in my itinerary a visit to Dr Nambisan in Kodaikanal. Manob warned me that he was difficult to contact as his horticultural station was tucked away in the hills.

The next day Manob invited me to join him and his family on a trip to Auroville, which had been a brainchild of the Mother, an 'experiment in international living'. There were thirty settlements and six hundred and fifty foreigners including children. We drove along lanes shaded by cashew trees and Manob pointed out a banner: 'Promesse, Esperance et Ermitage'. Each settlement ran a project involving alternative technology, in agriculture, handicraft, computer research or the environment.

We went straight to the Matri Mandir, a huge meditation hall still under construction and intended to become the spiritual and physical centre of the community. We wound our way up wide, spiralling stairs until we reached a circular chamber of white marble. In the centre of the room was a crystal ball, one and a half metres in diameter. People sat in silent meditation. I felt a vibration from the play of light that fell on the crystal from an opening in the roof above. I focused on the vibration and was able to experience the 'presence' between my thoughts much as I had learnt to do in yogic practice with a candle flame.

Outside again, I sat just beyond the drooping branches of a huge banyan tree. It was the biggest Indian fig tree I had encountered. The long sprawling branches dropped tendrils to the ground, some of which had taken root and thickened into sub-trunks. The tree splayed over a large area, its shade preventing anything else thriving. I decided that I disliked personality cults and the worship of individuals because they seem to overshadow individual creativity.

Before leaving we picnicked from the boot of the Ambassador under some eucalyptus trees. There was sweet tea and Calcutta sweetmeats – soft milk fudge, which, remarkably, had not melted in the day's heat. The sunset was so strong that I could feel the warm orange-red glow like fire embers.

The following day on my departure I acquired a retinue to make sure I got on to the bus. Mr Supremanium had reported on both Sunday night and Monday morning with impeccable manner and timing. Manob had arranged for the ashram mini-bus and driver to take us to the bus, and Ranjan and he came with us to find our seats, wedging my bag into the overhead rack. In parting Manob hugged me.

I had a bottle of water and my tape-recorder as my essentials to get through the five-hour drive back to Madras. I was prepared for a hot, dusty journey and was glad at first that I had the window seat bringing the benefit of whatever breeze there might be. However, once we left town, there was nothing but hot air and dust blasting at me. After only forty minutes the bus stopped and passengers clambered off to stretch their legs and buy refreshments. A putrefying stench of rotting fruit, excrement and ammonia-smelling urine hung in the air. Mr Supremanium asked, 'Do you want some fruits only?' I declined.

Next to my open window I could hear a gas burner that was keeping a *chai* saucepan hot. Buses swept past and sent stagnant pools of foul water swilling into blocked gutters and spewing out again to slop up against the pavement corners and buildings. Closer to me, perhaps a hand's reach away, there was the frequent but irregular clang of metal hitting metal. First a lid scraped back, then there was a plop as a tin cup hit water. A general splashing and throaty gulps confirmed that water had been drawn from a metal water butt, and finally the tin cup clanged against the side of the butt to which it was attached with a chain. For moments afterwards the cup danced and dangled, knocking against the butt. People snorted, gargled and spat. Every waterborne disease from typhoid to cholera flowed through my imagination – and most likely through the butt as well.

I wanted to go and pee but the thought of stepping out into what smelt like an open sewer and the embarrassment of asking my guide to find me a toilet – which probably did not exist – was enough to make me decide to last until the next stop. Hopefully, there would be a cleaner bus stand.

I cursed the half-litre of water I had already drunk. Perversely, I went on sipping, indoctrinated by the lectures I had received about not drinking enough. The bus bumped along the road jolting my bladder mercilessly. A mix of potholes and no suspension bounced me until I felt ready to burst. An hour passed and still there was no stop. Then another hour, and I went from discomfort to pain. I asked Mr Supremanium in, I hoped, a cheerful voice, 'Is it much longer now?'

He neither nodded nor shook his head which was a sure sign that he did not know. I tried again: 'Do you think there will be another rest stop?' I noticed that a nervous squeak had entered my voice.

He both nodded and shook this time so, miserably, I gave up. The roads became smoother and wider and we increased speed, which made me think we were very near Madras. I tried to hold on and think about something else. A meaningful twinge in my bladder and the inevitable was clear. I said, 'You have got to stop the bus. I don't feel well. I've got to get down.'

He did not react straight away so I turned and yelled, '*Now*!'

The bus stopped. I imagined that the other passengers probably thought some lily-livered foreigner had literally fallen by the wayside, unable to tolerate the conditions. We got off and scrambled down a bank over a wall and into spiky undergrowth of brittle, razor-edged grass. I was charging ahead with my escort lurching behind trying to grab me out of the way of dangers. I signalled to him to stay back and turn round but was too desperate to check whether he obeyed. I squatted and snakes slithered through my thoughts, but the relief was sublime. Afterwards I felt ridiculous.

We were forced to get a rickshaw to take us back to Peerooze's office. On arrival there was an almighty altercation about the fare. Palani turned up and joined in, and it took some persuasion before he allowed himself to be extracted so that he could drive me to Susan then on to the station in time for my train.

Susan was as pleased to see me as I her. She fed me on papaya and loaded me with with curd, biscuits and fruit for my journey. 'I don't need all this,' I argued.

'Shush, you never know,' was her definitive reply.

With Susan's help, catching my train at Egmore station was easy. She called a red-coat, an official porter with a turbaned head on which he placed my bag, and he found my train, coach and seat. Once in the carriage Susan flew round to tell at least three people that I was blind, and asked them to help if necessary. She discovered that the woman, Radha, sitting opposite me was a railway official and also travelling to Trivandrum. This seemed to convince Susan that I was safe, so she left with a final reminder, 'Plenty drinking.'

The train departed on time and I settled back for the seventeen-hour journey ahead. It was already seven in the evening and dark outside. As I was in an air-conditioned sleeper all the windows were sealed shut, and I was dismayed to realise that I would cross a slice of India in a vacuum with no open window from which I could gain a sense of the changing landscape.

The plastic bench seat slid out to make a wider bed. There was also a bench against the wall above my head, which could be pulled down to make another bed. When a man came around calling for orders Radha asked for a non-vegetarian meal. I smelt the starch of clean linen and was reminded of nights spent in stiff, crisp sheets at my uncle's house in the Cotswolds. Radha paid for a bundle of sheets and blankets, which were so inviting I regretted that I had already got out my own sheet sleeping-bag.

Radha explained that the food orders were written down, tied round a stone and flung out while passing through a station. They were then telephoned to the next station down the line where the food would be prepared. At about nine thirty metal trays were carried through the train and people settled to eat. At every station a horde of food- and drink-sellers shouted their wares and walked through the carriages with crackly bags of salted and sweet snacks, or rattling tin buckets of crushed ice and canned drinks. The constant clamour persisted through the night and muddled into a hectic dream as tiredness overtook me and the rocking and swaying lulled me to sleep.

In the early hours I came to enough to realise that we had been stationary for a very long time. People were getting off the train and hanging around beside the track. Radha explained, 'We are delaying only. You see, this is single-gauge track and a goods train is derailing from the other way. Now it will take time for it to come through.'

As time passed it got hotter and hotter because the air-conditioning stopped working while we were standing. I decided to try out the toilets at the end of the carriage. There were two, one squat, one western. I opted for the squat one as I had converted to the idea that it must be more hygienic to hover. Judging by the smell coming from the western toilet and the relative cleanliness of the one I used, I guessed my choice had been right. In the gangway I was tempted by the fresh air outside. I was fed up with being meditative, drowsy and patient, which seemed to be the state most passengers adopted to survive the boredom. To the horror and amazement of those entrusted by Susan with my safe-keeping, I made my way to the doors and joined the people at the track side. 'No, I don't need help, I am just cooling off.'

By the time we were under way again the seventeen-hour journey had turned into twenty-seven hours, and I was increasingly grateful for Susan's ample food and drink supplies. She was familiar with the necessary precautions for Indian travel but I was aghast at the irregularity and inefficiency.

I worried that the delay might prevent Vijay and Padma, my hosts in Trivandrum, from being at the station to meet me. What would I do if they weren't there?

TRIVANDRUM: FOOT MASSEURS VIJAY AND PADMA

'What shall I be doing with her if no one is bloody coming?' the station-master at Trivandrum railway station asked Radha, as if I was an article of lost property that would not fit behind the counter. I sat on the chair to which I had been steered and left them to decide where to send me next.

Radha said, 'Someone will come. Make another announcement on the loudspeaker. I will leave my number in case no one is coming.' The official position that my travel companion held in the railway hierarchy had served me well in the course of the longest railway journey of my life.

Just as Radha left, Vijay and Padma burst into the office. Vijay was small and solid, his movements swift and concentrated, like a juggler's, while the energy from Padma was dazzling. She was excited and relieved to find me. 'You are here. We have been looking up and down the platform. We saw you but you don't look blind so we walked right by.'

Vijay hid his poor English behind silence: he spoke little during the ten-kilometre taxi ride to their home in Valiavila. Padma, however, babbled proudly and enthusiastically, 'Our house is called Karma because it is our *karma*. We have built it ourselves and it is a round house.' Her flow was only hampered by bouts of giggling and interjections expressing her alarm at my delay and not finding me on the train when it eventually arrived.

We were greeted by their children, Chachou and Maki, aged eight and two. Chachou darted around us while Maki wrapped herself coyly in the folds of the long skirt of a servant girl who stood staring silently. Every so often some material flapped back and Maki peered out at me. Padma placed a garland of jasmine flowers, the traditional welcome of Kerala, around my neck. It made me think of Pacific island movies and I could see similarities between the dancing, singing, fun-loving characteristics of those island people and Padma. She was so voluptuous, round and effusive.

Once in my bedroom I was left to shower. The atmosphere was moist and heavy from the abundant tropical vegetation of the area, and had coated my skin with a clammy wetness that glued my shirt to my back. I was glad to peel off my sticky clothes.

The house was as curvaceous as my hostess was shapely, and she revolved around Vijay, her silent fulcrum. I found it difficult to get my bearings because I was confused by the lack of straight lines or right angles. These are usually good sources of echo and therefore, location. Instead my orientation was limited to listening to everyone's movements and using these as reference points on the internal map I was piecing together. Nevertheless, I was more like a meteorologist than a cartographer, as the information I charted was forever shifting.

While Vijay and I ate some vegetable and *chapatti* served by Padma, Maki was whisked off to bed and Chachou raced a toy car on the floor. I tentatively broached the arrangements for and financial terms of my stay. I had come here to learn about the traditional foot-pressure massage that Vijay and Padma taught and practised. I arranged for a two- or three-day break in the middle of the time I spent with them as I intended to make the trip to Kodaikanal to see Dr Nambisan.

This idea had germinated into a sometimes sturdy, sometimes wispy plan. I was simultaneously enervated and invigorated by the prospect because I realised that the only way of getting there and back was by bus and alone. I would have to keep this a secret from both Goutam and Peerooze, to whom I talked regularly on the telephone.

The next day Padma took the day off from work at the bank where she was a clerk to take me into Trivandrum, show me around, explain the bus routes, and to find Sudesh Desai. Sudesh was a student of ayurveda at the government college on Mahatma Gandhi (MG) Road, and Dr Renade had given me her name: he thought she would happily show me around her college and the Triveni nursing home, an ayurvedic orthopaedic clinic.

Padma and Vijay travelled everywhere by bus or rickshaw as they did not have a car and driver. It was a wonderful opportunity for me to experience public transport and the people who used it. Trivandrum and its suburbs are built on seven hills and the buses swung and sped around the curves that snaked up and down the terrain. My initiation on the buses with Padma opened a whole new world to me. If seats were to be had, there was an etiquette to be observed. The men sat in the front and also on the left at the back, while the women took the seats at the back and right only. However, there were no rules about personal space. Every inch of standing room was crammed with people hanging from hand loops, bodies so closely compressed that I often felt strange leg muscles contracting against the jolt of frequent braking.There were moments when I unexpectedly found myself wearing part of my neighbour's sari.

There was also a code of conduct regarding children. Mothers handed their babies to any woman who had a seat, and who was not loaded down with children or bags of her own. Little kicking legs brushed past my front as children passed noiselessly from one set of unknown hands to the next. I was seldom passed a child, either because permission was asked and granted by eye-contact from which I was excluded, or because I was a foreigner and not considered party to local understanding and expectations of these Keralans. The children never wailed in protest: they knew instinctively that acceptance was cooler and more comfortable.

The absence of unpleasant body odour was the most amazing thing about the entanglement of bodies. I often travelled with my head trapped in someone's armpit, but never had to hold my breath. All the Indians I had known were fastidious about showering whenever they returned home. They lounged around in loose gowns or pyjamas and always dressed in clean clothes to go out. In the buses there was always a heavy, heady smell of jasmine. I remember the first time my face brushed against a young woman's shoulders and I discovered that south Indian women pinned fresh jasmine flowers into their long, black, braided hair. I was smothered in an opiate-like fragrance.

At each stop there was a scrum to allow those who wanted to get off to unravel themselves from the skein of limbs. Some were pinioned against seatbacks while others scrambled for freedom. Then there was a slapping of *chapples* along the road as more people dashed to leap aboard before the driver pulled away. Some jumped on to the first step to find there was no room even to squeeze up to the second, others swung up on the door rail and dangled dangerously for the roller-coaster ride into town. Somehow the conductor pressed his way through and extracted his fare from the pulped passengers. The human morass splurged out when we arrived at the main stop in the centre of town.

After my first bus journey with Padma we wilted in the sun while a street-cobbler stitched a rip in my canvas rucksack. I concentrated on each drip of sweat that gathered in the nape of my neck and ran in rivulets down my spine. There was a voice coming from a nearby booth, gabbling so fast that I thought it was a wireless in a bookie's. Padma told me the lottery was being called. Men walked hand in hand and pushed past us in their pairs rather than break their fraternal grip. I could tell by the restricted step or the sound of cloth being rolled and hitched that most men were dressed in *dhotis*, long sarong-like wraps that hung from the waist and could be folded up between the legs. I imagined they looked like giant, sagging nappies. Once my bag had been mended we went on up MG Road to the bank and to the ayurvedic college.

After much asking we found Sudesh standing outside a classroom in a wide corridor full of tall columns. Dr Renade had not written to her about me, but she was obliging and ready to accompany me to where I needed to go. She was a friend of Dr Suresh Kumar, the director of the Triveni nursing home, and we agreed to meet the next day.

We walked up the continuation of MG Road, passing an assortment of small food shops. The whiff of roasting peanuts mingled with the spicy smell of curry. Padma stopped for some fruit juice. We took a giant step up into one of the small hutch-like shops – no more than eight feet square – and immediately met with a waist-height glass display counter that held platters of sweetmeats. The zesty aroma of cardamom pervaded the shop. Then we tried pharmacies galore for hair oil Padma wanted. Taking the giant step into each tiny shop became normal, and in the end I could have led Padma to every ayurvedic pharmacy by the pungency of the herbs and mephitic oils that impregnated the entrance to these brewers' dens. Soon the smell of leather accumulated in my nose as we passed shoe shops, and finally the smell of metal polish betrayed the utensil outlets. Traders clustered according to type, and the intensity made it easy to discern what they had to offer.

At the top of the road, outside the municipal building, a protest demonstration, consisting of people sprawling under canvas and on mattresses, was taking place. Head to foot, criss-crossed, asleep and awake, some shouted, others rattled collection tins. It all seemed rather languid but I suspected that the siege approach dented bureaucracy more effectively than any bombardment. I remembered reading that Kerala and Calcutta were the two Indian states containing a successful Communist influence with lively political activists. Kerala had been the first place in the world freely to elect a Communist government, in 1957. On the bus journey home we were delayed by more chants and stamping feet, which Padma informed me was 'Only All Indian Radio out on striking again.'

The next day on her way to work Padma accompanied me to meet Sudesh. I carried a bag crammed with a towel and swimsuit ready for the beach. I intended to go to Kovalam beach, sixteen kilometres south of Trivandrum, after my morning with Sudesh. I only needed her to show me to the East Fort bus stop where I could catch a bus to the beach. It was best not to think about how I would get back.

First Sudesh introduced me to her professor to ask permission for me to visit the college and hospital. I was familiar with the formalities by now and prepared myself for the frustratingly restricted communication because of the limitations of language. I was also ready for the volley of questions about my blindness.

This time, however, the professor was young and attended by a group of deferential students. I suspected he was telling them, rather than me, how he would treat my condition. He authorised my visit with Sudesh but asked, 'But what can you be seeing in your visiting only?'

'There is quite a lot I can pick up through other means if I can get close.'

The professor offered me some herbs to try and told me that if I noticed any improvement I should return for a course of treatment.

Arup, a male student and friend of Sudesh, accompanied us to the massage area. We walked along high, vaulted corridors, which opened into cavernous halls then narrowed into dim passages. The halls had beds around the pillars and I heard patients moving, stretching and moaning while they tried to rest or make themselves comfortable. The bustle and stir of these exposed wards receded as we entered another wing of the building.

Here we sat in a lecture room while Sudesh explained the principles of ayurvedic practice until I persuaded her gently that I was acquainted with them. In eastern medicine the patient is treated as a whole being, taking into account the physical, spiritual and mental interplay – an approach that owes its origins in part to classical Greek medicine. Hippocrates or, later, Galen would have recognised more in this system, which aids the body's inbuilt ability to recover from sickness, than they would in modern medicine's germ warfare. The blitz against bacteria may annihilate the invading force but often leaves the body a devastated battleground.

In common with ayurvedic practice, alternative practitioners in the West support the concept of treating the whole person, and generally resist practices that cure the disease but damage the individual. Most of my patients come to me because they feel their orthodox treatment has been fragmentary, overlooking the entirety of their state; they also come to combat the side-effects of steroid, cortisone and antibiotic treatments. Both Sudesh and I prescribe herbs and suitable massage applications, but we also involve our patients in a regimen of lifestyle improvements such as dietary, exercise and rest routines.

I encouraged her to show me pulse examination, or *nadi pariksha*, which is an important form of diagnosis in the East. She placed three fingers on my wrist below my thumb and concentrated on the strength of the beat. After a studied silence and an occasional lifting of one finger then another, she concluded that the *pitta* in me was dominant. I was impressed that the various alternative practitioners I had met had all reached the same conclusion.

The predominance of *pitta* was not necessarily a problem, but disease might be a complication of constitutional imbalance. I concurred with the idea that disease was not a factor in itself coming from outside but a product of lifestyle and constitution. I felt like one of my patients, who, while they know that they need to take steps to control certain unhealthy tendencies, find it too difficult. I knew that I should avoid unctuous or hot foods, and stay cool, but had not been very observant of this since my arrival in India.

Nadi pariksha is the examination of the arterial pulses in various parts of the body. In Indian tradition the wrist pulse is thought best, although practitioners like Kaluda in Pondicherry had clearly been influenced by the Chinese preference for stomach readings. The left hand of women and the right hand of men are taken to be examined. I asked Sudesh to examine my pulses again and tell me what she read. She placed her index finger firmly and softly at the base of my wrist while her middle and ring fingers fell in line next to it.

'We are looking for the quality, rate, depth, site, strength and regularity of the pulse.' Sudesh paused, then continued, 'You are frog pulse, you have *mandukagati*, resembling the movement of a frog. *Pitta* types are often wiry, taut and jumping, more bounding in nature. The motion is dancing, excited with high amplitude and sudden dropping.'

I removed my hand to consider this appraisal. If the pulse types were classified according to the movements of different types of animals I wanted to know what the *vata* and *kapha* types were like.

'The *vata* pulse has *sarpagati*, snake-like slithering movement. The pulse is hard to find because it has a tenuous, fluctuating manner,' Sudesh answered. 'It is subtle and changeable like the wind while *pitta* pulse sounds like the flaring up of fire.'

'Does that give the *kapha* pulse the quality of the movement of water, a kind of fluidity?' I asked, trying to make links with the cosmic qualities of the humours.

'Yes, the *kapha* pulse is said to have *hamsagati*, the movement of a swan. It is wide, broad and wavy like a river. Volume and rhythm are balanced.'

'In my work we associate excess *kapha* with too much phlegm accumulating in the body. This is mainly due to over-consumption of dairy products and mucus-forming foods. You would read this pulse as thick and rolling?' I checked out my interpretation, enthusiastic about the relevance of the comparisons.

Sudesh gave more examples. 'In liver disorders the pulse becomes more wiry and frog-like in motion. We say kidney disorders and general debility make the pulse weak and hard to find, thready like the snake.'

It made sense to me when she associated liver disorders with the excessive *pitta* pulse. I had never before linked my constitution and my liver weakness together so clearly.

The massage rooms were brighter, cleaner, less antiquated than in either Madras or Bombay. Sudesh spoke softly to a few patients undergoing treatment, and explained to me that the massage was given while the patient is moved between seven body positions. These included lying on both sides, back and front, sitting, standing and bending forward. It seemed exhausting. At home I put people either on their back or their front. Here the seven positions were designed to allow different tensions to pull in the muscles of the limbs and torso. A series of pops like blown bubble gum reverberated around the room. It was coming from under the fingers of masseuse who was pushing on *marma* points down each side of a woman's spine, and twanging the muscle between her fingers and thumb as she went.

Men and women were massaged in separate rooms although the wooden treatment benches were not secluded. The various oils were steaming and bubbling on hissing burners, but the pounding poultices were less thunderous than I had heard elsewhere. The contrast between Sudesh, modestly dressed in her beautiful sari, and her helpless naked patients struck me as yet another of India's extremes.

'Do you always wear a sari at college? I mean, do you ever wear *salwar kameez* – trousers and tunic?' I asked.

'The sari gives respect. It is what the doctor must wear,' she answered.

The calf-length skirt I wore felt suddenly inappropriate. First, it was tatty. Second, it was what young Indian girls wore before they adopted the sari at around seventeen. I would have been more appropriately dressed in knee-length shorts, loose trousers or a sundress, which are unmistakably western clothing.

Sudesh pointed out some apparatus designed to drip oil on to the skull and between the eyes. It was a modern version of the skull cap I had seen in Bombay. I asked whether it was used to treat insomnia and addiction. 'I have written a paper for my exams on ayurveda in mental illness. We are treating schizophrenia in this way.'

'And is it working?' I asked.

'Hard to say,' she replied, shyly and honestly.

We went by rickshaw to the Triveni nursing home and arrived at a less imposing, more modern building. Sudesh explained that Dr Kumar had been a fellow student and had taken over the clinic from his father. We went into what appeared to be a smaller version of an accident and emergency department in a hospital. The clamour of people rose and fell as they disappeared into rooms then emerged to sit and wait in the corridor. I could distinguish the medical staff from the patients by the confident stride of an attendant or doctor or the hesitant step of a patient.

I remembered that I had not drunk anything that morning and asked for some water. I was given a form of yogi tea. I had already tried it at Vijay and Padma's and knew it was boiled water with a herbal powder added to purify and cleanse both the water and the drinker. The one Sudesh gave me was also recommended as good for temperature control, blood circulation and preventing fainting. It tasted bitter and dried my mouth.

Dr Kumar called us into his tiny office and we squeezed into two seats in front of his desk. The door was left open and people popped in and out. One clanged a swab tray down on the desk, another came in wafting an X-ray as if it were a fan. Then I heard a man pull up his shirt front and Dr Kumar plopped a stethoscope onto his chest. He spoke to Sudesh about his findings, but ignored the man, who remained silent and passive.

'We are having an X-ray machine now but we can diagnose a fracture by feeling. We are keeping up with the times,' said Dr Kumar.

He flicked a pen to point at the X-ray and started a conversation about it with Sudesh, but was then called to an emergency by a buzzer on his desk. He invited us to follow, and we entered a small room in the centre of which a man sat cradling a fractured arm. Dr Kumar stepped over to a sink where he washed his hands, while Sudesh and I leant against a window-sill opposite the door. Two male assistants were cutting strips of lint, and I heard the squishing of sodden cloth being wrung out.

Dr Kumar explained, 'We are using splints and herbal wraps. A bone is healing this way in three weeks. Muslin is infusing with herbs and bound over the splints. Every two days it is removed for checking the bone knitting.' He handed me the bamboo splints he was going to use to strap the broken bone after straightening the arm. All the while the man sat motionless.

'He fell off a roof on a building site,' Sudesh whispered.

Dr Kumar was already telling the assistants to hold out the arm firmly. I winced with empathetic pain but the man did not squeak or squirm. I shifted my position and tried to concentrate on considering the amazingly short recovery time and how sensible it was not to use plaster-of-paris in such a hot climate, and to ignore the wrenching of the man's arm. The patient displayed the same unquestioning faith in a doctor's absolute authority that I had seen elsewhere.

These thoughts faded as I became aware of a strange sensation. My head had begun to fizz like a freshly shaken bottle of lemonade. I wanted to tell Sudesh that I was feeling peculiar, but I was too busy trying to control the mounting insurrection of my senses. I was sweating profusely and lost my orientation. I felt myself slipping, panicking, and disappearing...

'Are you all right?' someone was asking.

I knew I was lying on a bench, but I did not know where I was or who was talking to me. I did not answer. I could not answer.

'You passed out. You have been out for a while and your lips are very blue colour,' Sudesh told me. Gradually I placed myself and immediately felt embarrassed by my lapse as if it had been a *faux pas* that I might have prevented.

'Has she got any condition? The colour is very strange,' Dr Kumar asked Sudesh, who seemed at a loss.

I struggled to get up and, feeling dizzy but determined, said 'I'm fine. I just fainted, that's all.'

'Drink this. It is a herbal tonic for excess heat,' Dr Kumar instructed.

I obeyed unhesitatingly and gulped down a thick sweet liquid, which tasted like a fruit punch. Because of my liver problems I cannot drink alcohol and it occurred to me that this was kill or cure. I sensed the presence of the injured man by an absence of space between the window and myself and realised with horror that I was occupying the bench where he should have been.

Sudesh and I moved to the cool corridor, and Dr Kumar went to take a telephone call. I began to feel a little intoxicated, which helped to alleviate my embarrassment. I reassured Sudesh that I must have had too much sun and not enough water. I reflected on the homeopathic principle of 'proving', whereby a substance given to cure symptoms in a sick person will cause those symptoms if given to a healthy person. Yogi tea trickled into my mind as the most likely culprit.

Before leaving Dr Kumar suggested that we see the physiotherapy and massage work of the clinic. Treatments took place in individual rooms with one or two therapists per patient, and far more emphasis was placed on the massage movements and manipulation of joints than I had observed elsewhere. In one room an attendant was massaging a man lying prone.

His movements sounded like a stampede of galloping horses. I would have adopted much the same approach but perhaps slowed to a trot, given how sore the patient was. The masseur halted, caught his breath, then explained to me that he was using the palm of one hand with additional pressure coming from the other hand placed on top. The patient had an injured chest, diaphragm and rib-cage from a mugging, but his whole body was being massaged to increase the circulation and stimulate healing. The resinous smell of herbs was heavy in the room and I guessed he was using a lot of root oils. The weight of the aroma dragged at the air, making it thick and stale, verging on rancid.

Dr Kumar explained that the wood from which the massage tables were made had a therapeutic quality of its own. I touched the side of one: it felt warm and pulpy, like a pliable body.

Sudesh and I returned to the college by rickshaw to pick up Arup. She invited me to join them for lunch near where they lived in East Fort, and said that afterwards she would take me to the bus stop. We rattled along the road telling Arup of the morning's events when a tremendous avalanche of incongruous sounds thundered down upon us. The rickshaw swerved into a gutter, tilting at sixty degrees on one wheel in a failed attempt to about-turn. I could hear the whine of cars reversing furiously, and doors were slamming as people got out and ran for cover. The thwacking of feet against *chapples* and *chapples* against tarmac smacked the air. The source of danger was not clear to me but everyone was acting in unison as if battening down the hatches for a storm. The iron-grid shop shutters clattered down. Occasional shouts scarred the tense air.

Our rickshaw-wallah signalled for us to get out and disappeared hastily. Abandoned on the street, I became aware of glass smashing as stones were hurled through windows. Some rebounded on to the road and up again to splinter wooden carts and roadside shacks. People scurried everywhere, some trying to escape and others to join an oncoming, congealed mob moving with one mind in one direction. Policemen were hacking away at the people on the edges with their *lathis,* or batons, provoking more frenzied bellows to rise above the cracking and thudding of wood against bone and flesh.

The crowd was moving fast towards us. Arup grabbed my arm and tried to pull me into a side alley but lost his grip, and I was engulfed in moving bodies sweeping forward. I was aware that I needed to keep my footing and tried to move with the momentum. A woman to my side screamed as she toppled and rolled under the stamping feet. Her wails fell behind me, then ceased. I stumbled over something soft, grabbed for the nearest person and found myself clutching some feathery haunches. Momentarily bewildered I withdrew my hand, then heard the squawks of a hen, tucked under the arm of the charging man in front. I knew that my only escape was to get to the side of the throng, but this risked an encounter with a flailing lathi. My only hope was that my hair colour would make the policeman hesitate. Before I could attempt escape, a small rough hand pincered my neck and jerked me backwards. A hissing voice spat something unintelligible into my ear and the hand forced me down. I crouched among the forest of moving legs pulling my skirt around me. I remember being concerned about it riding up. Although my feet were still on the ground, I could not stand and was soon flung to the right. I instinctively rolled up like a hedgehog. Then came a thump in my back, which impelled me to move and I crawled frantically to the side. Away from the legs, I thought I was safe until a hand took my shoulder. I froze.

'This way, quickly. I lost you.' It was Arup's voice.

Before I knew how, Arup was steering Sudesh and me down alleys just wide enough for two people abreast. The front-door steps jutted almost into the middle of the alleys. I caught my ankle on the concrete corner of one. I was advised to take a huge step to cross the open gutter by the side of a house, and Sudesh announced, 'We are safe. This is where I live.'

We entered a dark, cluttered downstairs room, left our shoes and climbed up a narrow, wooden staircase that hugged the side wall of the house. The attic room, with two tiny square windows and no head room, was Sudesh's rented studio.

It began to rain, the drops pinging like gunfire on the tin roof turning the noise from the main streets into a distant rumble. We listened and waited until we thought it was safe to venture out. I fingered a small tear in my skirt, and ran my hands down my legs to feel for abrasions. I was shaken but uninjured. Sudesh and Arup had no better idea than I about what had ignited the trouble, but were astonishingly incurious about it.

Outside again, the roads were slippery with water and crunchy with glass fragments. The mob had left debris of wooden posts, sackcloth and roof tiles strewn about. Shopkeepers were tentatively raising their shutters and assessing the damage. The storm had purged the air of the usual cooking smells, so the acrid odour of smouldering fires and the fetid scent of tear gas were more piercing than they might otherwise have been.

Slowly, normality reinstated itself. People emerged, toppled stalls were hauled upright and children chattered. The bell around the neck of a passing ox tinkled, and I was drawn by the mouthwatering smell of coriander leaves, which were tied in bundles and loaded on the cart the ox was pulling.

Lunch was in a canteen where *thalis* arrived on stainless-steel plates with sections for chutney, sambar – a soupy, fiery dish, rice, vegetable, curd and raw onion. A man walked around flinging or spinning *chapattis* like frisbees on to our plates. I was given some curd rice, a boiled rice mixed with yoghurt, in case the curries were too hot. We ate in silence. I could still feel the breath of that man on my neck, and I shuddered.

A huge crowd of people was waiting at the East Fort bus stop and more western voices were percolating through the crush than I had heard since my arrival in India almost a month before. A cavalcade of rickshaws stood at the head of the group. The rickshaw-wallahs were profiting from the absence of buses – they were still in the depot following the troubles – by offering their services at Monopoly prices.

Arup confirmed there would be no buses for another couple of hours. The rickshaw-wallahs pushed and pestered so much that I resented giving in to their bullying. One driver offered a modest price reduction to share the ride to Kovalam beach with a woman who was already sitting inside.

People turned hopefully at the noise of a bus engine coming round the corner, but the greater noise of its screaming passengers made it clear that this was not a regular bus. 'It is the black bus,' said Arup. 'The bus for those taken prisoner.' The screeches from inside sounded insane and terrifying. Like caged wild animals, the inmates beat at the bars and shook their handcuffs violently as they passed.

'You should take this rickshaw. She is a foreigner too,' advised Sudesh.

I said my farewells, and sensed that Sudesh was anxious for my well-being as a lone traveller. As we moved off, a hefty Indian woman clambered in on top of us at the behest of the rickshaw-wallah.

'*Enfin, on y va. Alors,* where are you from?' asked the woman next to me.

'England,' I answered. 'What are you doing here?'

'I am staying at Kovalam, the beach, to rest as I am exhausted after eight years of travel,' she responded rather grandly.

The Indian woman squeezed in between us so that conversation became stilted by the compression on our lungs and her plait stuffing my mouth.

By the time we reached Kovalam, Sylvie, the Frenchwoman, had invited me to join her on the beach for the afternoon. She suggested walking to her hotel and sitting on the beach in front of it. I wondered when I was going to tell her that I was blind. I had described my journey through India briefly, and she had talked of the 'travel worm' that kept her backpacking.

After half an hour we stopped, and Sylvie gave the driver twenty rupees. I handed over twenty too on the basis that we were sharing. The rickshaw-wallah said, 'Twenty rupees still.' The Indian woman was slinking off, so I pointed and asked, 'What is she paying?'

Sylvie had also moved away and the rickshaw-wallah insisted on the rest. I glanced after her, realising what a wily traveller she was, and paid for my ingenuousness. I pulled out my white cane and listened to look for Sylvie's step. I was too infuriated to care, hesitate or falter over my usual inhibitions. Besides, I wanted to make her feel extra ashamed.

Sylvie turned, and I said, 'I forgot to tell you I'm blind. You will have to lead the way.' Then I changed the conversation to something banal and casual.

It proved almost impossible to follow Sylvie's voice and step at the same time over rough, steep, unfamiliar terrain. I was not going to ask to take her arm, so was forced to navigate the sandy descent to the beach; I did so with a dexterity of which I had not known myself capable.

'Let's walk in the seawater to get there,' I suggested, as I guessed there would be fewer obstacles like sunbathers, loungers or boats at the water's edge. 'It will be cooler than the sand.'

We picked our spot, spread our towels and went to cool off in the water. The waves were fairly ferocious and I remembered my guidebook saying that one or two people were washed out to sea here by the strong currents each year. As I plunged under a wave I imagined it to be a huge tongue, rearing up, curling back over me and flicking me down into the body of the sea where I would be lost in the depths. Half frightened and half exhilarated by these macabre thoughts, I let the breakers knock me down and toss me for a while longer until Sylvie called from the shallows that she was going to have a 'sun bath'.

On the beach we were joined by two people Sylvie had met in the hotel. Jessica was Scottish and Rob was from Yorkshire. They were evidently hardened travellers like Sylvie.

'Yeah, take a good look, don't mind me, go right ahead. Got nothing better to do?' Jessica jeered, at a group of men who were ogling and kicking sand in our direction as they sauntered up and down in front of us.

'They have nothing better to do than come and stare at the white women on the beach because they're topless. Their eyes nearly pop out of their heads. They're so repressed that they're disgusting,' she sneered.

I had only a swimming costume with me and was not topless, but I still felt shivers run down my back because of the male shadow hanging over me from one side.

'It's a bit like being a chimpanzee in Regent's Park zoo. Never mind. Are you getting the coffees today, Sylvie?' Rob's toes poked past my head to nudge Sylvie's leg and stir her into action.

'*Mais non, c'est a toi.*'

'I can't,' said Rob. 'We will be over our limit of two hundred a day.'

'You live on two hundred rupees – four pounds – a day?' I asked, incredulous.

'That's both of us,' Jessica said, with a hint of masochistic self-satisfaction. She added, 'Two pounds for the hotel and two for everything else.'

'Papaya, papaya, papaya, only ten rupees, very cheap, very good, papaya, papaya,' cried a girl circling our group.

'No papaya,' said Jessica.

'So very cheap,' the girl persisted.

'No very cheap,' retorted Jessica. She turned to me and said, 'We worked in Hong Kong to get the money for this part of the journey. You can't make money out here in Asia. Here it is sun and sand, and we'll just hang out cheap until the money goes.'

Rob added, 'It's made worse by all these flashy tourists who spend money like water because everything is so cheap to them. The locals get used to it and expect it of us too. The whole economy gets distorted.'

'Look, scoot, I don't want any bloody papaya, beat it.' Jessica's voice had risen as she arched into a sitting position.

The girl wandered off crying, 'Papaya, papaya.'

'Pineapple, fresh pineapple,' shouted the next hopeful fruit-seller. The citrus smell of the cut fruit was deliciously sharp. He got the same abrasive dismissal as the papaya-wallah.

A rustle and a rolling that flattened to a slap against the sand by my head caused Sylvie to moan irritably, 'We don't want mats.' She did not even glance at the offending party. She might have been flicking a fly off her leg; it was an automatic, dismissive reflex.

The bamboo oblongs dangled over the man's arm and swished in my face as he swung into action; 'For you fifty rupees only, special price forty rupees.' Beaten by silence he moved off, but came back ten minutes later followed by an onslaught of cashew-, necklace-, statue- and tender-coconut-wallahs.

'I'd better get going because the people I'm staying with will be waiting for me,' I said.

'I will show you to the bus because I go to sit on the rocks on the other side for the going to bed of the sun,' said Sylvie.

I was surprised and gladdened by her generosity as until then I had felt myself to be on the periphery of an egocentric world. These travellers acted like balls bouncing in space – colliding with other people's lives, making indentations but never sustaining any themselves.

On the bus I tried not to think of how I would find a connecting bus to Valiavila. I knew that I had to cross a very wide road to reach the main bus station but had no idea from which part of the station my bus departed.

The man in front of me turned and said, in good English, 'I lost everything on this bus two days ago. Someone took a knife and slit my bag, and all my money, my papers, my passport are gone. Here, look at this. This is the letter from the police.'

It was thrust into my hands, and I pretended to scan it because I saw no reason to burden him with more complications. I returned the letter and asked, 'What will you do, and where are you staying?'

His long thin hand was shaking a little as he took the letter. 'Every day I am at the police station. They do nothing. I am a doctor for the World Health Organisation and I must get to Nepal. I need my train fare.'

I was not convinced and suggested he contacted his employers to ask them to send some money. I could not help visualising him as a bloodhound rather than a white-coated medic.

'It will be very long and I am sleeping in the station. I must live and I must get back,' he said.

I tried the Indian solution to most problems and said, 'Why don't you contact your family?'

'I have no family here. They are in Malaysia.'

I was surprised. By then he had moved round and was standing over me, bending and swinging with the jolts of the bus as a lanky willow tree sways with the turn of the wind. I had thought of Malaysians as smaller people and had judged him to be a north Indian from his height .

When we reached East Fort I asked him to help me find the bus to Valiavila. He agreed and I followed him off the bus by maintaining the lightest of fingertip contact on his loose clothing. Keeping up with him in the crowd through which he slipped easily was difficult because he had not realised I was blind. He thought that I was just a foreigner unfamiliar with the bus timetable. We waited shoulder to shoulder in an area indicated by a bus official.

At last he asked falteringly 'Can you give me my train fare?'

I wondered whether his apprehensiveness was the skilled ruse of the master swindler, but I could not dismiss the possibility that he was in trouble. I gave him my telephone number and told him to call in three days if he was still without his fare.

Once on the bus I asked repeatedly for Valiavila among the passengers around me so there was no chance of anyone forgetting. I decided not to rely on the conductor alone as in England there have been too many times when conductors, busy ticketing, have overlooked my stop. Indian conductors had four times as many fares to collect and were therefore more likely to forget. However, the response from my fellow passengers was disconcerting because every time I said, 'Valiavila, I want Valiavila,' the person I addressed smiled, nodded amiably and repeated a word that meant nothing to me and did not resemble 'Valiavila'. As the whisper of a word not even beginning with V hissed its way around the bus I perched, disquieted and tense, on my seat. At each stop I looked around enquiringly but was met by silence until one time when the silence seemed to last for ever, and the bus did not move although no one was getting on or off. A chorus of voices began to chime like clocks, not quite in sequence, hands waved and I became confused.

'Valiavila?' I asked hopefully. Voices assailed me. Some people stood up and sat back down. I could make no sense of it. The engine revved. I decided to try a straw poll of vocal excitement to decide whether or not to get off. 'Valiavila?' I asked again, vigorously pointing outside. Again a wave of voices saying different things. I decided to get off and take my chances.

The bus pulled away in a flurry of dust and I was alone. I tried to make out any familiar audible landmarks. I heard a hollow hammering from my right, which was unsettling for I could not recall any such sound near to where I was staying. The air was hot and still. Something rustled along the ground near my feet. I started walking in the same direction as the bus had been travelling: I knew that should be the way back – assuming, of course, that I was in Valiavila. I followed the road round with one foot on the scrub and the other in the dusty edge: this kept me to the side. The sun troubled me: I felt sure that it should be behind me, yet I could feel it on my face. I turned and walked back in the other direction. On I went, in the optimistic belief that I was on the right road and in the right village. The more I walked, however, the more doubtful I became. I did not remember it taking so long and considered turning round again. I also did not remember the sweet smell of English summers in the air, and soon found my feet entangled in a freshly harvested mattress of hay spread at the roadside to dry. I tried wading through it, not wanting to lose track of the roadside, but it was too thick and springy. It seemed to go on for ever and I was forced to divert into the middle of the road. There had been no hay laid out previously. Maybe this was the first day of harvesting, or maybe I was in some farming area miles from Valiavila. I wondered what I would do. Nobody was around, not even a passing rickshaw and, even if there had been, I could never have made myself understood. 'Get yourself out of this,' I chided myself.

I continued, for want of any other option or plan. Determination was declining and so was the hope of recognising the sharp, right-handed hairpin bend that wrapped around Vijay and Padma's house. When I dipped suddenly into a left hairpin, I stopped, pivoted on my heels, causing hay to twist around my ankles, and decided to take the chance that this was the bend from the other direction. I retraced my steps, broke right instead of left as I would normally have done at the outermost bulge in the bend, and descended triumphant to the enormous wrought-iron gate of Karma. Clearly I had gone one stop too far and the bus had passed the house.

I felt like Scott of the Antarctic returning elated from a successful expedition, and could have done with a reception crowd cheering and waving banners. There was nothing more sumptuous, however, than an energetic hostess relieved to have me back safe and sound, and ready to indulge me with a foot-pressure massage. After the day's stampedes, the idea of Padma padding over my body with her soft, supple feet was divine.

I stripped completely and lay supine on a wide, plastic-covered massage couch. Padma painted oil lavishly over my whole front then asked me to turn over so that she could oil my back. She climbed on to the couch and straddled me, standing erect and reaching up for an overhead rope, which ran parallel to the ceiling and which she used for balance because she stood on one leg throughout.

She began the massage with a ceremonial Sanskrit mantra or chant. It started as a rumble coming from her belly, then rose and resonated through her throat and mouth. The sound was a primordial thanking of the gods for the act she was about to perform.

She circled each of my shoulders, tailing off down the arm and returning up to circle the shoulder again, forming a letter p or q. Then she heeled down my spine, and hugged her way down the back of my legs with the arch of her foot. She went back up my legs once more and to my shoulders. This full body effleurage was an introduction, repeated several times.

Rhythm and repetition were the key, unlocking the tension in my hunched shoulders, slightly stooped back and tight chest. My body was closed and clamped from the trials of the day. Now I was settling into a relaxing release. The movements became more delving and precise over my spine, buttocks and thighs. My muscles were kneaded then lengthened under the weight and pressure of Padma's flexible feet. I felt as malleable as a piece of dough as I turned over and Padma repeated the effleurage. This time she circled my breast then slid up and down one arm, over my rib-cage, up and over my hipbone, down and up the leg on the right; then she repeated the process on the left of my body. Around my neck her toes dipped in and out of each crevice between my collarbones and sternum. I sat up to have my head and body massaged by hand. My head felt as if it was popping and exploding under the pummelling of claw fingers. In a daze I went to shower while Padma prepared dinner.

During the next morning Vijay told me that he had checked the route to Kodaikanal. It would entail a seven-hour bus journey to Madurai to catch a bus up to Kodaikanal, which would be another five hours. He advised against such a difficult journey. Since Dr Nambisan had still not replied to my letter, I decided to follow Vijay's suggestion and delay the trip. I wondered whether I would ever get there. At least, I had nothing extra to conceal from Goutam when he telephoned. I had already omitted to mention the few local bus journeys, the riot, my black-out and my encounter with a possible con artist.

The man I had met on the bus did telephone to ask for money, claiming he was still stranded. I arranged to meet him at the Kovalam bus stand on my way to the beach, which had become a regular afternoon outing. If his claims were genuine, I wanted to help. If I ever found myself in that position, I would hope that someone would bail me out. He said he only wanted enough for his fare to Madras where he could get a traveller's cheque. I did not ask him to explain further, but decided to give him Peerooze's address to which he could return the money. The amount was insignificant but I wanted to know how gullible I was or how honest he was; the return of the money would decide that. The money never arrived. Con artists deter altruism.

On Sunday, the only day when Vijay and Padma did not work, we went to the beach together. I knew that we would not leave early as nothing in India ever happened until the day was nearing its end. I could no more pin Padma and Vijay to a departure time than I could pin up the hem of a skirt. For most of the day they were languid. Padma watched almost as much television as the servant girl, who was glued to a sugary Hindi film – her Sunday afternoon treat. There were a lot of earnest male speeches and tearful female interjections against a backdrop of crashing waves and seagull cries. The music seemed to run in a permanent crescendo and the regular absences of any dialogue were filled by this and many deep sighs.

'I thought she didn't speak Hindi,' I said to Padma.

Padma giggled and said, 'She is stupid girl. She watches just like that. No matter.'

'Where does she sleep?' I asked.

'Outside there is a shelter. She is not wanting anything else. She is lucky to have that. My mother is sending her here because she is too useless for them. She is not cooking and not very good with the cleaning. But she is very good to Maki so I keep her,' explained Padma.

Padma indicated the maid's quarters, outside the kitchen door. Around it were piles of carelessly tipped rubbish. A cockerel and a hen scrabbled a living from it. Further back was an outside fire in a pit on top of which stood a large cauldron. The girl was often hunkered down, grinding spices on a smooth stone next to it or hacking at coconuts and gourds. It was under this cooking shelter that she slept.

Resignedly, I went up to the flat roof of the house. Only mad dogs and Nicola would go to the beach before sundown. There I sat and waited among the high branches of the trees, which seemed to belong to the sky rather than to the jungle below and behind me. The house was built into the steep slope of the hill so that the roof was almost level with the tallest treetops. The branches of coconut palms swayed and arched just above my head, and their giant elliptical leaves partnered the wind in a floating, mesmerising dance. The sun glared through the few gaps in the dense canopy. A dry branch occasionally ripped the air like a firecracker as it snapped and crashed into the undergrowth. The detonations sent parrots screeching and monkeys clamouring, as did the backfiring of motor-bikes, which sped along the road at the front. Dogs barked, cats yowled, lorries rumbled by and momentarily blotted the constant distant voices. Myriad sounds billowed into the sky and gathered to cloud my mind until I dozed.

There was a huge jackfruit on a tree outside the front door. I had longed to taste it because I liked to think I was a connoisseur of fruit as others are of wines or cheese. I fingered it every time I went out of the house. When Padma's sister and two daughters arrived and we left for the beach, I had my photograph taken beside it. The fruit would not be ripe until May but the plant was edible as a vegetable. 'Tomorrow we will have jackfruit curry,' consoled Padma.

Vijay and Padma's house was semicircled by verdant forest-like foliage and almost disappeared into the abundance and abandon. This jungle plot could hardly be called a garden but it provided the family with coconuts, bananas, custard apples, chillies and mangoes at various times of the year. In return they supplied their surroundings with plentiful waste. There might once have been a time when most waste was organic, but this was plastic, paper and polystyrene. Anything from dead batteries to nappies was flung out of the back door into the jungle.

Once at the beach I was amazed when Padma and her sister went into the sea in their saris. I would rather strip off my modesty and plunge unencumbered into the sea than have to go home bedraggled in wet clothes. Then I wondered if coyness, not modesty, was at play, and that they found it worth the discomfort to emulate Hindi film heroines with wet saris clinging to alluring curves. I still thought they must have felt more like washing-lines. However, it was clearly an accepted practice because even girls of ten and eleven pulled off only their dresses before skipping into the water with their petticoats flying. When the women had finished, they stood in soaking saris on the sun-deserted beach, while globules of sand dripped from the folds in their clothing.

We got back to the smells of cooking, blaring music from the television and a deliriously happy servant, intoxicated from her afternoon of non-stop romantic movies. Padma was soon laughing and telling me that the girl had makeup smudged all over her face.

Most evenings after my massage, Padma's father, a farmer, came down from the fields to read his newspaper and eat a mountain of rice, an ocean of dal and a vast quantity of spiced vegetables. I knew he was stick thin from the weight in his step, which was that of an undernourished fairy. When the food was served, and to whom, was a random affair but the order in which it was best eaten was strictly observed. The spicy vegetables and fiery sambar – made from lentils and a blend of spices known as sambar powder – were taken with rice, and then came a second serving of rice mixed with pickles, curd and poppadums. This bland, soothing course took the heat out of the first one. Sometimes there was curd and papaya too, or *dosas* with their concentric ridges, which felt like contour lines on a tactile map.

I tripped over the servant girl one day when I was taking my empty plate into the kitchen. She was squatting on the floor by the sink eating her meal. I wanted to help with the washing-up if only to prevent her taking the plates, rinsing them under cold water and leaving a film of grease for the next meal. My offers were always rejected.

In the mornings, at six before it was hot, Vijay and I practised yoga. He walked around with an incense stick streaking a trail of sandalwood after him. His *dhoti* flicked against his ankles, and I heard him fold up the cloth between his legs to sit cross-legged in front of me. We began with a series of stretch and balance exercises to warm up then moved on to *kriyas*. These were a series of cleansing exercises using breathing techniques: breathing in through the nostrils, then one only, blowing out through the mouth and pumping air in and out using the diaphragm. This control of the breath was then carried into the *asanas*, or yoga positions.

My afternoon excursions to the beach were more pleasant now: there were fewer men to linger and leer in crowds because I had been shown a new area on our Sunday outing. There was a section with lifeguards, and two hotels catered for middle-class holidaymakers rather than travellers. I could also swim in safety: most Indian men only ever doggy-paddle, with an excessive amount of splashing and spluttering to stay afloat, which meant that I never swam into anyone as it was impossible not to hear them coming.

One day I made friends with an Indian Airlines crew, and the next, a group of German tourists. There never seemed to be a reason or a right moment to tell them that I was blind. I talked about my work and my travels, and enjoyed practising my German. Sometimes I feel my blindness makes me more glamorous than I really am: it can be difficult to make quick, easy friendships if strangers know I am blind, because they tend to take a step backwards in order to absorb the revelation. The distance leaves me as cold and lonely as a stone monument. It was nice to be an ordinary human being for once. When a woman commented, 'You're extraordinarily brave to come here, a woman all alone,' I smiled smugly to myself.

I became better at travelling alone on the buses and used an increasing variety of survival strategies. I learnt to commandeer people to my cause without feeling I owed them an explanation. For example, when I changed the bus at the main depot, I floated with the tide crossing the four-lane road and trusted the pull of the current of people in the direction of the main group of buses. Strings of women would knot together, their fingers entwined, at the edge of the road, making a secure safety-net for the very old and the very young. Then they all crossed as one and it was not difficult for me to attach myself, or abnormal to touch some stranger so intimately.

It has always felt safer to fit in as just one of a crowd than cause confusion by standing out: if I stepped off the bus with a white cane in my hand, I attracted attention as a single white blind woman and the crowd dispersed. People were not necessarily moving out of my way, but away from what they considered an oddity. Sometimes they did not know what my cane symbolised, at others they knew and were paralysed with disbelief and fear. Consequently I preferred not to use my cane because it seemed to alienate more than it encouraged people to respond with help. However, if I stood looking helpless and unable to find the correct bus, like any other bewildered foreigner, people tended to steer me in the right direction.

In the street, pedestrians moved out of the way of a blind beggar stumbling and tap-tapping along the road, but they could barely believe, let alone know what to do about, a blind foreigner seeking their assistance. Disabled people in India are either left to fend for themselves and rely on charity, or closeted in back rooms and discouraged from activity. An able disabled person is a challenging concept.

On one occasion only, an attempt to use my cane summoned understanding. A boy and a girl in their late teens came up to me and offered assistance with diplomatic graciousness and an unassuming desire to be helpful. I placed them as children of embassy staff because of their Oxbridge accents, good manners and charm. They were too well mannered to be nosy so I was not overrun with the usual questioning that comes my way in exchange for help. They waited silently until my bus arrived and saw me on safely.

Finding the right bus to Valiavila from the stand was proving about as difficult as asking for Valiavila itself once I was on the bus. After that first journey alone, Padma had armed me with a scrap of paper on which were written her address and the bus route in Malayalam, the state language. All the destinations written on the bus fronts, she explained, were in Malayalam not English. Valiavila, the English name for Padma's village, did not mean anything to the majority of the bus-travelling public. That was why people had responded with guesses of place-names in Malayalam to my flustered utterances of 'Valiavila'. I found the Malayalam word for the village both unrecognisable and unpronounceable. The piece of paper and Kerala's reputedly high literacy rate became my only hope of getting back each day.

On the festival day when there was no work, Vijay, Padma, the children and I made a trip to a siddha ashram to stock up on supplies of massage oil. The Samaja Ashram's members produce herbal medications and health products according to the siddha tradition, which is another form of ancient herbalism. First there was a long, winding bus ride into the hills and the remote countryside behind Trivandrum. From an outlying junction called Kadakal, the five of us crowded into a rickshaw, which panted and chugged its way further into the hills for another hour. Despite the remoteness of the countryside, there were sounds from dwellings every couple of hundred yards. Sometimes a lorry ran us into the side of the road, when the wheels of the rickshaw crunched over palm leaves stripped from their branches and laid to dry in the sun for thatching.

Men's voices floated down from the tree tops where they were tapping for rubber, letting the liquid latex bleed into upturned coconut shells attached to the trunks. Beyond the plantations, the foliage became less dense, opening into mango groves and tapioca fields with a wet, fertile smell. Oxen with bells around their necks plodded along, their carts piled high with sweet-smelling freshly cut hay. Forced into the side of the road on this section of the journey, we spun in a cloud of coconut dust that rose from the piles of discarded broken shells. The coconut flesh was spread out to dry for future oil extraction.

Finally we swung up a steep incline to the ashram and skidded over the gravel drive up to a veranda running around the concrete building. Sitting on the low wall a teacher was lecturing and reciting from scripts to an attentive pupil. They did not stop to greet us. Someone else came and chatted to Vijay in Malayalam. No one spoke English and I relied on Padma to be both guide and interpreter.

We were welcomed with a spread of food washed down with salted buttermilk, which we ate at rustic tables and benches, with a metal trough for washing our hands. I was aware of women with young children rustling in their skirts and old men leaning on sticks watching us from the corridors behind.

We were led to the 'engine room' of the ashram where all the herbs were sorted, prepared and stored. It smelt like a granary. I coughed and sneezed at the dust in the air. Padma scooped the many different seeds and powders from their sacks and put them into my hands to sift through my fingers. Some were hard, others crumbly or soft. I recognised cinnamon bark, nutmeg kernels, cloves, cardamom pods, fennel and coriander seeds, but there were many I could not identify.

I took a packet of Parimala bathing powder, containing sandalwood, musk, vetiver and turmeric, as a skin scrub to help remove some of the oil from my hair and body after one of Padma's extravagant massages. Parimala was also a treatment for heat conditions and infections with itching, like ringworm. I found some tooth powder, containing *neem*, a powerful antiseptic, and decided to convert to it paste.

Padma saved me from tripping into several holes dug in the concrete floor. They contained palm fronds and coconut husks, which were lit to heat cauldrons of herbs to make decoctions. In the background there was a permanent roar from a grinding machine that pulverised the seeds and leaves into fine powder, to be mixed according to siddha recipes and crudely packaged for sale in town pharmacies. Hessian sacks bursting with seeds and roots were piled on wooden slats and polythene bags of ready-mixed herbs were heaped on the floor, while brown medicine bottles crammed the shelves.

We stopped at Kadakal junction on the way back and my nose

informed me that almost every roadside shop was a siddha medical store. After consulting one of the many siddha doctors offering their services at the shops I procured a medicine for constipation. I had thought everyone got upset stomachs, diarrhoea or fevers from travelling in India, but I was the bunged-up exception. That evening I took the medicine nervously, but it tasted vile and did nothing. I repeated the dose twice the next day, expecting an explosion, but still nothing. Dispensing with all caution, I downed the rest of the bottle. Nothing.

I was also becoming anxious about my hearing. Sometimes I felt as if a dust bowl was accumulating in my ears due to the frequency with which I hung out of bus windows to appreciate the scene. In addition, there was a tidal whoosh every time I turned my head, which I associated with being knocked down by so many waves of polluted seawater. My ears itched and were blocked with eczema and small ulcers, either a reaction to the dust and sea or a consequence of my allergy to oily food, which I was never able to avoid. I suffered from varying degrees of deafness according to the level of inflammation and infection. I syringed warm oil and herbs into both ears daily, which relieved the pain and the blockage, but there were times when, worryingly, I felt doubly estranged from the world.

Just over half-way through my stay with Vijay and Padma I made a trip to the nearby Sivananda Yoga Vedanta Dhanwantari ashram in Neyyar Dam. I knew of its existence, some thirty kilometres outside Trivandrum, because it is in the network of International Sivananda Yoga Vedanta centres of which there is one in Putney, South London. It was founded by Swami Vishnu-devananda, a disciple of Swami Sivananda. Swami Sivananda was a doctor who renounced the world for the spiritual path, bringing the authority of his medical background to the teaching of yoga. In India, yoga is practised more as physiotherapy, not just as a sport or relaxation activity as it is in the West.

The route to Neyyar Dam involved travelling back into the hills by various buses, followed by a two- to three-kilometre walk. Padma insisted she should accompany me because in this remote district it was likely to be twice as difficult to make myself understood and to find help.

We left before five thirty in the morning because she wanted to get back for work. At the point where the public buses terminated, there was ferocious competition among private minibus companies to ferry passengers to the outlying villages in the hills. We crammed into the back seat of a minibus along with twenty or more others. Bags, buckets and tied bundles bounced as they landed on the roof, a clatter of feet climbed up the metal ladder on the back of the bus and thumped above our heads. When there was no more room on top for people or belongings, more baggage and bodies were stuffed through the windows and on top of us. Two knocks on the roof signalled to the driver to set off. At times the suffocating atmosphere was frightening and it was hard to keep calm.

The road ended at Neyyar Dam where there were a few *chai* stands, with branches of fat bananas hanging above their counters. Just above was the dam and from there a tarmac road twisted into the hills. We trudged along the road and soon began to sweat, despite the early hour. The surface turned to sand and dirt, full of potholes and gravel.

The ashram was built on a terraced hillside overlooking the dam. A series of flights of steps and concrete paths, lined with pots with flowers tumbling down their sides, brought us up to the offices, meditation hall and reception area. My arrival was greeted with the usual, noncommittal 'Please be sitting' from a *swami* in the reception office. We sat and waited and, as usual, I was the first to become impatient and fidgety. I seemed to worry more than Padma that she would be late in returning for work.

I went to the counter again and said, 'I think you are expecting me. I telephoned your office in Trivandrum to arrange to stay here for two days.'

'We are not having people for two days only. This is very short,' replied the *swami*.

'It is a bit late to be telling me that now. No one said anything when I telephoned,' I said.

'Just sit, please sit.'

After a while even Padma showed signs of agitation. I urged her to see what she could do. She explained that I was blind and that she would like to leave knowing I would be looked after.

'Where is her helper, then?' The *swami* was perplexed. 'Please be sitting.' We sat without knowing why, until I went to the *swami* again. 'Look, I just need to share a room and have a little help seeing around the place for a couple of days. I cleared it with your representative on the telephone when I arranged to come.'

'But where is your helper?' he insisted.

'I may be without a helper but I am not helpless. If you start by giving me a little help to know my way about, I am sure I will manage. Maybe one of your foreign guests will be willing to give me a hand.'

'Please be sitting.'

I persuaded Padma to go, and assured her that I would find my way back in a couple of days. I was both angry and anxious, desperate for the *swami* to propose anything other than 'Please sit.'

At last he called me to a large meditation hall next to the office. He stood on the entrance steps and his voice spread over my head like a black cloud: 'You'll be sleeping in here. Have you a mat?'

The thought of being alone in a meditation hall, not knowing how to get anywhere and isolated from the other visitors, was more than I was prepared to tolerate. I felt like a leper who had to be segregated.

'Why don't you let me share with your foreign students? I am quite happy to share a hut with them. Isn't that what they do? It would be easier for me to get around if I could make contact with some other people. Easier for you too. I won't bother you then.'

Somehow or other I had cracked the code, said the right thing. A boy took me to a hut and the padlock on the door was unlocked. There were two cots in the hut and I was left to wonder which one to take. Freda, my German roommate, entered and demanded, 'Who are you?'

Explaining to Freda was as effortless as letting an ice-cream melt in the sun. She simply suggested we get something to eat. I took her arm and she led the way.

Food was served in a large open-sided barn. Long, narrow rush matting was unrolled and people sat cross-legged with a metal tray in front of them. Other students walked around and plopped vegetables, rice and salad or ladled sambar on to the trays. After all the swishing, swirling, dolloping and pouring had finished, the talking stopped and a chant began led by a *swami*. Then we scooped up food with our hands while the servers wandered around to refill the plates. The food was plain because spices and garlic were considered to interfere with meditative practice. At the end everyone rinsed their metal plates under cold taps at the other end of the barn.

'We eat at ten thirty in the morning and at six in the evening. There is tea at two thirty.' Freda explained the running of the day to me. 'We rise at five and go for meditation and chanting on the meditation platform overlooking the dam. I have *karma* yoga now for one hour. You know this means to do jobs. Afterwards I will take you to the dam. Do you like swimming?'

The ashram was a rare haven of silence in India, tucked away from the tidal roar of traffic crashing relentlessly even through small villages like the one where Padma and Vijay lived. Only the activities of daily life reverberated in the air. The sonorous crash of the gong, summoning people to attend the next meal or class, wavered and vibrated, the sound unchallenged. As I rested in the cool hut, I listened to the chores being completed: the beating of rugs and the slapping clean of wet clothes to the sounds of chanting and lingering laughter. The time for ablutions was the noisiest and least delightful: running water from a shower or a toilet was accompanied by snorting, spitting and throaty gargling of catarrh.

The dam was enchanting, set among grassy banks and below dense jungle. We swam in clear water, floating and chatting, until I remembered that Padma had mentioned crocodiles. Instinctively and pointlessly I drew my legs up into my stomach, felt myself sink, thought better of it, stretched out and swam closer to the bank. As casually as I could, I asked Freda, 'Heard anything about crocodiles in these waters?'

'Ach, *ja*, they are only on the far side. They are not bothered with us.'

Perhaps she had consulted them. I thought about their swift, silent approach and decided to get out.

Real fear set in during the night after a conversation with a *swami*, who confirmed the presence of crocodiles in the dam because of a farm lower down. The smell of bloody water and the feel of cold amphibian skin crawled through my sleep. Realisation dawned in the early hours that I had narrowly escaped. I often seem to experience more fear about what might have been than I ever do about what might be to come. Despite my anxiety-ridden night I reflected that at least if I worried with hindsight I would not stop myself adventuring and exploring.

During the course of my stay I attended the *asana* and *pranayama* – exercise and breathing – classes. The *swamis* did not adapt their teaching to make anything clearer for me, and I was fascinated to watch them operate as wise sages imparting wisdom through tired metaphor. They lectured by delivering colourful but simple concepts, like a child paints by blobbing blocks of primary colour on a board. So, a *swami* would conclude, after two hours of circumlocution while we swatted away flies: 'A deep mind is peaceful like the waves that roll in deep water while shallow minds are disturbed by choppy thoughts.'

During my second evening there was great excitement because Swami Vishnu-devananda was visiting. He was confined to a wheelchair and escorted by an entourage of disciples. A musical evening, given by local tabla and sitar players, followed a group meditation. I went to bed to the sound of Indian music and rose at dawn to the sound of chanting coming from the platform above the dam.

When I was ready to leave the ashram, the *swami* at the office refused to take any money for my stay. He was warmer than he had been at my arrival and other *swamis* came to say goodbye. I felt I had succeeded in removing some blinkers and letting them see that there really was nothing from which to shy away.

Freda walked with me down to the bus to make sure I got on the right one to the junction. We waited ages. She bought a cold drink in a screw-top bottle, drank a third and stopped. She held the bottle to the light and declared, 'Just look! It is cloudy, no good.' She paused and continued, 'Oh, I just forgot you don't see it.' She demanded her money back. The

Goutam and Aunty with their dog at home

Peerooze with his two sons

'Trying the local delicacies.'

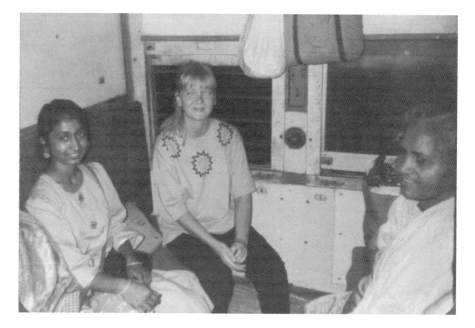

On the train to Trivandrum

Sunset at Kovalam Beach

Meeting new friends

The modes and comfort of transport changed

The contrasts of the market bombarded all my senses

drink-wallah was battered by her indignation at being cheated. He gave her a peanut and honey bar from a glass jar instead of money as compensation, but she was even more annoyed to be appeased like a child having a tantrum. She opened the lid of the jar and helped herself to two more bars to make up the value of her drink. Back at the bus stop she spat out a mouthful of peanuts and gave the other bars to children shinning up the poles of the shelter. 'It is dried out. No one takes any notice of the sell-by dates in this country,' she said. The children ate gleefully, proving her point.

At Kadakal junction I pulled out my cane, rather than pointing vaguely at my piece of paper, in the faint hope that someone might get me on a bus to Valiavila. A voice said, 'There, that way.' I tried to follow the direction in which he had pointed his voice and kept walking. I got on the first bus I came to after listening for feet climbing up steps. I sat and the bus filled. I checked once, twice, three times that the bus went to Valiavila. I stuck my paper with the magic translation under people's noses. The fourth person I asked said, 'You get down now. This bus no good.' No one else had murmured a word, so I trusted this instruction rather than no instruction at all.

I was ushered on to another bus by a man winding on a ticketing machine. My confidence was flagging, however, and I asked a woman, 'Is this bus going to Valiavila?'

She did not reply but after a while I sat down and she tapped the shoulder of the person sitting in front and spoke in Malayalam. The person turned to me and said in staccato English, 'White Express. Tirumalei. White Express.'

'That's good,' I said cheerfully. I knew that Tirumalei was the village after Valiavila, even if I did not know the meaning of White Express.

There followed an increasing burble of voices conferring in the bus. I knew from the excited pointing and covering of eyes that everyone knew I was blind. Someone had recognised my cane when I first got on. The chatter was noisy and seemed to be agitated as it travelled up the bus row by row until it reached the driver at the front. He slammed the door and his voice boomed back furiously at the collective drone. I could not imagine what message the driver had received to make him so angry.

'What's up?' I asked the person in front.

'White Express,' was the answer. I began to figure that an Express bus might not stop everywhere, and that it would go straight through Valiavila. I made a move to get off but my neighbour raised a hand and rested it on my shoulder in a firm command to hold on. I realised that the commotion had gathered force and it was all about me. I sensed tongues flicking in my direction as people glanced over and continued to plead my cause with the driver. The passengers were vociferous, but their clamorous appeals to the driver's rigid back to stop at Valiavila were meeting with steadfast obduracy. I gazed out of the window and pretended it had nothing to do with me.

The irate driver revved the engine, crunched the gearstick and swung the bus out of the station. There was sudden and total silence. We careered around bends and sped recklessly downhill. The driver accelerated and braked alternately like a crazed rider spurring the flanks of his horse while simultaneously wrenching its head.

He finally jammed on the brakes and we were at a standstill. No one spoke. My instinct was to get off. I felt everyone willing me to get off but no one told me to do so. I made for the doors, fumbled to open them, climbed down and stood in a whirlwind of dust left by the bus wheels spitting out sand as they spun away. In my experience, it tends to be the grumpiest London cabbies who know London best; they always drop me precisely where I want to be. So is it with Indian bus drivers, for I stood at the gates to Karma. How he knew I will never know.

My departure from Valiavila was now imminent and I telephoned Mr Joseph, a friend of a friend in England, to make arrangements to get hold of his sister, Leela Abraham, in Ernakulam, Cochin. Mr Joseph offered to pick me up in Trivandrum because he travelled there frequently on business. I declined because I wanted to go by the traditional route to Cochin – by boat through the backwaters. Coastal Kerala is interlaced with an intricate network of inland waterways, and it takes a day to navigate as far as Alleppey. Mr Joseph agreed to send his car and driver to fetch me from his cousin, Mr Paul, who lived in Alleppey and would meet me off the boat.

Before I left Valiavila I decided to visit Kanyakumari, the Land's End of India. I would join a bus party led by a tour guide who was Vijay's cousin, and Chachou was appointed my guide for the day. Young children in India are often responsible for looking after tiny siblings or disabled members of the family, but although I thought this made them less selfish than western children, I was not entirely comfortable about using an eight-year-old as my eyes for the day. The night before he lost his nerve and decided not to go with me.

On the bus I befriended a Dutch couple and amazed myself by being open about my situation at the first opportunity. They promptly invited me to spend the day with them, which was refreshing after the wiles and manoeuvres I had been employing to get where I wanted to go. I spent the next two and a half hours relaxed in the surety of companionship and help for the day. We stopped to visit Padmanabhapuram, a pagoda-shaped palace, which had been the seat of the Travancore rulers during the seventeenth and eighteenth centuries. The earlier part had been built in the early sixteenth century and it was still possible to imagine the lives its inhabitants must have led. It was entirely of timber construction, with shutters and ornately carved pillars. There was even a massage room, with steps leading down to a large concrete bath full of stagnant water and green slime.

Karin and Waldesar, my Dutch friends, accompanied me round the palace, and we were joined by Betty, an Indian woman. Then I had three people's descriptions streaming my way. My mind's eye flicked through them as if they were a series of photographs. Waldesar sat beside me for the next leg of the journey, and gave a running commentary on the fleeting pastiches of life that came into view as the bus rushed on into Tamil Nadu and to Kanyakumari. Having Waldesar describe what he saw as he saw it was both affirming and alarming. On the one hand, I was pleased to hear that much of what I perceived was accurate, and even extended beyond what he noticed. I pointed out, for example, the sweetly aromatic curry-leaf trees, which he had not seen. On the other hand, he slotted many

131

missing pieces into a jigsaw picture I was putting together of the countryside around me. He told me about the lotus flowers floating on patches of water, and of how the houses with their whitewashed concrete walls and red-tiled roofs became coconut-thatched mud huts as we entered deeper countryside. Tin shacks stood within yards of pompous villas, which had often been built by wealthy Indians who, having worked abroad, returned home to build neo-Georgian mansions in their native state.

When we crossed back from Kerala into Tamil Nadu, it became apparent from the quality of the roads, the dust and the debris that it was a poor state. Kerala's lush bounty, with its fecund soil and plentiful harvests, dwindled to a few paddy-fields as our journey continued. It made me appreciate how every stretch of land in Kerala was shaded by trees or moist with vegetation.

We stopped at the Hindu temple of Suchindram. Non-Hindus were allowed to visit it providing men wore *dhotis*, and women were in long skirts or saris. The most striking thing about it was the volume of noise inside. The ecclesiastical solemnity of the churches in England is far removed from the convivial atmosphere of temple life. Silent reverence, I was beginning to learn, is not something Hindus consider necessary to the observance of their religion. Children ran, skipped and played. People rang bells and milled around in large family groups as if at a car-boot sale. There was a buzz of fun, and the gladness of people on an outing rather than the hush and still of Christian worship.

Once in Kanyakumari, Waldesar, Karin and I made the pilgrimage by boat to the rock out at sea where Vivekananda, a famous Indian philosopher and religious crusader, meditated. The water was confusing and choppy as we dipped in and out of maelstroms and eddies. It bubbled like a huge jacuzzi bath, erupting with sudden spurts. The water here is kept in swirling motion by the pressures of three seas joining at the tip of the continent. While everyone was meditating in the overcrowded meditation hall, built as part of the memorial to Vivekananda, I sat and listened to the chaotic energy of the sea. I was drawn to the vortices, and imagined that a century ago, when Vivekananda meditated for three days on this rock, the swell and noise was just the same.

Back on the mainland we wandered around the town, which was full of sales gimmicks for the tourists and begging *sadhus*. We retreated to those establishments catering for the non-vegetarian, drinking, smoking, gambling citizens. We moved from den to den, picking our way down concrete steps and arrived in smoky cellars with the smell of open whisky bottles and the sound of cards being flicked on to tables. The herbs I smelt were somewhat different from those I had investigated so far...

I dozed for most of the journey back to Trivandrum. I was aware of how different the night smelt from the day as we neared town. In the daytime, aromas are like cotton-wool clouds that billow in the sky; they waft momentarily past the nose. In the evening, they gain weight and hover inertly in the dark; they hang heavily in the nostrils, occlude, and clog in the night air. The smell of paraffin from lamps lighting the shops and hutch-like dwellings on the streets, the acridity of wood fires or noxious gas burners formed a solid backdrop to the pungency of cooking spices, which tarry, and eventually embalm the dead of night.

The next morning I left at five with Padma for Quilon and stood for three hours on the bus. When we arrived the Quilon boatmen tried to lure us on to their boats, regardless of my ticket. I assumed that once I was on board and we were under way they would reject it and charge me again. Padma was wise to the possible pitfalls and we walked some way around the lagoon's edge to search for the boat on which I was booked. She asked directions several times and always got the reply, '*Sidha sidha*,' meaning straight on. But she turned and twisted left and right regardless. I asked why. 'These people are very joking. They fooling about. They are not knowing.'

I was always amazed by this Indian compulsion to send people off in the wrong direction. It was a slight comfort to know that no discrimination was involved in this quirky behaviour. All foreigners, whether Asian or European, were equally misled.

Padma found my boat, a small wooden craft with a diesel engine. She steered me across a rickety plank and down some steps into the cabin.

A Dutch couple and a French girl were already on board. While the boatman took our tickets four other westerners got on. Padma explained to the incredulous boatman that I was to be met at Quilon and that I would need help on arrival and at the lunch stop. He scrutinised my ticket as if searching for a way out or for a clue to solve one of life's mysteries. He stared at me as if needing some confirmation. I stared back, held his gaze precisely, confusing him even more until my hello jolted him into action and he finished his ticket collection.

I said an emotional farewell to Padma, overwhelmed as I recognized just how kind she had been to me.

COCHIN: A FAMILY OF THE PLANTATIONS

S lowly, we chugged our way through the waterways of the coastal countryside. As elsewhere in Kerala, the vegetation on the islands and banks on either side of the channels or surrounding the lagoons was dense and tropical. The boat crossed many wide lagoons, which narrowed into networks of intricate waterways and opened again into large areas of flat water. Vultures skimmed the mirror-like surface, before shaking strong, wide wings and soaring into the sky again where they cruised in the air. I listened to them fluttering in the overhanging palm fronds when we slipped down the narrow channels under a canopy of branches, shaded from the fierce sun. The scent of mimosa rose from the dark green foliage and I imagined how its blossoms dotted the verdant greenery like yellow fairy-lights.

Along the banks, children waved and ran to keep up with the boat. They shouted, 'Pen, please. One pen, please,' and repeated, 'Hello,' ceaselessly. We were as much an attraction to the locals as they were to us: spectator and spectacle gradually merged.

The Dutch woman knew that I could not see. I had registered her listening to Padma's conversation with the boatman at the outset. She nudged her partner to make room for me when I clambered up on the cabin roof where all seven passengers perched, best to view backwater life. Her volunteering of succinct and useful descriptions made my impressions clearer. She commented on women threading coir, a by-product of coconut, and then on groups of people picking snails from the stone walls built down the banks. A picture of small fishing communities, supplementing their income with mat-making and snail-farming, was painted delicately in my mind. The huts were mainly made of mud with no electricity cables in sight. There were no modern amenities. She described how at the end of villages, small Punch-and-Judy-style cabins jutted over the water: people backed into them and defecated straight into the water. I heard youngsters splashing, women plopping pitchers, men urinating, and people of all ages washing themselves behind cloth screens.

When she picked out the cantilevered Chinese fishing-nets, I nodded as if I already knew what one of these looked like. I could have asked for a more detailed description, but I am always slightly embarrassed to admit to the excruciatingly simple gaps in my knowledge, which are nearly always of things I have never had enough sight to see for myself. If I was shown a clear picture of something as a child or given a full description, I can rely on memory or imagination to understand and re-create it. Cantilevered fishing-nets are missing.

By the early afternoon there was more traffic on the water. Small boats stank of fish and larger barges were heavy with hay. A quacking, and I pictured dark paddling patches of ducks, each family glued together so that they appeared like a dark puddle on a road surface.

Suddenly our engine spluttered into ominous silence and we drifted in the middle of a lagoon. It was rather peaceful, at least in the short term, floating dreamily without the smell of diesel or the constant rumble of an engine while the boatman and his boy crawled under boards with a large wrench and loop of rusted wire. A few of the passengers lay down on the cabin roof to snooze in the sun. They sat up again quickly when they heard a shuddering, dragging grind that shook the boat and rattled every bone. This scraping resistance was followed by the large snap of a sudden release. I felt sure that this noise was disappointing to the boatman. The boat grounded, snapping its propeller, then floated free only to slide to a halt again, this time more softly. The depth of the water varied greatly in the lagoons and we were in a particularly shallow part. The boatman produced a long pole, which he pushed into the mud with a squelch, shoving a large squashy jellyfish out of his way. We were marooned until the next boat came by to pick us up. Most of us felt indolent in the heat of the day and were resigned to loll about while the boatman ran around stringing engine parts together.

Eventually the Kerala Tourist vessel motored up. The boatmen negotiated a price and we offloaded from one boat to the other. The Kerala boat reminded me of the type of craft used for passenger trips down the Thames or the Rhine. We squeezed uncomfortably on to crowded bench seats. Our boatman came to reassure me that he would stay to see me off safely at Alleppey. He did not offer anyone a refund even though the tourist boat tickets were half the price of ours.

The noisy throbbing of the larger engine and the diesel fumes obliterated all the sounds and smells of life on the banks. I was like the screen of a television set that suddenly goes blank because transmission is cut. Blind in all but my imagination, and with nothing better to do, I visualised trees silhouetted in a rosy red sunset. I switched to a memory station, and to an evening some weeks back in Auroville when I had enjoyed a burning orange sunset on my face. The surrounding eucalyptus trees still glistened silver and cool in my memory, but I pictured the trees on the banks of the filament-thin waterways looming black and threatening as dusk fell.

The Dutch woman, one of the French passengers and our boatman were all ready to help me when we disembarked at Quilon. As they bade me farewell I suspected they were worried about the difficulties I might encounter when they were not at hand to intervene. It was hard for me to trust in serendipity, but my experience thus far had been encouraging. People had tended to appear unexpectedly just when I needed them. The goodwill and supportiveness I had met fuelled my optimism.

Mr Paul met me on the jetty and shook my hand. He was taller than most south Indians, with a gangly gait that made him seem doddery and frail. I let him lead me to his car, using my bag to shield myself from the jabs and scrapes of the crowd. He had been waiting for an hour and a half because of the delay and I felt anxious that he had been standing all that time.

At his house I was greeted by his daughter, home on study leave. They showed me through to the sitting room where a television talked to itself, and into the bathroom where I was left to freshen up. Then the girl took my hand and led me to the back of the room where a table was laid with snacks and tea. Fresh pineapple, fried banana and *ros malei*, spongy gram-flour balls in syrup, had been prepared for my visit, and I felt like an esteemed visitor instead of a gate-crasher, with father and daughter sitting to right and left, listening to my account of the boat trip, and encouraging me to eat and drink.

Now Mr Joseph's driver was waiting outside to take me to Leela Abraham's house in Ernakulam, the mainland section of Cochin. Although Mr Joseph, who was no relation to Susan Joseph with whom I spent time in Madras, had assumed responsibility for arranging my visit, I was to be the house guest of Leela, his recently widowed sister, because it was through friends of her son that I had been put in touch with the family.

I said farewell once again to people who had shown me kindness but whom I was unlikely ever to meet again. There were many people whose kindness overwhelmed me, sometimes after only a momentary interaction, and who added a unique quality to my trip, which I came to value more and more. I was learning how true generosity costs something but expects nothing in return, not even a promise to meet again. People had given me their time and their food and shared their homes without any expectation of reward. I came to believe that Indians had a greater sense of integration, of being part of a whole, than we individualistic westerners. Giving seemed to be a self-perpetuating way of life. My inclination was always to present my benefactors with some material token of thanks, and sometimes felt that this was a poor, misplaced attempt to repay them. I needed to do something more. I learned that the best gift is to become more generous and selfless as opportunities present. I discovered what hospitality and kindness are all about from my Indian friends.

I leant back in the rear seat of Mr Joseph's Ambassador and appreciated the suspension after the hours I had spent standing on the bus and sitting on the ferry. I opened the windows and was glad that no one was in the car who preferred the windows closed and the air-conditioning running. Interestingly, most of the drivers were happy for the windows to be open: they relaxed with one bent arm wedged on the window frame, more accustomed to the heat than their wealthier passengers who could afford to control even the power of the sun. I simply wanted to see what was outside, and needed the windows open to do so. I smelt the brackishness of coastal waters mixed with the putrefaction of dead fish.

I thought more about how much I had come to value the help that had been one of the main reasons why I had survived the trip so far. It had been in India that I had started to experience different feelings about the dependency on others that resulted from my blindness. I began to understand that the requests I had to make created opportunities for others to feel good about themselves, to feel that they could contribute to something beyond their usual sphere. It is not that Indians necessarily practise great acts of benevolence, but in a country with so many mouths and so little money it helps to have so many helping hands. It is almost an ingrained code of conduct comparable to our 'British reserve' and 'sense of fair play'. Indians have a great sense of 'family' and the concept extends to friends, who are soon called Aunty, Brother or Sister. People are made important in a land where they die in large numbers due to a lack of other resources.

My hosts were a wealthy Syrian Christian family of the tea and rubber plantations, of which there were many around Cochin. Following the death of her husband, Leela had come down from their tea estate in the hills around Monar to live in Ernakulam for its safety and convenience. She spoke nostalgically of the estates and her previous life, but Mr Joseph now headed the family interest in tea. George Varghese, Leela's younger brother, and his wife Shyla lived on and managed the family rubber estate outside Calicut, 219 kilometres north of Cochin.

I arrived at Leela's modern, comfortable villa to an assembly of her closest family members as well as various nephews and nieces. That first evening I was struck by how everyone spoke immaculate English – which was much less tiring for me – and how large a part their religion played in their lives. After dinner we gathered in the sitting room where we stood and joined hands for a reading and a prayer.

It wasn't until I settled into bed that I worked out some of the things that made Leela's bungalow different from other houses in which I had stayed. It was somehow more lavish with frippery, like soft furnishings in the bedroom and bowls of perfumed soaps in the bathroom. My mind turned to the prospect of going to visit a company called Synthite in the morning. Despite its unlikely name, it extracted and produced natural colourings, flavourings and oils from plant products, and I was always on the look-out for new suppliers of good quality essential oils that I could use in my work. I was to have Mr Joseph's driver for the journey and was pleased that I would be otherwise unescorted. I was wondering how I would be received as a blind customer without a companion when I slipped into sleep.

I wound down the windows and smelt wealth in the air throughout the drive out of town and into the rolling hills to Kolenchery. Everything seemed cleaner, more organised, crisper, sharper than other places I had been to, and when we turned into tiny winding country lanes, with high banks of hedges and flowers almost leaning into the car, we were still, surprisingly, on tarmac surfaces and not bumping in and out of potholes.

We passed through smoothly swinging metal gates and into the building's forecourt. The driver left me in Reception and I sat on an ergonomically designed office chair. I recognised the echo of glass and guessed there were huge tinted windows from floor to ceiling. Mr Jacob, the founding owner and director of Synthite, came out to meet me.

During our introduction I told him I was blind and asked for the guidance of his arm. I found the declaration and request difficult to make because they always distract attention from the business at hand. However, Mr Jacob was only briefly taken aback. He took me into his large office with cool floor tiles, air-conditioning and more modern furniture. He ordered coffee, and asked, 'How will we be doing this if you are not seeing?'

At first his directness augured well, although later I was discomfited him when he broadcast my disability to each employee as we met them. For the time being, though, there was the bonus that I understood his English. I answered, 'Perhaps you could start by giving me your sales documentation and price lists for natural essential oils. I will ask someone to read them to me when I get home.'

'You are only interested in natural oils? We do synthetic products as well for the food and fragrance industry.'

'I am searching out plant and spice oils for their medicinal value.'

'What oils are you wanting?'

'I would like to smell your range and take some samples home with me.'

We strolled across to the research and development laboratories. Mr Jacob explained that since he had started his business twenty years ago it had grown from a few farm buildings into a family concern. He employed both of his sons and his two sons-in-law. The laboratories were impressive, and the quality-control function seemed capable of the sort of detailed analysis that I required.

We moved into a large boardroom and I sat at the oval end of a conference table, while Mr Jacob had a boy bring racks of stoppered test tubes containing sample oils. I smelt spiky lemon-grass and tangy orange as soon as I passed the thin strips of blotting paper impregnated with them under my nose.

'I am not knowing much about the medicinal use,' said Mr Jacob, 'but this lemon-grass, you are so rightly knowing, it is very traditional in India. Very antiseptic. It is also chasing insects and bad smells away so very much used in the home.'

'Yes,' I agreed. 'I find it effective against infectious illness and fevers. It is very cooling to have a few drops diluted in a bath for someone with glandular fever or flu.'

I made a mental note to take a sample of the orange oil because it smelt particularly round and warm. I was treating a patient at home who had picked up a bad dose of amoebic dysentery while abroad. It had proved resistant to the normal antibiotics used and he had suffered with severe stomach upsets for almost two years. Abdominal massage with orange oil was the only thing that settled his stomach. I needed to stock up.

Mr Jacob anointed a succession of strips with a small amount of oil and waited for me to identify them, like a quiz-master. 'And this one?' he asked.

The next odour was pungent and sweet, reminding me of Christmas and mulled wine. Clove. Coriander was unmistakable – I had become so used to the bundles of its limp but powerful-smelling leaves piled high on carts heading for market. I was surprised to find the watery smell of celery when I had been expecting more exotic aromas. It was an oil I had never used while the ginger, full and juicy-smelling, and the whiff of pepper, like a blast of heat, were vital to my range of most-used oils. Ginger is invaluable for nausea, especially in pregnancy, either used like a smelling salt or in a massage. However, its main use stems from traditional Chinese medicine where it is prescribed for conditions where the body is not coping with moisture, whether the moisture comes from within the body or without; I use it with people suffering from diarrhoea, catarrh or bronchitis, which are all examples of complaints from internal moisture. Rheumatism is the most common example of the body's difficulty with external moisture: here, the fiery properties of ginger can combat the ache of a condition made worse by winter damp, as can the warming effects of black pepper. The best way to administer these oils is by massage or compresses on the painful areas. As black pepper is also a tonic, I prefer to use it when muscular pain is associated with fatigue. I have several clients who are athletes and benefit from black pepper massages before training because it stimulates the blood supply, so oxygenating the muscles and preventing stiffness and pain. My treatments to prepare runners for the London Marathon have been the most successful.

The nutmeg and cinnamon oils conjured up memories of milk puddings, while cardamom was cloying and reminiscent of Indian sweetmeats. Curcuma was the only one whose smell fooled me: it was so flowery and camphorous it made me think it was in fact camphor. I chose eight samples to take back for testing in England.

Mr Jacob bought his spices from farmers who gave him a sample of their crop to test before each sale was agreed. However, the standards required by the food and flavourings and perfumery industries are different from those of the medicinal world, so I would need to have the properties of the various samples analysed. While they were being packaged, we went down to the grinding, rolling and distilling buildings. In the distillery the tiny gallon drums collecting each essential oil stood next to giant vats that held a ton of the dry raw material. It emphasised the vast amounts of herbs and spices necessary to produce even a small quantity of oil. Mr Jacob was keen for me to climb ladders and walk along platforms around and above the vats and condensing pipes, so that I could witness the immaculate functioning of his units. It was during this tour that he could not resist sharing his amazement with his employees: 'She is not seeing, you know, and managing all this so brilliantly.'

'Your premises are very clean and tidy,' I complimented him.

'How do you be knowing this?' he marvelled.

The clues were easy to pick up: there was no grit or dust underfoot and no stale smell, but mainly there was the beaming pride of Mr Jacob.

In the fields around the buildings there were various spice crops. Black pepper vines clambered tenaciously up mango trees under which we stopped for shade. The peppercorns clustered together in bundles like bunched-up necklaces. Mr Jacob explained that they were not yet black but green, and walked me over to a platform of palm-leaf mats from which he gave me a handful of shrivelled berries and said, 'Now that they have dried in the sun they have darkened.'

Nutmeg hung on trees like golf balls, ripe and splitting open, surrendering their fruit and their curls of mace. Cardamoms stayed close to the ground, and I had to bend and delve into the bushes to feel the clinging pods. Cinnamon, clove and tamarind trees struggled for space and light, while ginger and turmeric plants sent their tuberous rhizomes downwards into the cool dark soil.

When I arrived back, Leela asked, 'What is your programme now?'

I seized on this as an opportunity to make arrangements for the rest of the day. 'I would like to squeeze in some sight-seeing, get to know Cochin a bit better, then go to the Kathakali dance evening here in Ernakulam.' I was hoping to track down Guru Kal, a teacher of Kathakali, Keralan dance. The dancers gave and received a strenuous form of foot massage as part of their training. Most Indian foot-pressure massage, such as the one Vijay and Padma's family had developed, was derived from the Kalari, Kathakali teachers, masters of footwork and massage.

Leela was suspicious about the traditional dancers, and uncertain about my proposed sight-seeing. 'What will you be seeing in Cochin?' she queried.

'I'll let you know once I know what there is to see.'

We booked a tourist taxi and a guide, who arrived within minutes. On his recommendation, we proceeded to Fort Cochin on the southern peninsula by crossing one of the bridges that connect the islands which make up Cochin. This was the older part, and consisted of winding alleys jammed with people and cars. There was a synagogue, Mattencherry Palace, and India's oldest European-built church, dedicated to St Francis. They were all closed, which delighted me because I preferred to wander around the narrow lanes of Jew Town, passing antique shops that smelt of brass polish and old leather.

We returned to Ernakulam for the Kathakali dance. The gathering spectators sat under a bamboo porch and watched the four actors preparing for the performance, painting one another's faces with copious quantities of makeup. I could hear the dabbing and plastering of sticky wetness, the colours that came from powdered minerals and tree sap. There was no Guru Kal, but I spoke to the dance-master about the chances of finding a

Kalari dancer to give me a massage so that I would know what it was like. He warned me that it was a firm massage, concentrating the work of the feet on the buttocks. It was given mainly during training in the monsoon when the dancers rise at four in the morning to practise. When they were saturated with sweat, they were pliable and ready to take the pressure of the massage to spread the pelvis and encourage the feet to splay outwards. The aim was to become duckfooted because this was the position they held in their dance movements. I was a little concerned that the pressure would be unpleasant and unhealthy for my pelvis, but agreed to send a rickshaw the following afternoon to collect a masseur.

We were called to enter the room where the performance was to take place. There were rows of wooden chairs on grass matting and a stage at the front. Each scene was introduced with a brief explanation without which I would not have understood what was happening because the performances were entirely of music, movement and mime. The opening was a demonstration of a ceremonial salutation. Feet thumped, wrist and ankle bells jangled, the singer wailed, a sitar player strummed and the tabla was pounded until it all climaxed in a sustained frenzy of emotion. The actors' painted faces denoted the characteristic they personified: the virtuous one was green and the evil or powerful one was black. Their extravagant posturing indicated an emotional state, like jealousy, greed or anger. The sound of the feet banging the floor, the feel of the actor receding or strutting forward by relaxing or contracting muscular tension, the sound of the bells making a solid rattling or crazed jangle conveyed a wordless story of love, betrayal and death.

I arrived back to a message that confirmed Dr Rajeevan, who was known to Dr Renade, had agreed to accompany me to Kottakkal, the heartland of ayurvedic practice. I was staggered that this man, who did not know me, a doctor in the middle of a Ph.D., was prepared to travel over eight hundred kilometres from his home, which was north of Bangalore, to pick me up in Cochin, then onwards for another two hundred and fifty kilometres to Kottakkal. And this did not include the return journey. He had not only agreed but had set off without contacting me, on the instruction of his former professor. He was due the following night.

Before the family gathered to read a psalm and say prayers, Leela conferred with Mr Joseph about my massage arrangements for the next day. They were uncomfortable about a masseur coming to the house and suggested an alternative: the eldest brother, Mathew, knew a clinic in town where ayurvedic massage was given. I volunteered to cancel my Kathakali masseur, albeit with some lingering regret, but I did not want to offend my hosts – and there was always the possibility that if I went through with it I would end up permanently duck-footed.

Instead, the teamwork of George Varghese, Mathew and Daisy, Mr Joseph's wife, resulted the following morning in a visit to Dr Babu's multi-disciplinary clinic. It was in the main shopping centre of Ernakulam, a smart area with huge glass-fronted shops reflecting the sun's glare so blindingly that no one could window-shop. When we arrived none of the escalators in the mall worked and few of the shops were open, but the piped music played regardless. I could have been in any shopping centre in any capital city; everything was so anodyne, except for the tell-tale sounds of India – incessant hammering, chiselling and sawing. Indians are forever putting up buildings or pulling them down.

A homeopath, acupuncturist, naturopath, unani – a Muslim derivation of ayurveda – and an ayurvedic doctor practised from this clinic. Dr Babu Vasudevan, the founder, sanctioned my request for a treatment in the clinic's hospital but added, 'This is being very unusual. Normally we are having in-patients on courses only.'

My masseuse was as wide as she was tall. As I stripped off she scrubbed her hands purposefully. The room was private with an adjoining bathroom. She commanded me to sit on a wooden table and began by giving me a light head massage. Then she worked over my body, discovering the stiffness in my spine between my shoulders. She pressed the marma points in this area with a constant, drilling thumb pressure. She delved her fingertips into my muscles and released fibrous tangles with twists of her wrists and pinches from her two pincer-like thumbs.

After this painful but gratifying start I lay on my back while she swept up my legs, up and over my hipbones, down and around my abdomen, encircled my breasts and pulled down my arms, shaking each individual finger as if in farewell before she repeated the whole movement. She told me she was divorced with one child as she worked the heel of her hand into my belly. She chatted about the many western patients in the hospital and said, 'They come for reducing massage. Why you come? You don't want reducing.'

'Oh, I'm just interested, that's all.' As I was turned on to my front I asked, 'Don't people come for other reasons?'

'Yes, yes, very sick people. Bad backs, rheumatism. Many Indian people getting diabetes and hearts. So very much spoonfuls of sugar, everything with coconut, and salt in drinking and very many snacks,' she said. 'You take dry-heat bath now.'

I lay flat on my back in a sauna, a wooden box like a coffin with a hole through which my head poked. Steam swelled over my body, spreading into all my curves and crevices, settling in the bony dips like a creeping fog lingering in street corners. I was clammy with a sense of claustrophobia, so hot that fast-flowing streams of oil and sweat ran and pooled on my stomach or slid down my sides. The masseuse had gone. I tried calling but there was no response and I could not lift the lid. A salty droplet of sweat stung my eye. I knew that panic and struggle would make me hotter so I tried to stay calm. It took an enormous effort of will not to think about the unregulated nature of Indian equipment and the temperature control system... However, I was just beginning to remember film scenes in which people were buried alive in deserts with just their heads above the sand when the attendant returned and released me with a smile.

On our return we found that Leela had laid the table with papaya, banana halva, *rasgullas* and salty wafers. The *rasgullas*, curdled milk balls made from concentrated milk solids and steeped in syrup, were almost too sweet to eat but irresistible because they squeaked at every bite.

In the morning I was to leave early with Dr Rajeevan, providing he reached us in time. After we had eaten I showered, scratched at some mosquito bites and packed my bag, which was bursting because I was accumulating more and more things to take back to England. There were not only oil samples and documents, but a *salwar kameez* given to me by Padma and now a garnet necklace from Leela.

When Dr Rajeevan arrived, he was immediately invited to eat. Everyone gathered around him to serve, discuss plans and watch him devour his meal ravenously. I realized that I had been spoilt by the excellent English of the Syrian Christian community in Cochin: Dr Rajeevan gabbled a fast, Indianised English in the most unintelligible fashion I had so far encountered. I foresaw a problem. He swung a lanky arm across to a serving dish for more food while explaining to Mr Joseph something about his ayurvedic training in Kottakkal and current Ph.D work. He gnawed simultaneously on a chicken bone, which squeaked against his teeth. He did not address me at all.

'So you trained to be an allopathic doctor after your time in Kottakkal,' clarified Mr Joseph.

I was glad someone could understand his English. He gobbled his words as fast as he guzzled his food. Uninhibited, he proceeded both to talk about and serve himself for what seemed like hours. At last he leant back and raised his arms, palms flattened, in the direction of his hostess as a sign that he had finished. We moved to the sitting room, where an animated but confused discussion took place about how best to get to Kottakkal: how to travel, where to change from bus to train, train to bus. When to leave provoked even more adamant opinions and complicated justifications. Understanding little of the detail, but conscious of the entanglement of the men's ideas and egos, I left them to unravel the schedule.

At six the following morning Mr Joseph and I met Dr Rajeevan at the railway station, and got on to the train. The journey was tiresome: we changed from one slow passenger train that stopped everywhere to another because there was no direct line. My new guide lacked the imagination to steer me around people and obstacles: as we went up and down steps or along train corridors, I tripped or banged into other passengers because he did not think to slow down or allow room for the two of us. I was irritated and thought, childishly, that a doctor should know better.

The wooden bench seats on the train were uncomfortable, and the sun glared relentlessly through the window bars. Dr Rajeevan and I stopped and started awkward conversations. I was unsure if he noticed how little I understood of what he said: he made no attempt to intonate more clearly, despite encouragement from me. The language problem was intensified by the drone of the engine and the rattle of the wheels over the tracks. As an experiment, I gave up trying to follow anything for a while and Dr Rajeevan continued happily – indeed he seemed to gather more confidence and even greater speed now that my interruptions had ceased.

He persisted in talking throughout the train journey because he was keen to elaborate on his future plans. I grasped that he wanted to set up some sort of research centre to test the efficacy of ayurvedic methods scientifically. He was looking for foreign sponsorship to achieve this. When he told me this I could feel him studying me intently and wondered again about his motivation in travelling three days and nights for my benefit. The talk about herbal medical research developed, and I found myself hoping for once that I *had* misunderstood him when he advocated the use of people in testing on the grounds that his country was overrun with them. He cast a hand around the carriage and said, with disgust, 'Look at all these people.'

Despite the discomfort of the journey I was enjoying the vignettes of life that appeared on the train. Women clanked milk churns, families ate picnics, labourers smoked silently, clerks rustled newspapers, groups of men snapped and shuffled packs of cards and night-workers snored.

For the final stretch of our journey we took a taxi. Dr Rajeevan had fallen silent. Kottakkal was a small, hilly town that had grown up around the Arya Vaidya Sala, founded and run by the Varier family. I had been told this was the best-known and most established ayurvedic hospital and training college in India. Certainly, it was the first one I had heard about when I began my research into my trip in England. The director had replied to my letters with an invitation to visit. Unfortunately I had not been able to make contact to warn him of the imminence of my arrival before I set out from England.

We got out of the taxi and Dr Rajeevan wandered off, forgetting to offer me his arm. I was marooned, unable to hear where he was heading, and embarrassed at not knowing which way to go. It was made worse by my certainty that the taxi-driver was watching.

'Do you know I can't see?' I asked angrily, exasperated by his carelessness. We had not mentioned it until now and Dr Rajeevan had made no concessions or acknowledgement throughout the long, tedious journey.

He strode back and took a light plastic bag out of my hands, leaving me with the heavy rucksack, and said, quite simply, 'Yes.'

I could not fathom this man. His efforts to reach me had been greater even than I had imagined. Following a call from Dr Renade, he had travelled from north of Bangalore, where he was studying, to his family home north of Calicut; he had waited two weeks there for further instructions to accompany me to Kottakkal; when no call came he returned to Bangalore, only to depart the following day for Cochin when the message finally arrived. And all because, he told me, he felt indebted to his former professor. Yet he made little effort to establish any rapport with me.

After an indifferent lunch we went to the head office where we were told that no one could see us because we were not expected. As usual we sat and waited until we were told that N. K. Varier, the public-relations manager, would see us after he had taken his lunch and his siesta. We waited for almost two hours.

When he appeared N. K. Varier was very willing to give us his spiel but by then I was too tired and fed up to care. I had allowed only a day for the visit so still had the return journey ahead, and there was therefore no time to delve behind N. K. Varier's practised patter and see any treatments, students or patients. I had mismanaged it. We left.

George and Shyla Varghese, who had also left Leela's that morning for their plantation near Calicut, had invited me to stay with them, and Dr Rajeevan had agreed to accompany me there after our day in Kottakkal.

The bus to Calicut took a couple of hours. My blocked ears itched and burned. At the Hyson Hotel we telephoned George to come and collect me. He took us to a dining hall, which echoed like my old college canteen.

We drank tea and Dr Rajeevan devoured a *dosa*. He mumbled something about how he would organise a more beneficial itinerary if I returned and brought more professionals with me. I wasn't convinced that he would make a good group leader. He refused my offers of payment so I squeezed money into his hand as we said goodbye. I was still mystified as to his motives. Perhaps the feeling was mutual.

George was an enthusiastic host and immediately whisked me off to visit all his friends. We drank lime juice with one family and collected a large bag of fresh cashew nuts from another. Everyone was consulted about the availability of swimming-pools and Kathakali massage because he had remembered my interest in both. He was planning excitedly for me to speak at his next Rotary Club meeting that Friday night until I reminded him gently that by then I would be on my way to Coimbatore. I was exhausted.

His 1930s house stood in the middle of a rubber plantation. The rooms had high ceilings and narrow wooden doorways with lipped stairs to step up and over. Distinctive sounds gave shape to the house. Paddle fans thwacked the air and floorboards creaked without anyone stepping on them. The water tanks groaned and gurgled when someone was showering. The sitting room was sometimes filled with quiet voices, or the singing of psalms to the accompaniment of a guitar. Cast-iron pans and stainless-steel containers clanked or scraped against stone in the kitchen. This, the hub of the house, was always brimming with the sounds of vegetable-scraping, spice-pounding and the ever-busy pressure-cooker steaming in fierce spurts in the preparation of yet more *dal*. One of my favourite foods became soft spongy *idlis*, shaped like spinning-tops but flatter. To produce these, a batter of parboiled ground rice and split peas was left to ferment overnight. By morning there would be a head of bubbles, which frothed quietly. Shyla showed me a tall steaming cylinder containing moulds into which the mixture was poured. The *idlis* were then served plain steamed, dipped in oil with seasonings of nuts and seeds, or fried, either sweet or sour.

Susan, George and Shyla's daughter, had arrived from Cochin, and Laura, the Vargheses' other daughter, who was doing an MA in English literature in Calicut, was also at home. Shyla's elderly mother shuffled slowly about the tasks that kept up her involvement in the home. Shyla was a sound, sensible woman and the four women formed a strong matriarchy in which George basked, as imperious as an adolescent.

George was both principled and passionate. We walked the boundaries of the rubber plantation with his two German shepherd dogs bounding about and breaking the dried grasses. George explained how the rubber trees are tapped, letting me feel the scars on the thick trunks. My fingers soon stuck together as latex ran over them from the fresh cuts. They grew pineapples, chicos – an egg-shaped golden brown fruit – and custard apples in an exotic mini-orchard nearer to the house, while purple bougainvillaea and pink azaleas climbed their way up the whitewashed facade towards an old bee-hive.

In the evening before bed I joined the family to sing a hymn, read a psalm and say prayers on bent knees with our foreheads touching the ground. In the morning George and Shyla drove me to Calicut station for my train to Coimbatore where I had been invited to stay with Peerooze's parents. I expected to arrive before Peerooze, who was coming from Madras, so his mother would meet me. George and Shyla called a red-coat, an official porter, as soon as we got out of the car. I heard the fall of folds of fabric and the cushioned sound of expelled air as he pressed the weight of my bag on his turban. It was hard to keep up with him on the way to the train. We dodged around other people and crossed tracks by jumping on and off platforms rather than using a bridge. George and Shyla wished me well and left me on a busy commuter train, refusing to take any money for my ticket, which George had purchased in the rush. I knew they were waving from the platform as people automatically do, so I waved back.

I felt rested from the tranquil and peaceful stay on their plantation after the hectic few days' work in Cochin and Kottakkal, but it was reassuring to know that I would be back with Peerooze again for the next leg of my journey. Sitting alone on this train, which crawled to frequent halts, I began to feel how much I had missed both Goutam and Peerooze.

Beggars got on and off the train at each station. Some hobbled or hopped down the aisles, others murmured plaintively. Papers were thrust into my hands or dropped in my lap. I guessed the writers of these notes pleaded some good cause or other. My neighbour pushed his hips forward to slip his hand into his back pocket. He unfolded some notes and gave them to a woman, who was on her way back down the carriage to collect any donations and the scraps of paper she had handed out when she walked up the train. I asked him why she was begging and he replied, 'Her daughter is getting married. It is for the wedding.' I could hear that people were sympathetic to the cause, dropping coins into her bag. On a couple of occasions, coarse, smelly fibres brushed my skin as a bandaged limb was thrust into my face. I assumed that as I did not appear suitably shocked by the sight, the beggar was determined to attract my attention. On one occasion, a blind man made his way slowly up our carriage, tapping his stick and ringing a bell. There were not two but four footsteps. He was being led by his wife, who called for money by shaking a tin. She stopped by me, rattling her tin under my chin. She was more insistent than the rest, and I dropped an ironical few coins in. Then I realised we had little in common and felt pain and pity.

COIMBATORE: PEEROOZE'S PARENTS

'**B**ed tea for you, Madam.'

'Peerooze? Is that you?' I questioned, dragging strands of hair from my sleepy face. 'What time is it? When did you get here?' I took the tea and refused the salty biscuits he offered.

'It's five thirty in the morning. I have just arrived. I got the overnight train from Madras. 'What do you think of my bedroom?'

I looked around, as if I could see, to study the bedroom for the first time. It was an enormous room with an adjacent bathroom, and another smaller room with bunk-beds behind some curtains to my right. The fan hummed overhead. I stretched in the bed and my foot encountered Peerooze, flopped out at the far end.

'It's like a suite,' I answered. 'Do your boys sleep in the bunks when they come?'

Peerooze stirred enough to nod and asked, 'What do you think of Mummy and Daddy? Have they been looking after you?'

'Everything's fine. Your mother met me at the station yesterday afternoon. We came back here, had some tea, and I rested for a while before eating with them in the evening. I like your mother. She's been telling me about her cows, her school, her children.'

'I hope nothing bad about me?' Peerooze interjected.

'Well, I think you're the renegade,' I joked, then added more seriously, 'She worries about you.'

'She has quite enough to worry about with the next new calf about to be born, or a child coming for the first time to her school. She doesn't need me to worry about as well.' Peerooze dismissed his mother's concern as if it were an indulgence he neither deserved nor wanted. He said, 'I'll take my shower and then we'll see what there is to do. I'll have to work with Daddy, but only until lunchtime because it's Saturday.'

'Is there a swimming-pool where I can go until then?' I asked quickly. I did not want to be stuck in the house with nothing to do, and it was likely that Peerooze would be delayed well beyond lunch.

'There is the Coimbatore Club just around the corner. I'll have to sign you in. I'm not sure whether you'll be all right. You mustn't tell Daddy I'm leaving you there alone. He will think it irresponsible.'

'Tell him I'm a good swimmer. Please don't worry about me.'

He kissed me on the forehead affectionately as he left to have his shower.

I was ready long before anyone else and walked through the sitting room into the empty dining room from where I could hear the noise of servants moving pans and filling vessels with water in the kitchen beyond. Just as I was about to step out from the door leading into the backyard, a voice from the kitchen to my right said, 'Good morning, Madam.'

'Good morning, Alexander,' I said to the manservant, who I guessed to be in his fifties.

Once outside I quickly appreciated how dark and cool the house was. Someone climbed the wooden stairs on the outside of the house, leading to the second floor, which was set aside as offices for the family business. I wandered hesitantly over the sandy yard towards the back buildings. Since Mrs Hataria had already shown me around briefly, I had some idea that the shelter for her dairy cows was there and that the servants' quarters along with the schoolroom were further back to the right. I dragged my feet in the dust to make sure that there were no sudden dips or holes. When I heard servants' voices, I turned back in case I was intruding on their privacy. I also felt self-conscious about the confusion I might be causing: at one moment I was walking around holding someone's arm, and the next I was wandering free and easy. I knew that the servants stared at me, fascinated, from corners, corridors and doorways.

I decided to venture around the side of the house and circle the long drive, which swept in front of the house and back down towards the main gates. I managed not to trip over the various hoses which were spread about on the ground, but I nearly choked myself by wading into chin-high cow grass. The previous evening Mrs Hataria had explained its superb nutritional value, and I felt sure it was better eaten than shoved up the nose.

The area in the middle and around the edge of the drive was full of exotic plants in terracotta pots or in dry, deeply ridged beds, the earth curling up at the edges like a stale bread crust. I moved slowly from plant to plant, handling the leaves, and pushing my nose into the mouth of trumpet-shaped blooms. I inhaled the flowers' fragrance. It was exciting to discover how many of the plants I recognised.

Here, in abundance and in startling bloom, were all the difficult *Dracaena* and *Cordyline* plants I had tried and failed to grow. Curled, shrivelled leaves with tips like parchment, sagging stems, or leggy leafless sticks had been the result of my efforts. In this sunny plant paradise, the glossy foliage and spreading branches made me conclude once and for all how miserable my specimens had looked. There was a profusion of shrubby types, false palms, crotons clothed in colour from top to bottom, elegant jacarandas with lacy leaves, and fleshy succulents. Flowers rose out from between the strap-like leaves of some *Bromeliads*. I had thought until then that such extraterrestrial-looking blooms only existed in sophisticated plant-sales magazines. The urn plant's spiky flower-heads were soft to the touch and the tea-tree wore a crown of leaves on top of a single cane-like stem. Orchids clung to tree-trunks while pots of Indian strawberries and tinkling chimes hung from branches. There were so many clusters of starry, fragrant flowers that it was hard to tell what was what. But the jasmines were more delicate than the similar highly perfumed wax plants, like the hoya flowers with umbrella-like heads. Whenever I brushed by large gardenias, they made the air heavy with a delightful scent, as did lilies, sitting elegantly at the ends of tall, swaying stalks, dripping scent like debutantes at their first dance. I was not sickened by the clashing, confused aromas as I often am in a perfumery because here they blended naturally to produce a harmonious fragrance.

I turned a double loop like a figure of eight and halted at the front gates, listening to the traffic on a busy main road leading into town. I wanted to explore. I took a resolute breath and set off. I turned left out of the gate and, keeping well into the side, I trusted that the dust and grit, blown into mounds by the rush of traffic, would indicate the edge of the road. I walked slowly and cautiously, anticipating the inevitable collision with a road sign or telegraph pole. I am never too worried by injury: dented pride upsets me more. However, I was jittery, just as I had been in Trivandrum during my forays out alone. The fact is, I had not previously been out alone, without a guide or a dog, for years. It reminded me of childhood, when I first strayed beyond the 'allowed' boundaries of my home street into the 'not allowed' world beyond. In India I had moved from feeling threatened by the presence of a sighted guide to feeling threatened by their absence.

I sensed an open space on my left as the wall I was shadowing came to an end. A couple more steps and there was hard tarmac underfoot without the usual thick layer of dust. I took a side turning to escape the blast of the traffic. Dogs barked from houses set back from the road, hose-piped water splashed on concrete, a car door slammed, a telephone rang, someone was practising the tabla. My antennae tuned in to the domesticity of a residential backwater and I felt less tense, even if more conspicuous, than I had in the choppy, unpredictable flow of the main road.

On my return to the house I met Mrs Hataria in the dining room. 'Did you sleep well?' she asked in her distinctive high, hoarse voice.

'Yes, thank you, and I have been enjoying your garden since getting up,' I answered.

After breakfast Peerooze and I went to the Coimbatore Club. On the way he asked what I wanted to do and whom I wanted to meet while I was in Coimbatore. In Madras I had been advised to visit a Dr Arjunan, who ran an orthopaedic hospital just outside the town, and I wanted to sample another oil massage this time in the Coimbatore Ayurvedic Hospital. It was also my last chance to get to Dr Nambisan in Kodaikanal, and not just because I wanted to locate another oil supplier: Kodaikanal was the least visited and, reputedly, most beautiful of the three main hill stations of the south, and I was determined not to miss it.

Peerooze did not respond and I wondered if he had been listening.

At the swimming-pool, there was a bevy of staff, although I was the only guest. I heard a pool attendant padding around, a *mali*, or gardener, clipping a hedge, a sweeper swishing dead leaves into piles and a waiter wiping down tables. I prepared myself for an audience. Peerooze signed me in, talked to the pool attendant and promised to return later.

My delight in swimming again was intense. In England I swim every morning and feel tense and miserable without the release it brings. In the water I can move fast and free, independent, with almost no risks. It is a time when I unravel both the physical and emotional tangles I seem to spend the rest of my life weaving. I have no need for a guide because I can align myself with the wall of the swimming-pool, and I have developed a simple technique to avoid colliding with other swimmers: I swim in a fast, straight line with uncompromising determination, so fellow swimmers find it advisable to avoid me. Over the years the more I have felt the loss of privacy and independence, the more I have made swimming a daily priority. I had worried about the lack of opportunities to swim while travelling in India.

As soon as Peerooze left I plunged clean and deep, loving the watery, dark silence where no one could reach me. Finally I surfaced from the dive and revelled in my uninhibited strokes, slicing my way through the water. I went as fast as I liked while monitoring my position and distance from the sides by sound. The frustration of never being mistress of my own movements dissipated in each thrust of my arms or kick of my legs. I flipped on to my back and thought of how, earlier, I had been floundering out of my depth as a disabled pedestrian in the street. Now I was strong, a solitary swimmer, immersed alone in the water heeding no one and nothing.

For lunch Mrs Hataria organised a *biriani*, a dish normally served on festive occasions, followed by *kulfi*, home-made ice-cream. Mr Hataria grumbled openly and incessantly about Alexander while he served the various dishes and poured the water. 'Get out of my way,' he snapped finally when Alexander tried to serve him with more cauliflower. Alexander retreated into the darkest corner to take cover from the volley of vituperation that followed. 'I tell you,' he railed at the rest of us, 'he is stupid. He shouldn't be serving me before I am finished, only when I tell him to do so.'

Mrs Hataria placated her husband, agreeing with him and lamenting the loss of their previous cook and servant who had been taken ill. I tried to point out that Alexander was simply attempting to move the cauliflower out of the way to reduce the clutter of dishes between Mr Hataria and me. Only the previous day he had been chastised for not being more observant while serving at table; now he was blamed for being over-diligent.

'What are you people doing this afternoon? Your mother will want to know if you are eating here tonight.' Mr Hataria's question seemed to foreshadow another outburst.

'We're eating at the club tonight. We are playing bridge,' Mrs Hataria reminded him.

'That's fine, Mummy,' Peerooze said reassuringly. 'We are visiting Dr Arjunan at the Telungupalayam hospital, a bone specialist. Then I thought we would go and see Sanjay on his farm.'

After a siesta, Peerooze and I set off for the hospital. We called in on some of his friends before we left town. I was used to dropping in unannounced on neighbours and relatives, sitting for ten minutes, perhaps having a cold drink, then leaving to pursue the original reason for going out. It let me experience all sorts of families, their homes, their conversations and their rituals. I enjoyed the sociability, the casual and uncomplicated way people got together. At home I arrange to see a friend by making an arrangement days in advance. Indeed, it is so unusual for someone to drop in without first telephoning that I only answer the doorbell when I know someone is due. But however appealing and friendly the spontaneous visiting was, I found it hard to cope with the delay and disruption to other plans.

When we reached the orthopaedic hospital, a long, low building in a scrubby plain far from town, we were told that Dr Arjunan would see us immediately. A girl led the way through a narrow, curtained door. We left our shoes behind on the veranda where a group of limping but smiling children had gathered. Dr Arjunan, a stocky, friendly man, offered me a tiny stool in front of him and sat squarely on his, patting his knees with his hands. Peerooze remained standing and acted as interpreter: Dr Arjunan only spoke Tamil.

He quickly grasped that the way to explain his work to me was by demonstration, and invited us to follow him behind another curtain to where a man sat on a bench with his leg propped on a stool in front of him. There was a brief discussion between the doctor and his patient, Ranjan, who rubbed his hands, stopping only to point to his knees. Dr Arjunan caught one of Ranjan's hands and pulled it towards me while Peerooze translated, 'Look at the misshapen joint from arthritis.' I felt where the bone had bent and stiffened into an unnatural claw. A girl approached with an old-fashioned stone hot-water bottle. The doctor passed it to me to feel how hot it was before rolling it around over

Ranjan's knee. Although his leg was fully stretched, the knee was excessively humped. When it was warm, Dr Arjunan applied an oil with a deep heating effect that he said would penetrate to the bone. Another girl brought a metal bowl containing melted wax for the doctor to paste over the knee. It set within minutes but had to be left for half an hour. While we were waiting he showed me the medicated wax cakes that felt like large round soaps before they were melted. When he peeled the wax off Ranjan's leg, he rolled it into a ball and dropped it into a dish. He told us it was reusable. He finished the treatment by rubbing a herbal oil and soothing ointment over the affected area.

When I asked about the herb-infused wax and oil preparations, Dr Arjunan laughed and said he gathered the plants from the land and followed secret recipes handed down to him through the generations of practitioners in his family. He sent me away with a supply of wax cakes and oils to try on my patients at home. He recommended the hot oil and ointment applications to treat everything from an arthritic joint to ankylosing spondylitis, a rheumatic disease involving inflammation of the joints of the spine, which sometimes leads to fusion of these joints and a rigid back. I have since found them useful for treating very stiff elderly arthritis patients, who are sometimes not comfortable with essential-oil massage. They find the lubricating and warming effect of the medicated wax frees their joints enough to allow for some gentle manipulation and improved movement. I used to apply compresses steeped in essential oils to swollen joints, but I find the wax more successful. I still use herbal compresses to reduce inflammation in injured joints or muscles.

Dr Arjunan claimed success with problems like knock knees, bow legs, palsy, calcanial spurs, polio and Parkinson's. Any dysfunction of the bone, nerve and muscle seemed to fall into his area of treatment. I was passed a leather foot cast, which Dr Arjunan said would correct club-foot. Outside again, I realised that many children wore them. Congenital conditions, or the effects of illnesses like polio, are beyond my expertise.

After leaving, Peerooze and I headed deeper into the countryside to visit his friends Sanjay and Shanthi. We stopped to ask directions to their farm from a solitary villager walking in the roadside with a bundle of hay spiked on a fork over his shoulder. Within moments a crowd had gathered from the apparent wilderness. Men chattered excitedly about which way we should go, as if they were collectively solving a crossword puzzle. I could not imagine how Peerooze decided from among the many conflicting gesticulations which was right. However, he jumped down, opened the rear door, and ordered a man to get in. We were on our way again with the man hanging out of the back window, shouting his directions, and signalling with loud bangs of his fists on the roof. We dropped him, with relief, just before turning down a track that led to the farm.

'Peerooze, how will that man get home?' I asked. 'It's really nice of him to put himself out but we can't just leave him. It must be miles to his village.'

'He is happy to get a ride in a big car. Half of them have never seen one like this.'

We bumped along the track in silence until we arrived in a yard, which I felt was enclosed by buildings on all sides except for the gateway where we entered. Sanjay shook our hands and took us into a sitting area in one of the buildings, a small room with beds for seats on two sides. My head touched wooden rafters on the ceiling and I guessed there was a hay-loft or grain-store above. The room was one of several in a long line of buildings once used to house animals. I concluded from the uneven hard mud floor and rough unplastered walls that the eviction of the livestock had been recent. Sanjay, a solicitor in Coimbatore, had moved to the farm with his wife and two-year-old daughter during the previous year. For the time being they lived, squatter-like, with some electrical wires pinned up for lighting, gas bottles for cooking, and cold water from a well. They had neither heating for the winter nor electric fans for the summer.

I heard a curtain flick back and felt a warm rush of air carrying a sweet but stale smell of sheets mixed with powdered and perfumed skin. Shanthi came from the bedroom with little Mala, who was drowsy from sleep. Sanjay went to fetch some tender coconuts for us to drink.

After a cursory tour of the farm, we came back into the yard to be greeted by pipe smoke. A man was sitting in the shade of the grass-roofed veranda. He was the farmer who managed the land. Judging by Sanjay's inability to name the crops or identify the vegetables, he was crucial to the viability of the place. Everyone sat, drank beer and chatted while dusk gathered. By the time it was fully dark and late, Sanjay had invited us for dinner and Shanthi, who had minimal cooking facilities, had said, 'Really, do stay. It will be simple food but you're welcome.'

The men remained outside but I followed Shanthi into the sitting room, which sloped down through a pulled-back curtain into a cooking area. Like most western women, Shanthi did not have servants to whom she could delegate even the most basic preparations. I found her trying frantically to get Mala ready for bed while sorting and chopping vegetables. Two scrawny village girls appeared from the dark and played with the little girl on the floor so that Shanthi could grind fresh spices by hand. I offered to help, but she was concerned that she was not entertaining me. She fumbled to put on a cassette but had to switch to a crackling radio when the tape spilled out. The two girls reminded me of thin little old women. They crouched on the floor, playing some counter game with Mala. Every so often Shanthi asked one or other to clean, fetch or carry something. I tried to talk to them but Shanthi had to translate because their English was limited. They told me they were both ten, maybe eleven years old and that they were sisters. When I asked if they were twins, they giggled coyly and said in English, 'Two mummies, one daddy.' Shanthi explained that the village community was mainly Muslim and that many of the men kept two wives in one home.

It was late before Shanthi laid a gnarled, broad wooden table, served everyone except herself and scooped Mala off to bed before the threatened tears could tumble down the tired child's face. The village girls disappeared silently and abruptly, as if at the flick of a switch.

Driving back into Coimbatore I felt tired and melancholic. Suddenly I remembered my friend Laura who, after her brief stopover in Bombay, had come to work in an orphanage outside Coimbatore. We had both wanted to spend time in Asia after university but by that time I was in hospital. Laura's letters from Coimbatore would leave me torn between pleasure for and interest in a friend, and angry jealousy that she was doing what I wanted to do but could not. I remembered, with some shame, how despairing I felt when she told me about a dying child she looked after. My heart had shrunk and my despair was selfish. I wanted to be that child so much that the child became my enemy, robbing me of the death I sought. As I recalled the anguish of those bitter emotions my eyes stung, and I turned my head to the window so that Peerooze could not see the slight glistening.

On Sunday morning Peerooze and I went to the fruit and vegetable market because he liked to stock up for his parents before he returned to Madras. We entered the covered market and stopped at almost the first stall, which was loaded with trays and baskets of vegetables. Peerooze selected the ones he wanted and passed them to the stall-holder who thudded them down into the metal scales, then tipped them loose into one of the sacks Peerooze held open. He filled bag after bag, mixing everything, soft and hard, tubular and round, leaf and root.

My attention was distracted by the perfume of fresh flowers sneaking up behind me. I screwed up my eyes, inhaled, opened both eyes and nostrils wide, and turned round. I was two paces away from a flower stall. There was a tray at the front laden with carnation flower-heads and jasmine threaded on strings. There were no buckets full of mixed bunches like in England, just an ever-increasing pile of threaded flowers to fasten into the hair. A nimble-fingered boy was rapidly twisting and weaving the flowers. As he finished each string he dunked it in water and swung it on the tray, spraying me in the process. Peerooze bought three strings of the jasmine.

As we left the market, garlic flavoured the air. Its smell was so overpowering that Peerooze could not forget that he had promised the barrow-boy he would buy some on his way out. We made one final stop at a fruit stall surrounded by people and orange peel. The layer of fruit skin underfoot was so thick it was squishy. The choice of freshly squeezed juices from oranges, grapes, limes, pawpaw and pineapple was mouthwatering, but Peerooze advised caution on the grounds of poor hygiene. We left with a huge box of sweet seedless grapes.

The first thing Mrs Hataria saw when Peerooze,and I walked in was the huge box of grapes. 'What are we to do with so many grapes?' she cried, aghast.

Mr Hataria emerged from his bedroom and said, 'Peerooze, so much, always so much. Can't you be reasonable?'

Peerooze did not seem bothered by the outcry and handed all the shopping to a servant to put away.

That evening, Mr Hataria invited us to go out for dinner. I pinned lacy strings of jasmine from the market in my hair. Mrs Hataria wore a beautifully embroidered *salwar kameez.*

We went to a rooftop restaurant in one of the town's biggest hotels. I pulled *rotis* apart, which spread and fluffed like cotton wool. I folded the soft bread around vegetables and squeezed gently to glue the bundle together before I popped it into my mouth. I was sorry to realise, from the clatter of knives and forks on china, that most of the diners were using cutlery. I had come to prefer using one hand in the traditional Indian way. The meal was delicious but hot. In India it was generally considered a sign of refinement not to overspice food, rather like the British middle classes think it unsophisticated to overcook vegetables. Mrs Hataria criticised, 'Too much chilli,' and everyone agreed.

During dinner Peerooze triumphantly announced his plan to send me to Kodaikanal with a salesman from the office. He said A. K. Palanivelsamy had some work do to there, and would also be able to escort me to find Dr Nambisan. Peerooze could take us in the car as far as Palani, the last town before the climb up to Kodaikanal, where he had some business to finish. A. K. Palanivelsamy and I would take the bus onwards from there, stay overnight in Kodaikanal and travel the whole way back by bus. Peerooze would return the same day with the car to catch the night train to Madras. We were to leave early on Monday morning – the next day. Like a magician, Peerooze had transformed my frustrated intention to get to Kodaikanal into all but a *fait accompli*. I was thrilled. At every stage of my journey, the travel arrangements had worried me until they were sorted out.

Before I got into the car, I practised saying Palanivelsamy, but my tongue got twisted. I could not picture how to break the word into syllables because I had never seen it written. The pronunciation of individual letters rolled so differently off the Indian tongue that my confused ears behaved like a sighted person groping in the dark. In the end I decided to avoid addressing my new companion directly by name.

When we reached Palani after four or five hours, we had to rush for the bus to Kodaikanal as it was about to leave. Amid the impatient horn blasts, I kept thinking of how I would not see Peerooze again on this trip. My goodbye and thank-you were lost in the flurry of clambering aboard.

The bus left the plains and I leant out of the window as we climbed for four hours, passing rocky outcrops jutting so far out into the road that I could almost touch them. The air changed quickly to a thinner, sharper current. It danced in refreshing gusts around my face rather than lying languid and dense as it had over the hot plains. Coming from a cooler part of the world, I was more comfortable with the labile quality of the atmosphere in the hills than the still, immobile pressure that dominated the low country. As we got higher, trees swayed, leaves fluttered, water gushed and plummeted over precipitous rocks.

The movement of crashing water, the cracking of wood on the heavily forested slopes, men hammering stones for road repairs, and the high-pitched chirruping of small hill birds held my attention. I was still leaning half out of the open window with the air rushing through my hair in blissful appreciation of the changing scene when I heard a throaty snort. Horror! Wet stickiness was plastering my cheek. Then I heard another spit and clutched at my loose hair, but this time, splat! It hit the side of the bus. I withdrew into my seat, fumbling for a tissue to wipe my face, and heard the satisfied sigh of the woman sitting in front of me She had ejected a mouthful of red saliva collected from hours of chewing her *paan*.

As we approached Kodaikanal hill station, I thought I could hear hundreds of sails billowing and thwacking against their masts. I knew there was an artificial lake in Kodaikanal and asked my guide if we were passing a sailing regatta. He was baffled until I pointed out of the window in the direction of the sound and he explained, 'No, no, clothes-washing. All drying now.' It was not the lake but an open field with poles and stone walls covered with sheets and clothes. The walloping sound was simply the town's fiercely flapping laundry.

It was mid-afternoon by the time we arrived and A. K. Palanivelsamy seemed ready to put into action any plan I hatched. I suggested that first we should stretch our legs around the lake. During what turned out to be a two-hour walk, I learnt that my guide had never before spent time with a woman alone. He did not seem uneasy but I did, so I decided to walk next to him rather than hold his arm. Having circled the lake, we wandered back up the main street where the crowds of mainly Indian tourists and honeymooners forced me to hold on to him. I wondered if I was more self-conscious than he, especially in what was obviously a honeymoon destination. We stopped at a few shops and found that that there was only plastic and badly cut clothing for sale so strolled on to a viewpoint where queues of couples were having their photographs taken.

As it got cold and dark we headed for the Kodaikanal Club where I was to spend the night. Most of the ex-British clubs are affiliated with each other – the Bombay Gymkhana, the Coimbatore Club and the Madras Club have reciprocal hospitality arrangements for members, who are carefully selected. Membership is given for life if the family meets the requirements. I remember Aunty telling me that 'only good families' were accepted. As elitist now as they were in colonial days, the clubs, are maintained by servile Indians, managed by ingratiating ones and frequented by upper-crust ones with Harvard or Etonian accents.

My guide made sure that Peerooze's letter of recommendation was accepted before he left me to have his dinner and find a cheap room for the night. I ordered a bowl of tomato soup and waited alone in a drawing room that smelt of stale cigar smoke, wax polish and leather chairs. The soup was the only item on the menu that could be ordered without a day's notice, and even then I had to wait a long time for it to come. Unlike the other clubs I had visited, this relic of the Raj was decrepit and dowdy, down-at-heel, shabby and tired, like an old general who insists on wearing his threadbare uniform in his dotage. There was a ghostly presence of former glory.

The bedrooms were in an annex at the back of the old British-built stone and wood house. After dinner I was led through a porch into a sitting room and into my bedroom. Beyond this was a dressing room and bathroom. The furniture was plain wood with no frills, and the floors were cold and hard, except for a few scattered durries. The single bed was made with sheets, blankets and a candlewick counterpane. It seemed strange to pull all these covers around my ears in south India. There were even gas heaters in the corners for the really cold nights.

My suite overlooked rolling lawns edged with flowering shrubs and little alpine plants. When I went out in the early morning, the lawns were damp with dew, the air was crisp and smelt of the conifers and pines that covered the thickly wooded slopes all around. Even the tinkle of a distant cowbell made me feel as if I was in the Alps and not in southern India.

On our drive the next morning to Fairy Falls to find Dr Nambisan, I prepared myself for him not to be there. All my attempts to contact him over the past weeks had failed. We emerged from forests full of the sound of rushing water into sunny pastures. Here the road dipped up and down and I heard sheep bleating, the shepherds whistling and the dull peal of cowbells. The ever-present water babbled softly in brooks and rock pools.

The Government Horticultural Research Station where Dr Nambisan worked amounted to no more than a few wooden buildings sandwiched between two steep, terraced slopes adorned with tiny but colourful alpine flowers. Dr Nambisan was standing outside as if he was expecting us, and seemed pleased to have a visitor. I knew, without knowing how, that he was white-bearded and white-haired. He seemed like a country bumpkin, with his untucked shirt and floppy sandals, whose buckles scratched the ground as we followed him to his office.

Dr Nambisan and his team were researching the most favourable growing conditions in which to maximise a crop's yield of its essential oil. They grew a lot themselves and bought from hill farmers who grew their crops at a specific altitude or in a particular soil type. I took some *Eucalyptus globulus* and *Eucalyptus citradora*. Although these are both eucalypti, their oils smell and work very differently. The *globulus* is the more common mentholated smelling oil used as a decongestant for colds or sinus problems, the *citradora* smells more of lemon-flavoured cough sweets, and I find it most useful for treating arthritic conditions. I also bought some lemon-grass for the treatment of infectious illness and fever, geranium for the relief of fluid retention and pre-menstrual tension, and citronella for my own use as an insect repellent. These three lemon-scented oils are distinguishable because the lemon-grass has the aroma of fragrant lemon herb tea, the citronella smells like sherbet lemons and the geranium has a subtle, floral lemon overtone. I also use geranium in skincare preparations, because it is an effective antiseptic and astringent.

Dr Nambisan was interested to know whether I could advance the capital to grow the crops of my choice, have them distilled and sent to me in England. It was tempting to have my private supply of oils grown in such an idyllic, unpolluted setting, but the quantity would be greater than I could ever use. I wanted to remain a therapist rather than become a trader in essential oils.

Back in town, we rushed to catch the midday bus back to Palani. It hurtled down the hill and reached the plains just in time for the last bus of the day to Coimbatore. The heat was more vicious and wearing than previously. Dirty, dusty and tired, I arrived back at the Hatarias' late in the evening.

The next morning Mr Hataria offered me his driver to go to the Coimbatore ayurvedic hospital known as the Aryavaidya Chikitsalayam and Research Institute. I met the deputy director, Dr G. G. Gangadharan, in a modern, two-storey building. His office was in a partitioned corner of a lecture hall. The hospital was in the process of setting up a two- or three-year ayurvedic training course for foreign students. Little was known or practised of ayurveda outside India, and the plan was to make it more popular internationally, but I was becoming increasingly doubtful as to how realistic this was. Many of the herbal preparations used in it were peculiar to India, and the techniques so closely associated with a tradition and belief system alien to allopathic medicine that it seemed unlikely that many westerners would want the treatments on offer. Those involving fasting and purging, using enemas and emetics, were especially odious, but I thought there was a place for the oilings or massages. Dr Gangadharan was not too disappointed when I explained that I was focusing on these and I asked if I could experience the ayurvedic massage as given in the hospital. He directed me to his administrator, Y. P. Manjunathan, to complete the necessary paperwork. I knew then that I was in for a long wait.

The driver accompanied me to a prefabricated building that stood alone to the side of the hospital. The metal stairs leaning on the side of the building swayed dangerously as we clattered up them. We went into a busy office where I was told that I was expected and was asked to sit and wait. Two clerks hammered at manual typewriters. Someone was bobbing in and out of a corner room, fanning papers, sitting down and making sounds like a sink emptying the last dreges of water before springing up again. At first I thought the noise was a gurgling stomach, then realised the man was sucking the top of his biro. The flurry of papers, the scurrying in and out of the far door and the clerks' agitation told me that Y. P. Manjunathan was in the room beyond, keeping the papers flowing.

After a long while, I was asked to step into his office. I felt suddenly self-conscious because I could hear everyone behind me padding about barefoot and I had forgotten to remove my shoes. We shook hands and I resisted the urge to look down at my feet. He invited me to sit, only to tell me that he would give instructions for the paperwork authorising the massage to be prepared. In the meantime I was to wait outside again.

I could not understand why they had not set about the paperwork an hour ago when I first arrived since they knew the purpose of my call. Then it occurred to me that to keep someone waiting was a way to assert one's own importance. Perhaps a coded message was hidden in those familiar words, 'Just sit, please wait.' I amused myself with this theory until a clerk gave me a three-inch square piece of paper and said, 'I typing just two addresses for many places you go massages.' He instructed me to return to the main foyer where an assistant would come to take me for my massage.

It took place in one of a series of bedrooms in a duplex running along the side of the hospital. Each bedroom had an attached bathroom and treatment room, with a low massage table and worktop. The arrangements were clearly designed for in-patients following a course.

On command I stripped off and lay down ready for the indulgence as well as to learn some new techniques or movements. The masseuse squeaked and squelched some oil in the palms of her hands and ran them in one long stroke from my toes up to my shoulders and back down again. She did this a few times, stopped and said, 'Finish now, very good, you liking.' Without waiting for my response she left the room, saying, 'You bathroom, then you sleeping.' The few strokes were what I do as a preliminary to spread the oil and prepare for the massage. I could not imagine how the quick back and sides I had been given could cure anyone of anything. Yet the facilities had been so promising, compared to the rudimentary ones I had found in many places. Even the delay and complications involved in the necessary documentation had made me think something extraordinary was about to happen – and it had, in its own disappointing way.

Back at the Hatarias', I had to decide what to do next. I twisted the piece of paper between my fingers with the recommended practitioners' names that the administration clerk had given me. Mr Hataria had already read out the names and addresses of these massage specialists. A Dr B. Gokulan was in Pathanamthitta district and Sri P. C. Damodaran in Palghat district. Their names were magical because they were so foreign, and they lived in obscure villages so I could not contact them in advance. They would certainly speak only Malayalam and I could not begin to think how I would reach them, but their physical remoteness and professional isolation made it more alluring to do so.

During the rest of that day and the evening I tussled between the temptation to make further discoveries and an unwillingness to face the fuss over another trip beleaguered with practical travel difficulties. On my bed lay a piece of card printed with the name and address of a foot masseur, Sri Parameswaran Nambudiripad. I had been given the card in Madras and I had treasured the possibility of finally having a Kathakali massage. This address was also in Palghat district and I added it to the list of reasons why I should set off again. Against all this stood the attraction of continuing on my way to Susan's parents in Coonoor near Ootacamund, or Ooty as it is called locally.

When I was in Madras, Susan had promised to see me at her parents' house. She had to bring some of the villagers' furniture work and handicrafts to sell at a hill fair and intended her visit to coincide with mine. She would already be on the night train from Madras. I folded away the papers bearing the addresses, knowing I might never make those visits, and decided that I would meet Susan the following afternoon. I was travel weary and had less heart for the difficulties and detours involved in searching out more practitioners.

However, I still wanted to visit a specialist in flower oils based in Mettupalayam, the last town north of Coimbatore in the lowlands before climbing the two thousand metres up to Coonoor. This was on my way and easy for a taxi-driver to find.

Before I left I tried to settle my bill for the night I had spent in the Kodaikanal club. Mr Hataria refused. He had also paid in advance for the taxi to take me to Coonoor, and arranged for the driver to assist me at the flower oil distillery. Once again, I was overwhelmed by the spectacular generosity of my hosts.

Mr Hataria was fretful about where I was going after my stay in Coonoor, how I would travel and who would receive me in my new destination, and Goutam echoed this in several telephone conversations. Both men wanted me to go straight to Bangalore, the last place where I had business appointments in south India, and where they had colleagues and friends with whom they could put me in touch. However, after some deliberation, I decided to take a complete rest from my work tour and contacted Nalini Cariappa in Madikeri, a friend of some friends in London, to arrange to stay with her before travelling to Bangalore.

I was not sure exactly where Nalini lived in relation to Coonoor and Bangalore, but hoped that it would not mean going too far out of my way. My geographical memory had failed me so, without telephoning Nalini, I did not know the route or the distance involved in reaching her. Before I had left England, I had persuaded many friends to trace my finger round the outline of a map of India. Once I had the shape committed to memory, they would position my fingers on various towns, my hand splaying into triangles, quadrangles and trapeziums. My fingers had to contort to map the relation and distance between one place and the next. Unfortunately, the region of Coorg, of which Madikeri is the main town, eluded me at the time when I most needed to remember.

I decided to telephone Nalini and find out more about where she was and how to get to her. Neither Goutam nor Mr Hataria was happy with the uncertainty of my arrangements, but I tried to sound confident and reassuring. Goutam agreed to speak with me again when I was in Coonoor, and Mr Hataria waved me off gruffly but fondly the next morning.

At Encee Aromatics, the flower-oil distillery, I met R. Murali Babu. He showed me around the premises, which were surrounded by fields of flowers at the foot of the Blue Mountains. The company specialised in high-quality floral oils, which are used more in perfumery than in therapeutics. I could not resist the opportunity to sniff the floral fragrances even though their use to me is limited to relaxing massage or bath oils. I lingered over the heady scent of jasmine and tuberose, captured and concentrated in the two minuscule vials I was given. Encee also produced two non-floral oils: vetivert and Indian basil. Vetivert is a scented grass, liked by the perfumery industry and useful in my work to reduce anxiety without a sedative effect. The one I smelt was rich, dark and acrid like burnt wood with lemony overtones. The basil was disappointingly caustic, lacking the mouthwatering aroma of French-grown varieties.

I felt quite giddy and sleepy from the oils by the time I was back in the car, swinging up and around the hills to the high mountain village of Coonoor, just below Ooty. We were soon so high that I could sense the clouds clinging to the hills, the trees, the car. My head swirled and I imagined our car surfing through the rolling cloudscape towards my new hosts.

COONOOR: SAVED BY SUSAN

It was chilly in the Nilgiri Hills, or the Blue Mountains as they are commonly called. As soon as I arrived Susan sat me in her parents' garden and lent me a thick hand-knitted cardigan. She neither introduced me to her parents nor showed me into the cottage. I selected my spot in strong sunlight, warmed up in a matter of seconds and discarded the woolly.

Susan disappeared into the house to order some tea. I sensed someone hovering at the door and I got up to greet the frail presence of an old person. 'This is my father,' Susan said, when she reappeared. Dr Joseph murmured something inaudible and retired shakily into the house. A dog was barking, dragging and rattling at a chain that restrained it to the side of the whitewashed old stone house. 'The tea is nearly made. Do you want to see your room before it comes?' Susan asked.

We entered a porch with large glass windows, trapping the sun, then wound down several dark, narrow passages. I noticed the sudden drop in temperature and realised why Susan had left me in the garden in the sun. The house had low ceilings and flagged floors and the sun could barely creep through the small windows, recessed in the thick stone walls. I was comforted to discover the pile of blankets on the two single beds in the room where she and I were to sleep.

We followed the sound of a whistling kettle into the kitchen. Susan's mother struggled out of a chair to greet me. Her movements were cumbrous and I was not sure whether the chair or she creaked more. Dr Joseph swayed, wispy and insubstantial, by her side. He flickered like a dying candle flame before fading into his bedroom. Susan's sister flitted from sink to table to side. She was preparing food and stopped only briefly to nod in my direction. Her quickness reminded me of the way Susan scooted about her business, but Susan's haste was purposeful and her sister's tense.

Susan took me outside again to drink tea in the fenced flower garden. 'We can have a walk if you like,' she suggested. I agreed enthusiastically: there is no better way for me to get to know my surroundings than to meander through them.

I was glad to leave behind the dog, yanking at his chain and still barking. We joined the steep main road and walked up it until we crossed on to a track that led into pasture. It was strewn with small boulders and stone chippings, which slipped and slid underfoot. Since I was unable to pick the best way, I trod on them at awkward angles, sending them spinning in all directions. It sounded worse than it actually was and Susan flinched at my every skid. She suggested we should turn back, but I was confident. During years of rambling anywhere from the Scottish Highlands to the Irish coast, deep in conversation with a companion and my guide dog running free, I have subconsciously developed a technique to cope with tricky terrain. I relax my legs and let them bend like rubber, going with the fall of stones and any unexpected surface movements until everything settles. Then I can regain my balance, stiffen my legs and grip the ground with my toes again. Trusting to my own legs and balance in these situations is often safer than taking someone's arm for guidance. I may stumble, but I try to relax and stumble in style.

We descended into a slim valley with a rocky pool at the bottom. On each side of us were terraces with tea gardens and small allotments full of vegetables. Women carried baskets of freshly picked produce on their heads. When we encountered them on the narrow path, they would sometimes stand to one side to let us pass, plonking their baskets down beside them, making the most of a rest from their load. Other times they would trudge by regardless, and I would hear their heavy breathing as if the weight of their burden constricted their air intake. Goats and lambs bleated while tinkling cowbells mixed with the chatter of people working on the terraces. The occasional blast of a gun ripped through the distant forests. The sounds echoed and reverberated because we were enclosed on all sides by densely wooded, coniferous slopes.

The path opened on to a golf course. We climbed over a sagging wire fence and sheep scattered over the green. During the first hour and a half of the walk Susan and I caught up with each other's news. Then our questions and tales came in dribbles, until we settled to strolling in silence.

I began to miss Nan, my guide dog. It was not because I needed her but because it seemed strange to enjoy a country walk without sharing the pleasure with her. I never thought about working her in India since it would be impossible for a dog to guide anyone through the hurly-burly of Indian streets. In most towns there are no pavements running in straight lines with kerbs to indicate the edge of a road. There are more obstacles, people, livestock and street furniture, than there is space to squeeze through. A guide dog needs to be able to steer a course by working in a straight line in the middle of a pavement, and only deviates from this to weave around obstacles or people in the way. It is bad enough attempting to get down Oxford Street in London where there are often too few gaps in the crowd through which the dog can thread a path. If the mass of people is solid, my dog sits patiently and waits until there is room to continue without colliding. If we were in India, this would mean we would never move. I could see that what is difficult to achieve with a guide dog in Oxford Street would be impossible in the quietest Indian street. Also, in India many more people were available and willing to accompany me than I would ever find in England. Before I left I was surprised that so many people assumed that I would take my dog. The quarantine restrictions would have made this impossible.

We finished our walk by strolling through Wellington, the Army area. There were large buildings with parade and sports grounds, concealed behind high walls but revealed by yelled commands and running feet chasing a bouncing ball. Ironically, given my reflections on guide dogs, the roads in that area had a new tarmac surface with a sweeping broad pavement on one side.

By the time we got back to the house it was dark, and without the sun the cold took on a new, biting dimension. The kitchen was warm because food was bubbling in pots on the stove for the evening meal. The family gathered there because it was the only warm room. Susan's sister, who was a teacher, had returned from school to cook dinner. Susan scurried around to help out and a few sharp words were exchanged quietly.

I slept well that night, tucked up with sheets and blankets wrapped around my ears, curled around a hot-water bottle. After the many long, hot nights, sprawled naked with not even a sheet to cover me, I was glad of the chance to snuggle down as I do at home. The morning was less cosy because I had to brave the frosty room followed by a cold-water bucket bath. I was well used to houses only having cold water, but here it was icy, running straight down from the mountains. The bucket for the bath was like a fat kitchen rubbish bin. I could just stand in it, making the water rise up my thighs, but I had to get out on to the concrete floor to rinse by scooping water over my back, front and shoulders. Each time I took a plastic jug full of cold water, I cringed at pouring it over my shrinking body. Next time, I decided, I would be less heroic and accept Susan's offer of a few pails of hot water to add to the cold.

I had been syringing oil into my ears morning and night ever since they had first given me trouble some weeks previously. They still itched, burned and ached at varying times of the day and night, and I passed through periods of deafness when I felt cut off from the outside world, a prisoner in my own head. Luckily, these moments were short-lived and I kept hoping I would fight off whatever was causing the condition to flare up.

The Josephs' driver arrived mid-morning. He was as antiquated as their Ambassador car. Dr Joseph took the front passenger seat and Mrs

Joseph sat with Susan and me in the back. It had become a family outing to seek out the assistant director of horticulture in Coonoor. Although my interest was hardly horticultural, the director was my only lead to discover more about the oil-extraction business in the Nilgiris. The address I had for him read, 'Opposite Simp's (*sic*) Park'. Our hunt was like pinning the tail on the donkey. We fumbled around asking for directions until we parked outside a civic building opposite the park. With no sign or open door to take us to the director, we were baffled. The building looked closed for the season. I felt like suggesting that we should take a walk in the gardens opposite: a stroll through an alpine park would be a restful alternative to the irritation of chasing after a man who would probably know nothing about essential oils anyway. However, I did not want to appear faint-hearted or to trivialise our mission, to which everyone else seemed horribly dedicated on my behalf. We followed all the directions and advice we had been given for another hour until we arrived once more opposite the park. This time the doors to the civic building were open.

As we entered I was not too hopeful because the building had the empty echo of schools and town halls when all the staff have gone home. Susan and I pushed through swing doors and began to climb a flight of stairs away from the stench of urine seeping out from the toilets at the bottom. At the top, we found the assistant director, who occupied the whole floor but had no office furniture except his desk. He sat behind this like a pea to the side of an otherwise empty dinner plate.

Susan explained why we had come and I was astounded when he promptly pulled out from his desk drawer folders and files of information on essential oils. He handed me discussion papers and documentation on research carried out at the Central Institute of Medicinal and Aromatic Plants in Lucknow, detailing the chemical make-up and medicinal use of countless oils. He then read the title, 'Cedrus oil – A Promising Antifungal Agent', of an extract photocopied from the *Indian Perfumer*. He produced reviews on muskdana and spikenard oils. I was staggered by his familiarity with the subject: his understanding was not just of the general therapeutic value of plant, as I had found elsewhere, but specifically of essential oils.

He flourished a final wad of notes at Susan. She took them to browse through and said, 'These are his handwritten notes taken at a course on essential oils.' She read aloud some snippets: 'There is eucalyptus for common cold with cough and muscular strains. Geranium, citronella and *Eucalyptus citradora* are useful here too if there is fever. Clove oil is for digestion.' It says, "It is a good antiseptic and antibiotic." She paused and rustled through the papers. 'Here are the spices. "Nutmeg is a carminative and stimulant." It gives a list of things it can help. Flatulence, vomiting, sciatica and rheumatic pain".

'You keep it. All of them. Read later at home,' the assistant director interrupted.

I was flabbergasted. He was giving me his personal notes. Before we left, he advised Susan of a few local suppliers of essential oils. Most of the producers had united to form societies or co-operatives to distil and supply oil for the larger companies. The Tamil Nadu Khadi and Village Industries Board was one such group. It collected the oil from its members and sold it on.

We made arrangements to go up to Ooty in the morning to the Khadi Oil Producers Co-operative. Afterwards Susan had to catch her train from Ooty to return to Madras.

Back in the car Mrs Joseph remembered that every year a man knocked at the doors of all the houses, offering money in return for permission to strip the leaves from the eucalyptuses in the gardens. He sent young boys up the trees as a sweep would once have sent his apprentices up chimneys. Then the tree boys bagged up the leaves and took them to be distilled. With a little encouragement from Susan, Mrs Joseph managed to direct the driver to where the eucalyptus man lived. We parked at the end of a lane and Susan and I got out

The smoke that filled my nostrils smelt blue. It twirled and curled around my head and in my clothing. Beneath that wispy, wafting smell of eucalyptus smoke there was a more permanent acrid odour of burnt wood and charcoal. I sniffed and licked the air touching my lips. It was ashy, charred and delicious, just like the air in parks and recreation grounds on the day following Bonfire Night. We stepped through a gate from the rocky path we had started along, and crunched over a springy bed of half-burnt eucalyptus leaves. Dogs were barking in houses in the lane where the car was parked, but we were alone in an open area of wasteland, except for a child calling for her father. Her shouts bobbed in and out of my hearing as she darted her head back and forth into the hut where he was working.

A man who smelt like a bonfire, smoky and mild, came to help us across the ever-thickening eucalyptus bed. When I sensed that the wall of the hut was close I put out my hand to steady myself and regain my footing. It crackled under my touch. I glided my fingers across it to discover leaves rather than stone or brick. I pushed them through the brittle foliage to try to find the stone underneath, but there were only more eucalyptus leaves. These were packed tight and filled the gaps between several bent eucalyptus poles forming the domed structure of the hut. There were two such huts, one for living and one for the distillery. I was advised to bend down to enter the distillery hut, and had to double over on to my knees to get through the low door.

The father and son talked in Tamil to Susan. They explained their business by tapping on metal drums where the leaves were stored, then kicking at the ash left in a hole in the floor where a fire was lit each night. Nothing was wasted. After the oil had been taken from the leaves, they were recycled and burned as fuel for the next distillation. A pint-size glass jam-jar was propped on the uneven ground below a pipe to collect the distilled oil drop by drop. The father took my hand and manoeuvred me down into a dip so I could lean forward and smell the latest extraction. I reeled back, blasted as if by the recoil of a rifle. The terpenes contained in the eucalyptus were dominant in the oil and strong enough to disorientate me, and the eucalyptol made my eyes smart. The brutality of the vapours was like that of paint stripper or methylated spirit. Susan was more cautious when she inhaled from the jar. The extractions were collected in these crude, impure vessels and sold privately by the father and son team.

We stepped outside the hut to escape the overpowering fumes. The smoke was saturated with the decongesting, mentholated vapours that clear colds and blockages in my patients' heads, chests and noses when I give them eucalyptus inhalations.

The next morning the driver arrived early to take us up to Ooty. Once again Dr and Mrs Joseph accompanied Susan and me. Ooty is as high as Chamonix in France, maybe higher. The alpine smells and sounds conjured up a mental picture into which I placed French *paysans* more easily than I could imagine Indian women in saris. It was as though I had jumbled the pieces of two jigsaws and could not sort them out.

Before reaching Ooty we turned off into the countryside to find the oil producers' co-operative. Susan left us in the car while she went to find out if we could buy some oil. She was gone a long time, and I was not as patient as her parents. I got out to stretch my legs along the grassy lane. There were children playing while women chattered and scrubbed clothes against stone. Stepping to one side, I knocked against one of the cattle troughs used as both a sink and rubbing board. My head bumped against a branch, sending a flurry of jacaranda petals to the ground. I wished I could remember whether jacaranda flowers are blue or purple to complete the idyllic picture in my mind's eye

Susan returned with a man who was jangling a bunch of keys. 'They only have eucalyptus oil here,' she said.

We followed the man to a derelict house hidden among trees. He unlocked the door into a windowless room where he stored drums of oil in one corner. A boy ran for a rag which I could hear the man rip, knot and pull tight before dipping it into one of the barrels. The oil soaked into the cloth and evaporated into the room. He passed the cloth to me: it was dry, not greasy from the drenching in oil. Essential oils are non-greasy and evaporate quickly in the air. Strong aromatic particles pervaded the atmosphere in the room and obliterated all other smells

Susan and the man had a discussion ending in shrugging shoulders and resigned shakes of their heads. 'He is asking for our bottle, but we have no bottle,' she explained. Without a bottle we could not decant any oil.

I was not disappointed because I guessed this extraction was as crude and impure as the one produced in the eucalyptus hut in Coonoor so I could not use it. The pipes, jars and drums I had come across looked as if they belonged in a garage. The rag on which I had smelt the eucalyptus did not compare favourably with the sterile blotting strips I use for oil smelling. The individual distillers delivered their oil to a central depot before it went to the Cottage Industrial Society for further distilling, bottling and distributing. We decided to make our way to the society, at Honey House, Cherring Cross, to find some ready-bottled oil.

Honey House was a stone cottage on the corner of a busy road entering Ooty. Inside, clerks scratched pens across ledgers, slamming them shut after each entry. Typewriters snapped and rattled, their bells tinging at the end of each line. Metal filing cabinets shook every time drawers raced shut with a bang. Susan and I sat on swivel chairs and waited for a price list of available oils. The society had *Eucalyptus globulus*, either raw or double distilled. There was raw citronella, lemon-grass and *citradora*. I was not convinced by the quality after what I had seen so I bought nothing.

Ooty was a noisy, dishevelled, hustling town with overcrowded, narrow streets full of mountain people bartering for provisions, and honeymoon couples (the temporary inhabitants of all hill stations) sitting on benches around the racecourse, or gazing dreamily over the botanical gardens. We got caught up in a political rally, deafened by the loudspeakers and mobbed by the crowd, who seemed to treat the spectacle as light entertainment. The driver inched the car along, nudging people's backs with the bumper until they either moved out of the way or slammed a hand down on the bonnet as if trying to push the car backwards.

For the first time since my arrival in India I came across ponies. They were lightweight and unshod, trotting softly through the streets, pulling tongas twice their size. Off-duty, they could be heard grazing loose at the sides of the emptier roads on the outskirts of town. While we were stuck in a jam of people and hissing, squeaking rickshaws, pushing and shoving like penned farm animals, my attention was diverted to the snuffling of more hill ponies standing in a group. I realised this was the rank where they waited, chomping at nose bags, for their next passengers, their swishing tails warding off flies. I was so close I could just touch the flank of a small, scruffy specimen, who sneezed hungrily and snorted over the food, rushing in case my touch was a summons to more work and less lunch.

We stopped to take a look at a shop, the closest thing to a health-food store I had come across. Susan's mother decided to get out with us. The car dropped us outside the shop but Mrs Joseph could not make the giant step up and in until two men leapt to her aid. The shop had a counter open to the pavement and shelves to the back and sides. I picked up bags of dried fruits, nuts, seeds and flours. There were soaps and creams smelling of natural perfumes. I rattled pots of herbal tablets and swilled the liquid in bottles of herbal medicine. There were no bottles of essential oil. The storekeeper explained, 'All gone to Cochin.'

Later we pulled over for tea, stopping right outside the tearoom. I assumed this was so that the parents would not have to walk far. In fact we were so close to the tearoom that I thought we had driven right inside – as indeed, we had: from my car window I could hear muffled slurping and chewing from the nearest table. The driver got out and returned with a tray of china cups and saucers filled with steaming, sticky milk tea, which we drank along with the other customers, but still in the car.

Revived, we dashed to the station. There was no time for farewells as all the brakesmen on the train were blowing their whistles as if calling people to a circus. Susan whisked herself away, instructing her parents to ensure that I reached Mysore, my next destination, safely.

While staying with the Josephs, I had avoided discussion about where and how I was travelling next. I knew they would be as concerned as Goutam and the Hatarias about my plans to reach Madikeri. I had spoken to Nalini on the telephone and established that from Ooty I would take a bus to Mysore where I would change and travel on to her. Although Madikeri lay in the opposite direction to Bangalore, I still wanted to go somewhere that would be a rest from my work tour. I also wanted to meet the challenge of travelling to Mysore alone, and even staying there a few days without help before getting myself to Madikeri. Until then, I had been met and assisted at every stage, but now I wanted to do it alone. This was my chance.

Nalini had not offered to meet me in Mysore and had not even asked about my travel arrangements. I wondered how she thought I would reach her. I wondered too. On the other hand Goutam, whom I had also telephoned, had a series of questions the length of a shopping list for a wedding party. I lied. And I lied again later when the Josephs asked what would happen to me in Mysore. I told everyone that Nalini would meet me there off the bus from Ooty.

Nevertheless, the Josephs wanted to send the husband of their servant on the bus with me all the way to Mysore. He would take the day off work in the fields and hand me over to Nalini. Apart from blowing my cover, I could not bear to inconvenience anyone to the tune of fourteen boring hours on a bumpy bus. I insisted on going alone, but agreed that George, Susan's nephew, would accompany me as far as Ooty for seven the next morning.

My final evening was quiet, except for a strange incident. I was sitting in my bedroom with the door open writing some notes when I sensed the furtive movements of someone standing and watching me. I looked directly at the person by my bedroom door. I guessed it was the servant. She was brazen about her spying, probably thinking I could not know she was there. I gazed at her, feigning recognition, but she did not move, presumably confident that her stealth made her invisible. I returned to my writing and she continued to observe me unabashed and fascinated. Half an hour later, I looked up, smiled and asked her if she would bring me some tea. She vanished.

George was a bright, interesting companion on the bus journey to Ooty. He was a confident young graduate aiming to get to America for further studies. I was glad of his escort at the bus station when I took the precaution of using the toilet, which would be hard to manage alone later in the long day ahead. An old woman was in attendance, and when George explained that I could not see, she grabbed me with her rough hands and steered me into a cubicle with a hole in the floor. I hoped she had picked one with clean footpads and gingerly felt for the ridged surface. Open-toed sandals were a great disadvantage in this situation because excrement around the foot treads was unhappily common. However, I preferred the holes in the ground – better to subject my feet to the risk rather than my bottom.

I boarded the bus, grateful to George for his discretion. He was one of the few people I had been with who did not tell the conductor, the driver and dozens of passengers to watch out for me. I felt as if I had been given a clean licence, no penalties, no restrictions and no obligations other than to myself.

MYSORE: JASMINE AND ARNICA

'**W**hat is your good name?' eventually asked the man sitting behind me. He was young and fidgety. During most of the bus journey he had been tiresome, lolling across the central gangway, laughing and joking with his friend on the other side.

'Nicola,' I answered, and turned to gaze out of the window.

He tapped my shoulder. 'Are you being married?'

I could not help feeling irritated by what seemed like nosiness, although I suspected that Indians would have taken it for straightforward friendliness: they habitually launch into an inquisitive, persistent round of questions with strangers.

'No, I am not married. Are you?'

The young man hooted with laughter. 'No, no, I am at college only. We are going to a friend's wedding.' He was delighted with my interest and continued, 'How many years have you? Why are you travelling alone? You are having friends to meet you? Where are you getting down?'

I fielded the questions, wary of how genuine he was and how much it was safe to reveal. Finally I said, 'Look, if you don't mind I want to rest a bit.' The young man slouched back in a dejected heap, and I felt guilty about what must have seemed to him like one more cold, haughty westerner snubbing friendship.

My reprieve was brief because the man sitting beside me asked suddenly, 'Why are you coming here?' His tweed jacket flapped open against my leg. I felt his thick, canvas trousers and heard his heavy boots scraping on the floor whenever he adjusted his position.

I forced myself to be civil and answered, 'Because of my work. I have been seeing what oils, like eucalyptus and lemon-grass, are available.'

'I am knowing very much about these oils. I have woods for cutting. I am working only in these hills.'

It turned out that my neighbour was well informed about the nature and use of essential oils. He had a degree in chemistry and understood molecular structures and refining processes, including double distillations, which, he explained, altered the composition of oils. I could have learnt more from him about the grading of oils for quality than from many of the experts I had met formally. Unfortunately, his poor English blurred everything he said and the noise of the rattling bus, filled with the hum and drone of other passengers' voices, drowned his words. I was thankful when he said, 'I am getting down now. Here are my most superior woods. If I can be helping you further, please be having my card.'

I was left to a stretch of silence, in which my more anxious thoughts conspired to disturb me. Being alone on that bus was not so very different from the other journeys I had made until then, except there was no one to meet me at the other end, and I would be several days in a new town with no contacts. The few unaided ventures I had made while staying in Trivandrum and Coimbatore had highlighted how vulnerable I felt after nine years of constant guidance, yet I had arranged for there to be no help in Mysore: no tame driver, appointed guide or friend awaiting my safe arrival. Why was I subjecting myself to this? I suppose I felt that going it alone would be exhilarating not just bruising. On I went with my jasmine and arnica, and my stony resolve.

My attention switched back momentarily to the man's card, which was crumpled in my hand. I shoved it into my pocket where the little bottle of arnica pills was bouncing around. My tiny vial of jasmine oil, an aromatic solution to calm anxiety and uplift a faltering spirit, rolled between my fingers in the other pocket.

I was not sure how I would manage once I was in Mysore, or Sandalwood City as it is known, but I was committed to the experiment. Now I had the continuing distraction of the young man to occupy me, so irritation superseded worry. He darted into the seat next to me, vacated by the wood man, and directed more questions at me, and discussed my replies with his friend, who was still sitting on the other side. After a brief *chai* stop, the seat was taken by another man, who remained quiet for a surprisingly long time. The young man continued to pester from behind but it was easier to keep my back to him and ignore him.

We had dropped down out of the hills and were driving through a forest. The cracking of dry branches and crunching of animals moving in dead undergrowth made it very different from the moist, tree-covered hills. Feeling confident that the man next to me was not given to incessant chatter, I enquired, 'Where are we?'

'This is wildlife sanctuary, Bandipur,' he said. 'Elephants are here.'

I was not convinced by his answer because I did not think the bus route passed through Bandipur. I also knew that in India an answer, whether accurate or not, is the polite way to deal with a question. However, we had a delightfully brief conversation in which I warmed to him. He had just visited his daughter in Ooty and was now going to his son's wedding in Mysore before returning home to Bangalore.

'Maharajah's Palace,' called the bus driver, and the bus screeched to a halt.

Alerted to the fact that we were entering Mysore, I panicked. How was I going to find a rickshaw to take me to my hotel? This conundrum loomed darkly over me. At moments like this I feel the weight of the helplessness that casts a shadow over me. I decided to ask the man sitting next to me to help me find a rickshaw, but I could not bring myself to tell him I was blind when we had just travelled for three hours together. I had let him assume that I had enjoyed visually the landmarks he had pointed out.

When we arrived at the bus station I stuck to his every move. He got off first and immediately I lost him in the crowd. Everyone was in a bunch, trying to orientate themselves after climbing down the steps. Standing hopelessly for a second or two, I put down my bag and pretended there was some problem with the strap. My ploy worked, and he returned to offer to carry the bag. This time I allowed no more than a centimetre of air to separate us. I paced his step, I coincided my breath with his, I ensured that the suction in the tiny space between us was as adhesive as glue. Within seconds we were out of the bus station, I halted in line with the man and crossed the road to arrive beside a parked rickshaw. He and the driver talked to confirm the destination and fix the price. I thanked the man, who probably thought he had simply helped a rather inept foreigner, bewildered by the language and habits of a strange culture. He never knew that he had guided a blind woman through one of the busiest parts of Mysore. I felt more stressed and confused than blind.

My rickshaw journey ended under an arch in the cobbled courtyard of the Hotel Dasaprakash. As soon as the vehicle had juddered away, I could detect from the sound of telephones and voices that the driver had obligingly dropped me right by an open door leading into Reception. There were foreigners talking, door keys jangling from rings, and a fan whipping up the sticky air into swirls of wet heat. The sounds rose to meet me from a lower level, indicating I would have to go down several steps. I did not know how many.

Losing my nerve, I reached for my cane in my bag. I knew that it would not necessarily signal anything to anyone, and for me, it was still such a stark symbol of blindness – and blindness was synonymous with hopelessness. Ironically the cane sometimes disabled me: I fumbled more when it was in my hand because its association with hopelessness undermined my confidence and with no other source of help, I had no choice.

The drop of the cane confirmed the down step and I swerved right towards the voices. I stood still as soon as I detected the bottom of the counter. People stopped talking and looked over at me. I stiffened under the stare of an English woman who had just checked in. She frisked me with her eyes, searching for answers to the unvoiced questions storming her mind. Oddly, she turned and hurried out.

'Yes, what are you wanting?' the receptionist asked, unaware of anything more meaningful than another westerner parading the latest frivolous fashionable object.

'I want a single room with a bathroom for two nights,' I said.

'That will be seventy rupees a night. Please be filling the book.'

I gave him my passport and said, 'I am blind so I can't see to fill in the form. Will you do it?'

He took my passport and did so without showing either perplexity or understanding. 'Please be signing here.' He pointed with the pen, which he dropped on the page, and called for someone to carry my bags. By filling in the form for me he had seemed to accept that I was not able to see, yet must have presumed that I would regain my sight to sign it and follow the bag boy to my room. I scrawled anywhere, anyhow.

'Will you be taking English-language morning newspaper, Madam?'

I nodded. Things were becoming ludicrous.

The bag boy was an elderly, bow-legged man, who conjured up in my mind's eye an instant picture of a strong, sure-footed billy-goat. I folded away my cane thinking I could keep abreast of him.

We went into the courtyard, where I heard people walking on the open corridors above. There were three floors on three sides with open walkways. The bedrooms were on the far side of the building, or tucked down a warren of dark passages leading into the heart of the complex. I remembered that the courtyard was cobbled and followed the bag boy's every step, listening out for when his footfall became heavier, signalling that he had started up the stairs. Light-headed with nervousness, my stomach as tight as a fist, I stuck as close to him as I dared – not as close as one would be with a lover, but closer than with anyone else. I counted the flights not the steps – there were too many to remember – and jarred my spine each time I reached a platform and my foot fell unexpectedly flat. Trying hard to collect navigational aids as we progressed, I noted that we turned left and followed the passage to the end where we bent right. The light and air from the inner courtyard were always on my right.

The porter took the padlock from the door and switched on the fan. He walked to the end of the room and opened another door to show me the bathroom. I nodded dismissively, not wanting the charade of performing an inspection by walking over to take a look. I tipped him. He closed the door and I stood in a daze for some time. I was stunned to have pulled it off, and relieved to be alone.

Slowly I began to examine the bedroom. There was a single bed against a wall. I sniffed the folded top sheet and the towel. They smelt neither fresh nor stale, and they felt thin and worn. I looked for the telephone to call Room Service to come and change them. My nose and imagination are harsher judges of cleanliness than the most discerning eye and I was taking no chances. I found a metal table and chair, a Formica coffee table on which stood a Thermos flask of water and a glass. Above this was the only window, next to the door; it was barred and covered with a net curtain. The telephone was propped on the sill.

I followed the length of the wall to the bathroom. Some pegs were nailed in at shoulder height, which I bumped into on the way. The bathroom had a chipped tiled floor, a western-style toilet, a basin and a shower with a bucket underneath. There was a constant dripping sound and a faint smell of sewage. Only one tap at the basin and one at the shower worked; I was immediately doubtful about the claim that there was running hot water.

My head was aching. I felt battered and hungry but methodically began to unpack so that I could find my talking clock. It was two thirty in the afternoon and I had not eaten since six thirty that morning. I finished my last bottle of water, realising that my headache was due to dehydration, but knew I could not muster the spirit to venture out in search of more bottled water or food. The water in the Thermos would certainly not have been filtered, so I assembled the compact water filter I carried with me. Pumping the water from the flask through the porous filter and into an empty bottle was exhausting. After twenty minutes of toil I had no more than half a pint of water. I felt weak and my head pounded. My efforts might have improved the quality of the water but did nothing for its fetid smell and sour taste. Thirst forced me to drink anyway until I gagged and could face no more.

My shock was slowly yielding to distress about the complications and energy involved in getting myself so far. I dissolved an arnica tablet in my mouth and collapsed on the bed. I was mentally prostrate and so apathetic that, for the first time, I felt despondent and indifferent about my whole trip. Waves of agoraphobia eroded my intention to spend the rest of the day exploring Mysore. When I was first losing my sight I had experienced feelings similar to these. I would try to go somewhere with no help and exhaust myself in the process. Enervated from the stress and risks, I would return, disconsolate and morose about ever being able to do anything again. I did not see then, nor did I in those early weeks of my travels, that I needed to tailor my plans differently to change my destructive pattern of behaviour. I drove myself forward regardless, but my passage would have been so much smoother had I learned more quickly how to pace myself. Too often, my flyweight constitution was no match for my heavyweight resolution. True to form, that day I took a quick shower, allowed myself a forty-minute rest then goaded myself to go out again.

The arch forming the entrance to the hotel was on the edge of a small roundabout. There I stood – defiantly, doubtless foolishly – without my cane. I had decided, in my exhausted obstinacy, to go out and explore – just as other guests would. Such insane denial has brought me much misery, but also some triumph. The standard array of rickshaws and drivers waited by the stone pillars to pick up hotel guests. 'Where are you going, Madam?' asked one of the three drivers standing closest to me.

'I am walking,' I answered, knowing I would be hassled unless I moved off quickly, but not yet sure enough of the lie of the land to make my first move.

'No very good walking. Please be riding.' I knew the rickshaw-wallah was not just looking for a fare: he was unused to the idea, that people with money would walk anywhere. Most middle-class Indians hailed a rickshaw rather than walk a hundred yards. The streets were considered hot, dirty, dusty and dangerous, best viewed from the relative safety of a rickshaw or car, only stopping occasionally outside a shop to make a purchase. But I wanted to wander through the town, absorb the atmosphere and maybe discover a market or some interesting little side-streets.

I waved away the rickshaw-wallah and, I hoped, confidently crossed the roundabout, heading for the high buildings I could sense on the other side. My crossing was made to an excited chorus of hoots, squeals, screeches and squeaks, but I was not sure whether I was the cause or whether it was just part of the operatics of street life. As usual the traffic was noisy and congested. It bottle-necked down small narrow streets and popped like a cork with a surge of explosive energy at every chance of escape. The three-wheelers, hand-pulled carts and the odd aimlessly wandering cow or donkey blocked the roads so cars could not speed. Collisions were frequent, but high-impact smash-ups were rare. The rickshaws were apt to skid to a halt or swerve at the last minute. Sometimes they toppled over if they spun too sharply. On the other hand, the slower carts, pulled by two men at the front and pushed by one at the back, rolled on relentlessly and unmindful of what was in their path. Under the momentum of a heavy load, sustained by the bulging muscles of sweating, grimly determined men, there was no chance of them ever making an emergency stop, or performing a cunning manoeuvre to avoid crushing anything in the way. I just hoped it would never be me.

Reaching the buildings, I hugged the wall and walked down the side-street, stopping every few paces to assemble bearings and to identify any obstacles ahead. As soon as I heard footsteps I asked, 'Where is the market?' I had to inquire several times before I found someone who understood English. Everyone answered, of course, not wanting to appear rude, and pointed in various directions or collected other passers-by to add authoritative weight to their random signals. I waited until I found someone who did not just wave but replied in English, 'Devaraja Market by Statue Square, oh, so very close. You just be going down here and over Dhanvantri Road.'

I followed the man's voice as I knew he would be speaking and looking in the direction in which he was pointing. I continued on my way, but moved to the middle of the street after stumbling into a beggar who was lying against the wall. I'm sure I trod on his hand but he made no noise, just curled up tightly. In the middle of the street, I tried to trace the width by the sounds of hawkers and barrow-sellers who lined both sides. The drone of a rickshaw would start as a faint waspish buzz that quickly gathered intensity. Just as the noise zoomed into a frantic zinging, I would step aside, hoping not to barge into the backs of shoppers or gossiping youths. In this way, my confidence increasing, I picked my path, adrenaline my foolish ally.

The road I came to next was more hazardous to cross: It was one of the main roads through town. Wheels spun dangerously fast, and I could not sense the solidity of any buildings on the other side, which meant it was wider than anything I had crossed since leaving the hotel. I stood at the edge of the road and waited with a steadily enlarging body of people. The crowd surged forward as if in one choreographed movement and I let myself be transported, protected in a cocoon of strangers. This was becoming easy.

The crowd was thick and swirled in the open square on the other side. It acted like a blob of ink spreading on a piece of blotting-paper, and I felt that by staying in its midst I could safely cover every inch of this absorbing town. I relinquished my impaired judgement and let myself be guided by the collective mind, steering too many people down a narrow passage. I remembered a book I had read about crowd behaviour where it was argued that a crowd develops its own personality as if it were one creature, and that each person was a component performing a particular function. I wondered what my function was. Realising that I was probably just baggage, or perhaps a parasite, I decided to think about something else. We squeezed between buildings until we spilled out of an opening into a covered market. The crowd dissolved, becoming individual shoppers, haggling over prices and bundling away their purchases.

Then my nose assumed command and I drifted from perfume-scented melons to honey-smelling pawpaws. Remembering my hunger I bought some fruit. In the stimulation and chaotic charm of the market I soaked up more than the information necessary for survival. I basked in the bright calls and shouts. I wallowed in the hot, pungent odours that swamped the air. There were so many different shapes, sizes and textures, littering the ground in discarded piles or stacked on trays that I might have been attending a special-effects sound-and-touch show. As a consequence, my tastebuds and third eye conjured magical flavours and visions from the multitude of raw ingredients. Bitter-sweet, hard-soft, shiny-dull, wet-dry, sharp-blunt, sparkling-flat: the extremes, the contrasts bombarded all my senses, breaking their boundaries until I could see, feel, hear, smell and taste the musty, the piercing, the glowing, the bristling, the moist; the varied qualities of life at its most vibrant. Each one triggered each and every sense – what is dull or gleaming is as meaningful to the touch as it is to the eye.

I left the market and asked for Cauvery Emporium. I knew from the tape-recording I had made in England, listing each town's highlights, which I had played in the bus on the way to Mysore, that the town was renowned for its arts and crafts and Cauvery was the place to find them. It turned out to be on the main road I had previously crossed. There were wide pavements, partially dug up, chipped and broken. The crowd was no longer dense enough to carry me along and disguise my drunken movements, but it was sufficiently thick to be bothersome. I crept along, pausing constantly as if I was looking at something interesting, while in fact I assessed whether it was clear ahead. I longed for the crowd to become constant and streaming, to move like a caterpillar once again so that I could feel like an inconspicuous segment. Instead I was painfully aware that I attracted attention every time I tripped and bungled, or stared transfixed at a blank stone wall.

A calculated guess that the quiet swish of heavy doors and cool blast of conditioned air meant I was outside Cauvery was correct. Inside, a cathedral-like silence made me feel watched. I edged my way around carefully, assuming the artifacts to be in side and central displays. I discovered rosewood tables with heavily carved legs, and elephants intricately inlaid with ivory. I felt fraudulent, inching my way around, minutely examining each object, when this meticulous concentration owed more to the need to study a safe route back to the exit than to admiring the handicrafts.

I was too tense to contemplate buying anything. I left after completing a circle of the ground floor.

I also wanted to visit the Maharajah's Palace and Chamundi Hill. According to my tape these were both to the south of the town. I decided to return to the hotel and set out again so as not to lose the location of my base. I was thankful for my natural ability to orientate myself as I picked my way through the maze of streets back to Hotel Dasaprakash. I have always operated like a mole in an underground network of tunnels. I rarely lose my sense of direction. I imagine that if I surfaced from my blindness and suddenly regained sight, I would be dazzled and confused by all the extraneous information (like most sighted people, I often think) and would never find my way so effectively again. Perhaps the crowd would promote me from baggage to compass. Perhaps there really was a Pinball Wizard.

Mysore is big enough to be a significant town but not so big that I could not work out how to get about. It had an easygoing, friendly atmosphere, and the streets, although narrow and old, were fairly clean. A lingering aroma of sandalwood, rose, musk, frangipani and jasmine hung in the doorways and down side alleys. I was tempted to follow these smells, which piped up to charm me off course. Mysore is known for its incense manufacture, and small family-owned *agarbathi*– incense – businesses are scattered around the town. Clouds of fragrant smoke billowed down streets, or curled up my nose as I passed a solitary shop burning an *agarbathi* stick on its counter. However, I was already saturated with the sensuality of the market and worried about overstretching my sense of direction, so the attraction of an odorous orgy in the back-streets of Mysore palled.

Once back in my room, I was reassured that I could find my way without too much difficulty, provided I did not go off at too many tangents. I dumped the fruit on my table and left immediately. I double-locked the door, using the huge padlock supplied by the hotel and a smaller one I had been carrying with me but had never used until then. This new necessity reminded me that I was not as safe as hitherto because I was not only alone and unprotected but in less secure accommodation than anywhere else I had stayed. The corridors were more animated now that it was late afternoon and people were active again after their siestas.

I needed to take a rickshaw to find the palace, and moved down the line of waiting, beckoning drivers until I picked one at random. Within a second of climbing in, an outraged rickshaw-wallah approached, yelling at my driver who was hurriedly kick-starting his machine. Soon the others had circled us in an angry mob. We were not going anywhere and I sat helplessly, fearing a lynching, while fists were waved furiously and my driver shuffled and looked down stubbornly. I was considering how I could get out and negotiate my way through the pack when someone held out a hand and said, 'Please be coming, Madam,' A small, stout man escorted me through a change of vehicle. Judging by the way the crowd parted he was some kind of union official or squad leader. Peace returned, and we hurtled through town papping at everything in our way. I got down by the south gate of the palace and deduced from the sound of crunching gravel that the entrance lay directly ahead.

'Very nice flowers, see, please be looking.' A little girl ran persistently at my side as I walked quicker and quicker to shake her off. The unmistakable, intoxicating power of jasmine flooded my nostrils. As I took a deep breath, I slowed my pace. 'Please buy, take two,' she pleaded. Before I could stop myself, I reached out and gently touched the flowers in her basket. There were only two strings left. I said nothing but she kept up with me all the way to the entrance kiosk.

I paid, and followed the steps of other visitors to tour the sumptuous palace, built in 1907 on the site of the former Indo-Saracenic seat of the maharajahs of Mysore. Everything I touched, brushed past or walked over was an extravaganza of gilt, mirrors and stained glass. The mosaic and cold marble floors were slippery; some carved wooden doors were as thick as tree trunks while others were made from solid silver. The Durbar Hall was huge and full of fat columns.

At the back of the palace there was the Residential Museum. I removed my shoes as I had to enter the palace and stuffed them into my bag. The attendant objected, saying, 'No shoes.' He tapped the mat where piles of shoes cascaded over the edges on to the path where I was standing.

I had already trodden on some of them, and I had no intention of leaving mine when I knew I would never identify them among the disorderly tangle of buckles and straps. I pointed to my bag to reassure the man that I did not intend to wear my shoes. He mistook my gesture, thinking it an act of defiance, flew into a rage and rallied everyone around to support his condemnation of how I was about to defile 'this most honourable place'.

Amazed that my little size-three sandals might have the power to defile a vast palace, I glanced down at them with renewed respect but decided that they could do no harm tucked into my bag, and said, 'Fine. If you want to return my entrance fee, your "honourable place" can do without my visit.' I could not bring myself to explain the situation. At best I would have to cope with the astonishment, and at worst the disbelief that honesty often brings. He would think I was faking, finding an excuse. After all, how many blind visitors walk unaided around a palace?

With two rupees clasped in my hand, I headed back across the gardens to the main palace, leaving the bellicose attendant behind. I began to feel less cross, then shamefaced about my overheated reaction and the unnecessary confrontation. I did not like behaving like another bad-mannered westerner and should have been more conciliatory. But another, altogether more truculent voice in my head said, 'Why should I have to shout about my disability from the rooftops at times when I don't need help? It's hard enough having to grovel when I do.' I don't defend my attitude, I merely record it. Negotiating my safe passage was draining all my reserves, and I had nothing to spare with which to placate outraged officials.

'If you please, Madam, just be taking one picture only.' A young man pushed a camera into my hand.

I took the course of least resistance, smiled benevolently and asked, 'Where do you want it taking?'

The man consulted with his partner. They were a young honeymoon couple, wanting shots for their album. They moved off the gravel path and trod softly on a lawn. Then the man came over to show me how the camera worked, and to suggest that I should cross on to the grass as well.

I tried to move on to the lawn and knocked against a chain, looped dangerously at knee height. I stepped over it and called, 'Ready?' hoping their response would mark the spot. There came no response, and I could sense them nowhere. Not wanting to bring the camera up to my eye without the slightest clue where to point it, I yelled, 'Ready?' They answered, I swung round, aimed, clicked and sighed deeply as I lowered the camera.

Once I was outside the palace, back in the forecourt, the little jasmine girl joined me again. She was still trying to sell her last two strings of flowers. I gave her the two rupees, which had been hot in my palm ever since the attendant had returned them. 'No, no. One string ten rupees only. No two rupees,' she insisted. I heard her flick the fingers of one hand wide open into a star shape, once, then twice to make the ten clear. I was not thinking of buying the flowers, just offloading the two rupees, but I usually preferred to buy something, even if I did not want it, rather than give money to someone begging. Now I was waving money at a vendor as though they were a beggar, which I would frown upon in others. I paid gladly for my insensitivity and gave the child her ten rupees in exchange for the flowers, but I found it hard to squash a growing feeling of unease. I did not feel at home, I did not feel confident. I felt a fraud, ashamed, and wished I was someone else.

The little girl was still with me and we were soon by some railings, running around the perimeter of the palace and leading to the main road. I perched wearily on the concrete ledge supporting the metal posts. 'One more string only, ten rupees.' She made herself comfortable, hunkering down next to me, swinging the jasmine. The smell was addictive. She was as fragile as the flowers and as persistent as their scent. I was spellbound by the pugnacious way she ground her heels in happy defiance into the shingle, daring me to refuse her challenge.

It was getting late. People were leaving the palace and heading into town. I still wanted to go to Chamundi Hill but I needed another surge of adrenaline to fortify me. I handed the child another ten rupees and hung her last string of jasmine in my hair. She stayed next to me and began to make patterns with her toes in the sand under the shingle. 'You speak good

English. Where did you learn?' I asked.

'Many foreign peoples are coming here. I speak very much English.'

'How old are you?'

She flashed her fingers as fast as a lizard's tongue. Her knuckles clicked. 'No,' I said. 'Tell me how old you are.'

'I am having seven years.'

I got up and started to walk towards the exit. She skipped beside me and slipped her hand into mine. 'Have you brothers and sisters?' I asked.

'Many, very many.' She said no more, so for a while I asked no more questions. I felt comforted to have a companion again. I let myself be pulled like a thread by her slight tugs and twists as she needled her way through the crowd on the pavement. After a while I encouraged her to make her way home.

'No going home. Later going home,' she declared.

'What about your mummy and daddy?'

'Later coming home. Dark time coming home.'

I asked, 'Do you know where the city bus station is? Can you take me there?' Ushered across roads, around charcoal pavement fires, with pans sizzling and spitting, my sandals coming down where they would, my tiny guide tugged me on through people lounging in groups, and along the edge of main roads full of streaming, snarling, screeching traffic as predatory as the noises of the jungle. The darting and twisting were exhilarating, but disorientating. Her little fingers steered me, and with every turn the change in our relationship was cemented.

The city bus station was worse than the departure lounge at an airport when the package holiday flights are delayed. The crowd of people was so dense that the only way to get through was to walk in the bus parking area, and hope no bus was about to swing in or out too quickly. Suddenly my companion spun me round, loosened her grip, and said, 'Goodbye.' She vanished before I had stopped spinning and I stumbled a pace or two. A real-life Blind Man's Buff. I felt that if I walked forward, the crowd would titter and jeer, 'Over here! No! Over *here*!' My hand was cold and clammy with the paralysing panic of sudden loss. I stood, rooted to the spot, while buses beeped and throaty engines revved all about me.

I asked repeatedly for my bus and each time understood that I was gestured to go a little further towards the back of the station. I passed down the sides of buses until I reached the steps of the one that I had been told unanimously was going to Chamundi Hill.

I was dismayed by how long the journey took. Darkness fell half an hour before we even began the hairpin crawl up the hill, and I was worrying already about how I would get myself back to the hotel. The bus emptied its passengers in a car park at the top of the hill. I joined the crowd that quickly evaporated among an array of *chai* stalls and snack bars. Oil lamps and smoky fires choked the night, making it thick and inky. The flicker of flames from the wooden and sackcloth shelters danced across my face.

The Shiva temple topping the hill loomed solitary and sinister on the far side. All the priests had disappeared for the night and the usual crew of beggars, postcard- and souvenir-sellers were eating and drinking in the shanty through which I picked my way on the steep climb to the temple. It had a forty-metre, seven-storey high *gopuram*, a soaring pyramidal gateway tower, with a statue of the demon Mahishasura who was one of the goddess Chamundi's victims. I sensed the imposing height and enjoyed the cool and dark after the hot, festive atmosphere of the bazaar below. The holler and buzz of nightlife had receded as I climbed.

I shivered slightly; a frisson of exhaustion not cold. The last bus returned at ten but I decided to try to get a rickshaw to the hotel. I hoped it would be simpler than the bus. I was tiring rapidly and less able to rely on my third eye. I stumbled over some steps and whacked a shin on a small stone pillar. Tiredness always blunts my senses and heightens my emotions. I felt wobbly and fought back tears. Every time I heard laughter coming from the food stalls I believed, with the unshakeable conviction of the paranoid, that my clumsy progress was the joke.

As I expected, the rickshaw-wallahs were lined up in the car park and pounced as soon as I arrived. I haggled in the sure knowledge that the price started at three times the local going rate. We helter-skeltered down the steep, dark hill with the engine turned off to save petrol.

Tired and troubled, I sat back in the rickshaw. The day now seemed surreal; it had been so chancy and I felt unsettled that it had happened. I had achieved a lot, yet I felt not pride but shame. I had managed by fecklessly ignoring my disability, imagining that I could see and behaving accordingly. I had been so convincing that no one else had thought I was blind either. I had done this when I first lost my sight and it entrenched me in denial and danger. My path to recovery had been to denounce denial as my foe. Yet it was shocking how quickly I had slipped back behind enemy lines and become again a traitor to myself. I pretend, others believe and I believe them. I am the actress who can believe she is her stage character, if her audience can.

When we arrived at the hotel I jolted into action again. With not a trace of stage-fright I strode into the tourist office just inside the entrance to book a sight-seeing trip for the following day.

I was thankful I could speak German and eavesdropped on the couple in front of me, discussing the plans and a route suggested by the tour manager. They traced a map under a glass-topped desk and tapped at postcard pictures of places of interest stuck around the map. I memorised the names of the sight-seeing places around Mysore about which they were most enthusiastic. When it was my turn I tried to keep my request as simple and as short as possible in order not to draw attention to the fact that, for me, it would be a sound-hearing, smell-smelling tour.

'I would like a tourist taxi for one day to see as much as possible of the places around Mysore.'

'Very good, Madam. Will you be taking a tour of the town first and then Chamundi Hill, before going to Somnathpur and such places?' the tour manager asked courteously.

'Oh, I've done the town and the hill.' I waved a hand as if flicking the suggestion aside. 'I'd like to move on.'

'*Acha*, you are seeing Nandi bull then?'

'Well, now you come to mention it, I'm not sure I did. Where is it?' I grinned, quite happy that my pride should meet its comeuppance.

'Shiva's bull is there, near the top of Chamundi. So very big, one of biggest in India. It is having five metres and carved out of one solid rock. You can't miss it.'

Not unless you're me, I thought 'Okay, I'll go there first, then breakfast at the Hotel Lalitha Mahal Palace.'

'Very good, Madam. The car is taking you to the top of hill and is waiting for you at the bottom. You are taking thousand steps coming down and passing by Nandi bull.' He spoke and scribbled the driver's job sheet with a scratchy pen at the same time.

I thought a thousand steps was more than my arrogance deserved but continued, undaunted, 'I suppose places like Belur and Halebid are too far. I would also love to see the seventeen-metre-high statue of Lord Bahubali at Sravanabelagola as well.' My guttural pronunciation of this last destination bore a marked German influence. I had decided I should mention as many places as possible before he started to point to pictures and maps.

'Oh, so very far, Madam. This is not being very necessary. Somnathpur is having Hoysala temple complex like Halebid and Belur. As for Lord Bahubali, Monday and Tuesday, you be going to Sravanabelagola. Two days only.'

We finally agreed an itinerary starting at six thirty the next morning and settled on a modest price.

I flopped into bed like a rag doll. The impact of the day disturbed my sleep. I wriggled fitfully, anxious about bed-bugs, made all the more numerous by their invisibility to me. I yo-yo'd in and out of sleep: vivid colours lashed me, and I surfaced into moments of semi-wakefulness when I could hear men's voices, keys turning in padlocks and toilets flushing. A procession was making its colourful twirling way through the square as I watched: elephants bedecked in red and gold leading a unit of squat soldiers, tall princes and lithe, dark-skinned dancers. As each line of people passed, they turned to look at me through black eyes. Then I saw that their eyes weren't eyes but mouths, open mouths with thin straight lips. The Kali goddess appeared among them, black, beautiful and vicious. 'Why are they looking at me?' I asked her. She smiled with her eyes and said, 'It's your third eye, you're supposed to leave it at the entrance.' I ran through the air to hillside retreats and to squalid rat-invested hovels, where mouths followed me and thin smiles stared at me.

I awoke, feeling as enervated by the frenetic night as I had by the previous day. The morning newspaper was scrunched under my door. After showering and dressing I straightened it, put it under my arm and left. I set off in the taxi, still thinking about the visions of the night and comparing them to the pictures I had made of the sights of the previous day.

The thousand steps down Chamundi are made of uneven rock, carved out from the side of the hill. The most difficult part of the descent was to find the continuation as one group of steps ended and the next began. I directed myself by the approaching puffing and panting of people on the ascent or by the racing clack of leather on stone from behind as others descended. Locals jumped and skipped down five or six steps at a time, as nimbly as alpine goats. I found it impossible to estimate the fall of my next step let alone handle more than one at a time. I missed Nandi, Shiva's bull altogether, but encountered some intrepid and pert monkeys. They were squabbling over the remains of some stolen *prasad* – the offerings made to the priests who attended Nandi. Seeing me, they swooped into action and made a grab for my bag. Their presumptuousness and agility reminded me of Fagin and his pickpocketing boys. Their childlike cheekiness was very human. I had not encountered monkeys in such close proximity before and had had to rely on vague childhood memories for a visual image of them. Luckily, I had the strap fastened securely around my shoulder. They screamed and chattered indignantly as if they had been cheated.

My driver contrived to take me to 'one most excellent emporium' before we stopped for breakfast at the Lalitha Mahal Palace Hotel, an ex-maharajah's palace. I did not wish to begrudge him his commission so I found my way into the huge shop while he parked outside. When I had viewed everything reachable, I bought a small sandalwood *agarbathi* holder carved in the shape of a lotus flower. I stood outside, optimistic that it was customary for the driver to notice when his passenger was ready, and bring the car over. The car came. This was luxury.

Likewise the privileged guests of the magnificent Lalitha Palace were escorted from car to Reception, and Reception to room, restaurant or sun terrace. There was, therefore, no chance of getting lost, although the elegant splendour of palatial reception rooms with opulent furnishings and self-effacing minions gliding in and out would have been a choice setting in which to do so. I seemed to be the only guest and revelled in the attention. After drinking some lassi, a yoghurt drink flavoured with cardamom, priced as it would have been in a hotel in England, I summoned my car and left on the arm of the doorman.

We travelled forty-five kilometres east of Mysore in about an hour and a half to reach Somnathpur. I had not wanted to spend much time sight-seeing while I was in India but a few places attracted me. When I reached the north I intended to find out if it was possible to appreciate the Taj Mahal without sight. I also planned to see the Indo-Aryan architecture of the earlier Chandella period in Khajuraho in Madhya Pradesh. These stone temples are liberally embellished with sculptural decorations so intricate that the stories they tell are vivid to the touch. Although I normally gain little by trying to see things through feeling them, I hoped that some of this stonework would be the exception. The sculptures depict scenes from the *Ramayana*, *Mahabharata*, *Bhagavadgita* and the life and times of the Hoysala kings. I was glad to start now by visiting the Hoysala temples in the south.

When we arrived I listened for the murmur of voices to direct me to the entrance. The temple stood on a platform and was squat and star-shaped. I was not disappointed as every centimetre of the outside walls was covered with an endless variety of sages, stylised animals and Hindu deities. No two friezes were alike, showing agricultural, war, music, dance and hunting scenes. There were a few sensual sculptures, portraying other temple activities. This was a foretaste of the erotica of Khajuraho where I was to feel sculptural sexuality of *Karma Sutra* notoriety. Apart from enjoying the artistically exuberant adornments, there was something more feminine and attractive about the low, round building than the soaring phallic temples I had seen in the Dravidian south.

We drove in a north-westerly arc to reach Srirangapatnam. Much of our journey was through farmland and we stopped for flocks of sheep, herded by shepherds tapping hollow-sounding bamboo canes on the road. This was the first time I had come across sheep on the plains. I smelt goats among them and realised the bleats were not just from lambs. Even the countryside in India was shrill with the noise of people calling and going about their work.

We turned off the road and the driver announced, 'Daria Daulat Bagh.' We pulled into a car park and came to a stop under some shady trees.

'But I thought we were going to Srirangapatnam?'

'Yes, Madam, we are here now. First be seeing Tipu's summer palace.'

We passed most of the day in driving between the Sultan Tipu's summer palace and his mausoleum, the Gumbaz, and finally his tomb. We bumped along dusty unmade roads and I wound up the windows to limit the suffocating effect of the grit and sand. At one point we stopped on the side of the road and the driver encouraged me to scramble up a bank to the old ramparts from where steps led down to Tipu's dungeons. A man scurried towards me across the waste, like a scorpion scuttling out from under a rock. Although my driver was sitting in the car below, the place was isolated and desolate. I felt uneasy.

'Oh, so very good. Madam, I am your tourist guide. Very official guide to show you dungeons. Please be coming this way.'

His breath reeked of alcohol. From the ramparts there was nothing else to do but go down the crumbling stone steps to the dungeons. The British had made such a good job of demolishing Hyder Ali and Tipu's capital that there were hardly enough ruins worth visiting. The self-appointed guide, who had gone down the steps ahead of me, threw himself against a stone wall, outstretching his arms crucifix-style and slapping his hands back against the rough surface. Dramatically he declared, 'For forty days the great Sultan tied the British prisoners like this. No food and no water. Very terrible thing.'

207

Politely I ignored his extraordinary display and turned away. The place stank of urine mingled with his alcoholic breath. Then he crossed in front of me and flung himself to the floor, where he sprawled so that I nearly tripped over him. 'After this most terrible doing, they are like this and could not be walking,' he cried.

'I should think they were dead,' I said, and made to go.

'This way, Madam.' The man beckoned in the other direction and turned circles around me as if herding a wayward sheep. Whatever macabre and grotesque detail of the tale he wanted to act next was more than I could stand. I was able to walk quicker than he back to the car because he had a limp, which hampered his step. By the time he hobbled up and tapped on the window, demanding fifty rupees, I was seated. Since his performance had spoiled rather than enhanced the visit, I told the driver to go. The driver did not move so I explained that I had not wanted the guide and did not intend to pay for what I had actively discouraged.

The driver said, 'He is wanting money for parking.'

I exploded, 'First he claims to be a guide and now he is a parking attendant. How do I know what to believe? Anyway, we are on the side of an empty road in the middle of nowhere. I don't see why I should pay to park in a dust hole.'

The driver did not start the engine. I urged, 'Let's go.' He waited motionless. I began to wonder whether the parking costs I had incurred every time we had stopped during the day had more to do with an agreement between the local punters and the taxi-drivers than with the Karnataka Government Tourist Board as was claimed. I was suffering from the helplessness of the foreigner abroad, not wanting to be taken for a ride and not wanting to abuse local custom. I handed over twenty rupees.

Then I suggested driving to the mosque. The driver said, 'Sri Ranganathasway temple is better.'

I detected that my Hindu driver had an ulterior motive and insisted on going to the mosque as I had visited many more temples than mosques so far. He drove me there sullenly and slowly. On arriving he announced cheerfully, 'Oh, so very closed, Madam.'

Our final destination for the day was Brindavan Gardens, another hour's drive. Before long the driver said, 'Here is Ranganathittoo Bird Sanctuary coming. Will we be stopping?'

I had lost confidence in his choice of sights worth visiting, suspecting he was in cahoots with the exotic birds as well as the wardens, so I declined the offer. The unease I experienced about being so dependent on him engendered some of my distrust. I was relying on him to look out for me and pick me up at the end of every visit. I was frightened that he might fall asleep or disappear on business of his own, and that I would be marooned, which provoked some of my disproportionate annoyance over details like parking costs. In the course of the day I had become as irritable with him over small incidents as many of my Indian friends were with their servants. A harmless, cunning ruse, and I was full of suspicion.

Parking was free at Brindavan on a sloping gravelled surface, crammed with cars, that led to the entrance. I grabbed my newspaper from the back window shelf and got out. The turnstile creaked, and I found my way on to a long bridge, leading over the Krishnarajasagar dam across the Cauvery river, and trailed my hand along the railings running along the side to maintain a straight line. The roar of the water below, frothing and spluttering over man-made gullies, made it impossible to listen out for oncoming people, but most of the visitors were heading, like me, for the gardens, laid out on the other side of the bridge below the dam.

The gardens were harder to navigate than the Moghul ones belonging to Tipu's summer palace and mausoleum. I missed the mathematical design and geometric shapes. Flights of steps took me from level to level until I reached an artificial lake. Narrow strips of water ran from the fountains at the top to the square of grass at the bottom. It was parched and the flowers tired. Families picnicked on the lawns, groups of youths idled around, and pairs of young men sauntered hand in hand. They were never willing to let go when I approached them on the paths, nor did they step aside. Time and again I was caught in their arms. My embarrassment worsened and I seemed to drift from one tangle to the next. I must have appeared stupid to them but they were also a bit dopey, I thought. I remember being trapped in an uncomfortable and distinctly troilistic embrace from which my only exit was to prise apart some fingers. Unwilling to face any more, I escaped to a bench and opened my newspaper. It formed a hood of print shielding me from the sun and the demands of the outside world. This is the most perfect form of oblivion I know. Engrossed and content, I turned pages and whiled away the remaining hours of daylight.

'Will you please be having a picture?'

One of a pair of young men sidled up to me and I reached automatically for his camera. At that moment the other young man bent to sit next to me. He straightened his clothes, shuffled closer to me and called for his friend's sunglasses to complete the pose. A few words and laughs were exchanged between the pair and just before the click of the camera I felt his arm go lightly around me. He jumped up, thanked me, and the two linked up again to disappear along the path, chuckling excitedly. I dreaded to think what kudos and what tale would be attached to the showing of this holiday snap.

By lighting-up time the gardens were brimming with people, music and fairy-lights. I decided to leave, and back on the bridge I fought a torrent of visitors, still heading for the already overflowing gardens. I did not have to worry about walking straight into anyone because there was no space even if I could see to take it. I bumped from body to body, stemming the tide that would sweep me back into the music and fairy-lights I was trying to leave.

By the time we reached Mysore I was exhausted. The Maharajah's Palace was lit up on Sunday nights and we stopped by the gates to see it illuminated. I was too weary to get out but opened the door to let the air circulate. There had been such a constant series of shifting scenes unfurling in front of my eyes throughout the day that I was tiring from the exertions of my imagination. I dream infrequently, but when I do it is always visual and I am always sighted. Despite not seeing, my world is still very much a visual one with vivid mental images born of a host of non-visual clues. My imagination fills in the gaps. In my exhausted state, it was hard to differentiate between my day-dreams in the taxi and my experiences outside it. Images floated by me in a strange, unpredictable array over which I had no control. When I lifted my head, did I 'see' what was there or was it another memory or another dream? The world had become a phantasmagoric picture show in which I acted and spectated, but which I could no longer direct. As I sat, dazzled by the glow from the palace, I smelt the stirring power of jasmine. There was one last string in the hand of the little flower girl. I reached for it without ever looking or seeing.

Back in my room, hunger and thirst cramped my stomach. I had hardly eaten since arriving in Mysore. I found a glass and searched for water. The glass shattered between my fingers. There was no filtered water left anyway, and it was hard to resist drinking from the flask. I crumbled into bed.

In the morning I felt as if I had been at an all-night movie, but hunger drove me to the downstairs restaurant. A waiter gave me a menu and I skimmed over the piece of bent card as if I was reading. I ordered coffee, and gave up trying to think what else might be on the menu. I left and took a rickshaw to the Lalitha Palace Hotel. I thought it best to put a luxurious end to my stay in Mysore.

When I swam in the hotel swimming-pool, which had appeared so inviting and sparkling the previous day, I found it was green and slimy down the sides. Of course, I had seen what I had imagined a palace hotel swimming-pool should be like. I lazed in a lounger, twitchy and still high on the adrenaline and resilience that I had needed to survive the past two days. But I was beginning to sink. I was more concerned than usual about the absurdity and the delusion with which I lived as I settled to read the newspaper. I skewed everyone's vision of me so much that I ended up feeling out of focus and out of place.

I returned to my hotel, checked out and trudged to the bus station, asking my way every two minutes. Every step, every engine, every whistle made me jump. I was nervy and taut, walking into many more obstacles than usual. People must have thought I was drunk. At the station I was directed on to the bus for Madikeri. I stayed by the door, unable to enter any further because the bus was so full. My knees felt so weak that I could not bear the thought of standing for three and a half hours, so I got off again with no idea or care about what to do next except to sit down and rest.

I slouched on my bag in the middle of the station until a cry went up, calling people for the Madikeri bus. This one was empty because it was a deluxe coach with comfortable seats, covers and head-rests. During the journey we ran over a puppy playing in the road. The yelping and screaming tore through me and I dropped my head back against the head-rest, clenching my fists and shutting my eyes, hoping the pain would end.

As arranged I got down at the second bus stand in Madikeri. No Nalini. I stood and waited. There were two voices in my head. One said, 'Go and find a taxi, you've done it before, you don't need to show you're blind.' The other said, 'For goodness' sake, stop putting yourself through this. Use the cane. Ask for help.' After a while, I took out my cane. A third voice said, 'Missahib, you are waiting for Nalini Cariappa?'

A tall man with a square and upright frame, wearing heavy boots, was at my side and Nalini followed behind. She greeted me: 'Have you been waiting long? I was at the top stand but must have missed the bus passing.'

COORG: NALINI, THE FIELD MARSHAL'S DAUGHTER

Coorg was delightful. This discovery was doubtless much enhanced by my low expectations and perturbed state of mind. It was like popping into my mouth another chocolate from an otherwise predictable assortment and discovering a fabulous new taste. I felt myself wanting to return before I had even left.

Nalini drove the jeep home while the man who had met me, a soldier, sat on the back seat. I had seldom been with Indians who drove their own cars, let alone an Indian woman. Nalini had lived and worked in Delhi for many years, most recently as social secretary to the British High Commissioner. After two unsuccessful marriages, she had recently come home to her father Field Marshal Cariappa's house.

Roshanara was an old, eccentric-looking house, growing almost organically among the trees on the brow of a hill outside Madikeri, the provincial capital of Coorg. Nalini was occupying it until her brother, an Air Force commander, retired. She planned then to move to her own house, which she was having built in a corner of the forested grounds. When we arrived at Roshanara, the young soldier disappeared to the quarters he shared with another orderly. The Army stationed two men to maintain the Field Marshal's house and grounds. Field Marshal Cariappa himself was ninety-four, infirm, and had been moved to the military hospital in Bangalore. He was a revered figure in India: he had been the first Indian head of the air, sea and land forces after Independence.

Nalini had installed herself there with her two dogs, her cat and her manservant, Vijaysingh, with his wife and child from Delhi. The dogs, Sammy and Tuppie, jumped around us and the cat, Domino, pressed her sleek body against my leg as we walked through the door. Vijaysingh was nowhere to be found.

'Vijaysingh? Vijaysingh, where are you?' Nalini's voice penetrated the heart of the house and rumbled away thunderously into the kitchen quarters. She returned saying, 'I don't know what is happening with this man. Ever since we come from Delhi he is fooling around. He is gone now for the evening.'

She showed me to my room, lavishly appointed with soft furnishings unlike the more usual Spartan Indian homes, with the exception of Leela's house in Cochin. Both women had been exposed to international influences and lifestyles.

'You make yourself comfortable and then we will have a drink,' she said. As she left, I noticed she was smoking.

I unpacked a few things and walked into the bathroom to take a shower. The shelves were dotted with familiar-shaped bottles, bulbous, waisted, cylindrical and square. The creams, shampoos and soaps smelt of Marks & Spencer and Body Shop. I did not need to be able to read the labels on the plump bath towels to guess they came from Harrods of London. The shower was warm, and for the first time in months the soap did not smell of paraffin.

Nalini heard me come out of my bedroom to go downstairs. She called, and I followed her voice to the right. 'Did you find everything? Did you find the potty?'

I struggled to find a suitable answer, but fortunately she continued, 'The flush is not always working if the water is off. Vijaysingh fixed the potty today so it should be working. Come, sit, sit.'

Relieved to realise that the loo and the potty were one and the same, I obediently sat down on a chair to which she directed me. She was reclining on her bed in her boudoir. Curtains, cushions and covers softened the room so it felt pampering and indolent.

Nalini said, 'I have my TV here and now we have a satellite so I can have BBC and Sky. In the evenings I take my drink, my cigarettes and have my TV. I am very happy.' The cat purred seductively, pricking claws in and out of a cushion on the bed. 'Come, I will show you the house. What will you drink?'

She led me across a dark wooden hall and we went into a large, teak-floored reception room. I smelt the wax and accumulated dust, which I disturbed from furniture grouped to the right of us as we passed. We headed diagonally through the room and into a small, sunny parlour with a circle of sofas and chairs, mats on the floor and magazines piled on coffee tables. 'This is the Sulking Room, as my father called it. We would come here to ponder.' Taken with this notion, I immediately set about mentally allocating a room for this purpose in my house in London. I would sit in it. Friends could use it, had they not one of their own. Indeed, I could let it for the purpose of sulking.

Beyond this was a terracotta-tiled breakfast terrace. A large dining room led from the reception room and another small room, tucked to one side, was the memorabilia room, full of photographs, medals and books belonging to the Field Marshal.

The rooms connected in a zigzag and Nalini was concerned about how I would find my way around. The wooden floor in the largest room was uneven, sloping and dipping unexpectedly. I was charmed by the idiosyncratic character of the house and liked the idea of losing myself in its quirky personality. The central rooms were strong-smelling and male. It was the home of a noble Indian warrior. In the bedrooms, modern Delhi, and its partial fostering of late-twentieth-century British culture, influenced everything from the choice of bed sheets to china ornaments.

Vijaysingh appeared, and Nalini addressed him in Hindi. This was the first time I had heard Hindi spoken, despite having spent nearly four months in India. In the south, everyone had spoken either in English or in their state's language.'Does Vijaysingh speak English?' I asked.

'No. He understands a little but he is Nepalese and has only learned Hindi. 'These fellows are too lazy to learn English.'

'Would you like a *nimbu pani*, a lime water, or a *nimbu soda?*' Nalini asked. 'Do you have it with salt?'

'I'll have it as it comes. I haven't tried one yet.'

'Really! Where've you been, girl? What have you been doing?'

She suggested returning to her bedroom. She already had a gin by her bed and we spooned down Bombay mix to the sound of the BBC world news. The click of the cigarette lighter was a frequent and soon familiar sound. *The Bold and the Beautiful* began its evening showing. I remembered this soap from Aunty's house in Bombay. I sat through a few scenes in which the characters sounded so one-dimensional and flimsy and the events so implausible that I got annoyed. There was evidently a pain threshold to cross before you got hooked. All addictions seem to require a certain resolute and selfless perseverance to get past the initial unpleasantness. Throughout the programme Nalini encouraged me with odd character details to get me interested, and at the end she said, 'Do you know *Dallas*? That is coming next. We have *Dynasty* as well later.'

A thread of hope remained. 'Do you get many power cuts?'

'Oh, yes, many many.'

'What do you do? Rely on the candles? You have lots lying around.'

'I have my own generator which comes on automatically so there is no interruption,' she answered contentedly.

'Nalini, I am going to write some letters and go to bed. Do you mind?'

'No of course not. Your bed is ready. Vijaysingh has put in a hottie for you.'

I was glad of the early night after my previous sleepless ones in Mysore, but the sheets smelt damp. The whole house seemed more dank in the cool of the night than it had in the day. The wet left by the monsoon was not even mopped up by the rays of the hot spring sun.

I lay, hugging my 'hottie'. I had come to take a break from my research and could see that I would be wonderfully bored. I decided to devote my time to recording some of the events of my trip. My efforts thus far had been haphazard, but these tranquil surroundings stirred my mind so that I began to write without even needing a spell in the Sulking Room. Indeed, there was something inspiring to the creative spirit in Coorg – later I met a British artist through Nalini and understood why he and other painters came there. As a child, I was always writing stories but the pivotal moment arrived on my tenth birthday when I unwrapped a gleaming new portable typewriter. I sat rocking on my bed, clutching my machine, while a whole different life unfurled before me in my mind. I would write for a living. It was simple.

A few years, dozens of tedious adventure stories and hundreds of obsessive key-hammering nights later, my aspirations had evolved into an adolescent certainty that I would become a journalist, preferably a foreign-affairs reporter and ideally an intrepid war correspondent. By sixteen I was writing obituaries and wedding announcements for my local newspaper in the holidays. I wanted to sign indentures and start as a cub reporter there and then, but was persuaded that A-levels and a university degree in languages and politics would give me better credentials into journalism and foreign affairs. In none of these plans did I take into account the difficulties my already severely limited sight would impose. How, for example, could a young reporter work without a driving licence? This was something I would never have. How could I read quickly enough to meet deadlines? For me reading was a painstaking, two-inches-from-the-eyes letter-by-letter farce. I steamed ahead regardless, and masterminded a way to spend the university's obligatory year abroad gaining work experience in a German radio and television station instead of being a teaching assistant. Just before graduation, as I was experiencing the first signs of a serious deterioration in my sight, I had a series of interviews lined up with various newspaper groups.

By the year after graduation some of these interviews had resulted in second- and third-stage selections, but the unasked questions about the obvious practical problems formed a silent barrier to success. However, by the end of the year I had worked as a freelance reporter for BBC Radio and secured a place on a postgraduate course in newspaper journalism. I was also in hospital, with a nervous breakdown, following my total and final sight loss.

In the first two years I spent in hospital or as a daily outpatient, I held on to the hope and determination that I would take up my hard-won postgraduate place and become a foreign reporter despite everything. When I finally arrived at the university with my guide dog and recorder, I was a successful but unhappy student. It was an unequal struggle in which I did not even want to struggle, because I did not want to succeed within the limits of being blind. I had only ever pictured myself as a sighted journalist, never as a blind one. Attending Islington Town Hall to report on a royal opening of some new scheme with a guide dog felt ridiculous enough, let alone trying to cover some great event such as the fall of the Berlin Wall with a white cane and a dog in quarantine.

I had dug a hole of disappointment, too deep to let in a glimmer of hope or success. I refused to accept a literary prize I won for a short story I wrote during that time, and ignored a prize awarded by the German embassy for the best report on the Bundestag elections of that year. One day during my final placement in the offices of a national newspaper, I was leaving the building on an assignment. Walking down the stairs to the ground floor, I stopped. A cold truth came to me. There were no tears, no heart-searching, no self-pity, but when I started walking again, it was to leave the building never to return. I could not be what I wanted to be or do what I wanted to do, and was too youthfully inflexible to compromise. There was some initial relief in stopping what had become a relentless, demoralising struggle, but it soon turned into a feeling of emptiness. I existed in a desolate void for many months until I began slowly to build my life in a new way and discovered different interests. I wrote not a word for eight years.

In Coorg, I had no plan, no grand intention. I was simply writing lest I forgot what had been wonderful because it was interesting and special.

In the morning Nalini and I went to the only attraction in Madikeri worth a visit. We ambled through some gardens to Raja's Seat, the local scenic lookout point. I liked the fertile, wooded, mountainous coffee country. It was fresh and sunny but not hot, even though it was not as high as Ooty or Kodaikanal.

Many of the shops in Madikeri were built of disused railway sleepers, divided into sections and lining the side of the road. It was a climb to get in followed by a quick leap out when I detected a pestilent smell as if dead rats were decomposing in the corners.

We drove to several of Nalini's friends, winding up and down narrow roads overhung with trees, stopping at houses dotted in forest clearings and surrounded by dense shrub and flower gardens. A floral fruity note lingered in the air from acres of coffee plants. The region is as dark, rich and lustrous as the beans it grows. The tang of oranges from the many groves made me feel as if I was actually sipping delicate flavours not just inhaling air infused with the region's produce.

Nalini greeted the elders we visited in the local dialect and with the customary gesture, a downward sweep and bow to touch the feet and knees of those being honoured. I never attempted this myself, not trusting my aim. A strong sense of tradition flowed through Coorgi veins; custom was still the marrow in the bones of the community. Coorg is in the south-western corner of Karnataka where the Western Ghats start to tumble down towards the sea. It was a mini-state until 1956 when it became part of Karnataka, but it has maintained its unique identity. The Coorgis I met were fierce, like the hill people they had been, but respectable, like the coffee cultivators and gentrified farmers they had become.

We finished our round of visits by attending Nalini's uncle Tim's eighty-second birthday party. 'Eighty-second' refers both to his age and to the approximate duration of the celebrations. Uncle Tim put on an odd felt hat, stood up clutching his tea and exclaimed, 'Yum-yum', whereupon he sat down and the party immediately dispersed. The old man was the father of her schoolfriend, Pearlie, not a real uncle. We passed the time eating slices of local chocolate cake made with curd and meringues. By the end of the day I had visited many different clans and people who still lived their lives according to feudal inheritance and traditions.

On the paths or drives leading to most of the houses I was met by the hot, unpleasant smell of rue. On one occasion Nalini noticed that I wrinkled my face, trying to close off my nostrils. She laughed and said, 'No better thing to keep snakes away. We have snakes in these hills. The rat snakes come visiting.'

In the early evening we strolled down the wooded drive from Roshanara to where Nalini's house was being built. She pointed out guava, jackfruit, lemon, mango and wild fig trees.

'The monkeys have all the fruit,' she lamented, 'but we have jacaranda, and in December huge, glorious poinsettias. Can you smell the eucalyptus? That is the smell of my childhood. I remember coming home from school in the holidays to that smell.'

Her reminiscence was short-lived because she was soon yelling and chasing away some locals who had come to chop and steal wood; she complained that the soldiers did not patrol the grounds properly. We sloped off right, into the woods and to the spot she had chosen for her house. The bedroom had pride of place among the rooms. I could see Nalini holding court comfortably from an elaborately pillowed double bed. Her guests would just flop and laze around, stretch out, drink and gossip.

Nalini started to take an interest in where I would stay in Bangalore, my next destination, and where and to whom I was going later in my travels. She proved a vital link in making the next chain of contacts I needed for the rest of my trip. Goutam and Peerooze had both spoken of some business contacts in Bangalore who might be able to help me, but no firm arrangements had been made. Nalini arranged for her cousin, Sagarie, to meet me from the bus and help me settle into Bangalore.

She also busied herself with arrangements for the second half of my journey in north India. A Delhi friend called Nita, who had taken over Nalini's job with the British High Commissioner, Sir Nicholas Fenn, agreed to look after me when I arrived there. We were also invited to meet Sir Nicholas. Apparently he was fascinated that a blind woman was making her way around India alone. The curiosity was mutual because Nalini had spoken of this accomplished man, who held one of the highest posts in the foreign diplomatic service and who woke up blind every morning, only slowly regaining his sight through the course of each day. From the moment I began to contemplate the complications and confusions associated with his condition, I became one of his greatest admirers.

My plans for travelling in north India had been unformed until Nalini intervened. I had decided on a rough route, but given the lack of contacts, both professional and personal, I had wondered whether I would make the journey into the north or just fly back from Bangalore to Goutam in Bombay, then on to England and home. I was still undecided but it looked more inviting to press ahead.

One day Nalini tempted me further: 'Nita's husband, Paddy, does trekking in the Himalayas. Kulu and Manali. They will be able to organise all that for you.'

She had been so nonchalant about my journey to her, yet was committed to help me on my onward passage. This was partly because she had befriended me, and partly because, during our time together, she had seen for herself the difficulty I had in getting around.

She was delighted when I told her that Kulu and Manali were the very areas in the Himalayas that I would most like to visit. Also they just happened to be the regions where I had some oil distillers to see. 'Really? That's fantastic. Nita will be able to do all that for you,' she said.

The mist descended each morning, damp, clinging to the house and curling among the trees. We had strong dark forest honey for breakfast with *akki roti*, a *chapatti* made from rice. As we sat and sipped the home-grown coffee, Nalini would urge, 'Hush. Listen. Do you hear that? It is the whistling schoolboy.' The piercing carefree whistle coming from the woods at the side of the terrace sounded just like a cheeky schoolboy spying on us. On my penultimate morning Nalini said, 'I think the proper name is the Malabar thrush. And there goes the coppersmith.'

A typical lunch would be curd rice with tomato and butter fruit salad but Nalini said this was not the norm for most Coorgis. "They are big meat-eaters with rich sauces and home-made wines. I send the soldier boy down to the Tibetan community to fetch good meat when my relations come to eat. The Tibetans have the best meat.'

'You don't seem to eat any dal here,' I commented.

'Coorgis like their meat too much. If I put dal on the table no one eats it. Meat and rice with some drumstick chutney is what they want.'

I thought back to her reference to the Tibetans and asked more about them. 'They have done well for themselves ever since they settled lower down the hill some years back. It is fantastic there now. They have many good things to sell and are a very hard-working people,' she answered.

When Nalini left me on the bus, she instructed the conductor to help me during the refreshment stops. I could feel him shrink under the weight of responsibility, but another passenger rose to the occasion and offered to assist whenever necessary. I still felt diminished to the status of a child in those moments, but could not deny that it led to a more reassuring journey than the ones when I struggled in secret with my disability. It was only as Nalini climbed down that I noticed her strong, free stride and realised that I had never seen her in a sari; sometimes she wore a *salwar kameez*, but she was most frequently in jeans.

BANGALORE: A WOMAN'S WELCOME FROM SAGARIE

I felt the strong, kind grip of a hand on my arm accompanied by an intelligent voice that affirmed rather than questioned, 'Nicola.' This was Sagarie come to meet me after the eight-hour bus journey.

'Yes,' I answered. 'I hope you haven't been waiting too long?'

'I came an hour before the arrival time in case the bus was early, and it is an hour late,' Sagarie answered, in the most perfectly polished English I had heard so far, and without a trace of irritation. Standing there patiently in her flowing, silken sari, she seemed both elegant and dependable. The day was just losing the ferocity of its heat. There were neither seats nor shade but Sagarie was too gracious to reveal any sign of fatigue, despite the tedious wait for a stranger. Sagarie's driver took us to the Woodlands vegetarian hotel where she checked me in and, politely and clearly, made the reception staff understand that I was blind. On the way to my room, she commented on my surroundings in an informative and charming way.

She did not leave me until we had had a dress rehearsal to demonstrate that I could find my way without difficulty to my room from the foyer.

Solemnly, I took the lift down and back up again while Sagarie walked silently behind. In the lift on the way back up, I counted the buttons to my floor according to Sagarie's previous instructions. They were large and convex, unmistakable like the counters in a child's board game. We got out of the lift and walked along the corridor to the right. I counted four doors and turned my key in the lock of the fifth. The door was not locked but I could not remember if I had locked it. I turned the knob, stepped on to carpet and froze. My room had had a tiled floor. Sagarie, who had been peering over my shoulder, hauled me out and closed the door firmly. 'This is the wrong room,' she said, flustered. 'There are two men sleeping on the beds in there. We must be one floor down. I don't know how it happened.'

'I don't suppose the best calculations can account for a temperamental lift. At least I didn't climb into bed with them.'

When Sagarie left I felt gloomy, and the strain of remaining alert to every detail returned. However, Sagarie had invited me for lunch and was to return in the morning to collect me. In the meantime I had to organise a sequence of visits to the people and organisations I wanted to see in Bangalore. I selected the cassette that recorded their addresses and moved to the telephone. Before I could pick it up it rang.

'Hello, Nicola. It is Goutam. Did you arrive safely? How is your hotel?'

'It is very comfortable. Sagarie, Nalini's cousin, is very nice. She brought me here.'

'Where is she now? You sound very low. Are you all right?'

I lifted my voice and answered, 'Yes, I'm fine. I'm just getting my bearings, that's all.'

'Look, you see it is like this. I have contacted someone in Bangalore who is an office manager of Mr Hataria's business there. That is to say I know him too. His wife is English. Maybe you won't be needing them now but I could give them this number.'

'It is not that I won't need them, but I haven't yet made any calls to see what I am doing and when. I want to stay a few days at the Vivekananda Kendra, that's a yoga research foundation, and perhaps a day at Jindal, the naturopathic health hospital. Let me try and arrange these things first.'

'Fine. I'll call you in the morning, then. Have a good evening. What are you going to do?'

'Nothing planned,' I answered.

'Good. Get some rest. I'll speak to you tomorrow.'

It was reassuring to know that there was always someone ready to step in and befriend me. It was what had made my trip so special and the lonely moments more manageable. I finished making my arrangements and decided to go and explore. This time I made myself take my cane because I did not want the confusion or the strain I had experienced in Mysore by not using one. The doormen stood to attention as I passed and other guests turned to stare. The rickshaw-wallahs blockaded the end of the drive in case anyone should try to leave without employing them to do so. They monitored my approach but remained inert, bunched and unhelpful.

I asked, 'How much to MG Road?' During my conversation with Sagarie I had established that this was one of the main shopping areas and I liked to take a town's pulse in its arterial streets. One of the drivers tapped the side of his three-wheeler, signalling me to get in.

To most of the educated guests in the hotel my cane communicated my blindness, but to the street community it was as meaningless as the written word. It was too bourgeois for the mass of people to care about. In their lives, legless people walked on their hands, and blind people stumbled behind crooked sticks with bells or behind children with a hand placed on a small shoulder. Most of the disabled were disfigured and made infirm by their poverty in a way that I am not. The poor people could never see me as truly blind because blindness for them was more devastating.

I stood by the rickshaw and repeated my question. The man did not name his price but said, 'I take you for shopping. Very good shopping.'

'I only want to go to MG Road. How much?' I insisted.

'Twenty rupees,' he answered.

I was sure this was five times as much as a local Indian would pay, asked him to switch on his meter and assumed that he would not know that I could not read it. The broad, shady avenues of Bangalore were streaming with traffic. When we stopped he said, 'Twenty rupees, clock is very much broken.' I paid, got out and began to walk along what I thought was MG Road. It seemed odd that there were no shops on what was meant to be a shopping street. I was surprised to find pavements, but they disintegrated abruptly or ended in piles of upturned, concrete slabs. I negotiated my way with the cane to a large junction, and listened to judge the traffic. I was unnerved by how unpredictable, fast and noisy it was.

I asked the next passer-by to help me cross. Once on the other side, I released my finger touch on his bony elbow and stepped back to put a less cosy distance between us.

'Where are you going?' he asked.

'Is this MG Road?'

'MG Road, no.'

'Which way is it?'

'I taking you.'

Oh, are you? I thought.

'Why are you going to MG Road?'

'No reason.'

'You want shopping. I taking you.'

I took the risk and his arm. For a long time he led me along busy roads. Our conversation was limited because he spoke little English. As we walked, I wondered about risk-taking. Perhaps there is some sort of divine risk-ledger somewhere that accumulates points. Two risk points for taking a stranger's arm, three if it's abroad, four points for crossing a road unaided, and when you have accumulated a certain number of points you exceed your personal allocation and bingo! You die. I trawled through my mind for all the ulterior motives the man might have for escorting me so generously. I worried about where he was leading me and busily mapped every turn in an attempt to keep some idea of where I was. The roads became narrower and crammed with more people. I kept thinking it was not normal for someone to have the time and inclination to show a stranger their town.

'Here is MG Road,' he said at last. 'Which shop are you wanting?'

'No shop,' I said. I was beginning to feel he was genuine and struggled to think of somewhere to go because I did not want him to feel his efforts had been wasted. 'Let's have a lassi or a coffee.' Oh dear, more points.

Obligingly he guided me into a café and I invited him to choose something from the menu. He refused and appeared embarrassed. After dextrous coaxing he agreed to a glass of water. While we drank my suspicions subsided and I no longer feared that when we parted company he was going to demand money. It was a relief to enjoy his kindness. He was unusually altruistic, giving up his time and going out of his way with no other motive other than a desire to be helpful to a stranger. Most strangers who stop to help me do not want to delay longer than it takes to cross a road, or find a train or some items in a shop. Sadly, some, whether a passer-by or a shop assistant, are motivated by an invasive curiosity about where I am going next or where I have come from. On many occasions I have been questioned on my life story after making a simple request to be told when the red light turns green. This time, however, my temporary companion walked me all the way back to the gates of the Woodlands, shook my hand and departed.

At the end of my day's exploring, my mind felt blunted. When I got into my room I was almost beyond hunger as well as tired. I felt annoyed that I could not read the room-service menu and tempt myself with some delicacy. I tossed it to one side and climbed into bed. My imagination feasted on the events of the day until I fell into a dreamless sleep.

The following morning I was up before six, ready to walk in Cubbon Park, the lungs of the city. Bangalore is studded with large gardens and parks, earning its reputation as the Garden City of India, but Cubbon is the main one. Once I was inside, which was not difficult to achieve because it was close to the hotel, the neem and pipal trees screened me from the din of traffic that was already pumping through the surrounding roads. Tennis balls plopped to the ground through the still air while joggers pounded and crunched the gravel on the pathways. Office workers from the fast-growing computer, electronic and machine-tool companies were conscientiously performing their morning exercise routines. A crew of labourers squatted in a circle by a *chai* stall from which came spurts of steam, strong coffee and the clank of metal containers. There was a lot of slurping, snorting and spitting in the breakfast gathering so I politely refused the chair they offered me.

Back at the hotel, I was in good time for Sagarie to arrive, smelling exquisitely of perfume. She suggested I move to the Bangalore Club where the service would be more personal, and when I agreed she signed me in for the night, then arranged for me to return the following Monday for another two or three nights after my weekend at the Vivekananda Kendra. The accommodation was meant solely for visiting members or members' guests and the rates were cheap. The staff were attentive and observant but never obsequious or fawning in the hope of large tips as they often were in the five-star hotels.

Sagarie showed me around the club grounds, pointing out the squash and tennis courts, swimming-pool, gym and weight-training area, the shop and the beauty and hair studio. She introduced me to a couple of the beauticians and to the ayah who kept the changing rooms at the swimming-pool tidy and stocked with fresh towels. We returned through the marble-floored clubhouse. I heard people flipping cards on to the green felt tops of card tables, wriggling themselves comfortably into leather armchairs, rustling papers and tinkling little hand-bells to call for the waiter.

Before going to Sagarie's house for lunch, we stopped at the Indian Airlines office to inquire about my entitlement to the 50 per cent discount given to disabled passengers. I had been refused this concession on the flight between Bombay and Madras on the grounds that I was not a national, but with Sagarie's presence to encourage co-operation, an official confirmed that we would need only a doctor's certificate and I would be able to buy my onward ticket at the foreigners' price discounted by 50 per cent. Foreigners' tickets were always twice as expensive as Indian nationals' tickets. In effect I could fly for the same price as an Indian if I provided a letter confirming that I was blind. The letter had to be from an Indian doctor. My British blind registration papers were in doubt, as was my sighted appearance.

Lunch was a family event. Jaghan Muthanna, Sagarie's husband, was home from work; Deepa, her daughter-in-law, was occupied with her young son. The little boy was showing his great-grandmother, who was resting in a corner, a drawing he had brought home from school. Then he and his mother disappeared upstairs, where they lived with Nirad, Sagarie's son, to get their own lunch. Sagarie moved to where Jaghan's elderly mother was sitting and spoke loudly and clearly to her in English. 'We have a visitor.' She paused for a reply that did not come and started again: 'Are you having some lunch now? Have you already had your lunch?'

She was patient and persistent. I heard a sharp intake of breath from the old woman and a servant's shuffling feet as she was carried to her room for an afternoon rest. This was not the first or the last time that I was moved at seeing the very old cared for within the family home.

During lunch I discovered from Sagarie and Jaghan that Nirad, a wildlife photographer, was visually impaired and could not see the game he photographed. To take his pictures he was directed by sound, and guided by someone standing next to him. Then I understood that Sagarie's unusually natural and skilled way of guiding and giving me information owed a lot to practice. She talked about her son's schooling and how she used to copy by hand into large print everything he needed to read. The special magnification aids and support services for tapes and transcription are not available or affordable even to middle-class Indians. Sagarie had dedicated herself to finding resourceful ways to reduce and compensate for her son's disadvantages. I respected the understated but determined way the family seemed to cope with their problems, whether infirmity in old age or a sight disability.

I spent the rest of the afternoon wallowing in the water or by the side of the club swimming-pool. It was quiet until five o'clock when young children arrived to splash in the shallow end. By six, adolescent boys were squeaking by in their sneakers, dumping kit-bags on to empty tables and calling each other to the changing rooms in American college-boy accents. They had the arrogance and self-confidence born of advantage. Their bombast and joviality jarred, like a piercing strobe light on a romantic dinner for two.

One of my morning's telephone calls had led me to discover that Mr Atuna, a yoga teacher in Jayarnagar, had a class starting at seven that evening. After showering and changing, I wandered with my cane past the beauty salon on my way to the main gates. I still did not like the attention it attracted but knew that Sagarie had explained I was blind and that the cane was only reinforcing and spreading the word. One of the beauticians approached to walk with me. She was on her way home and asked where I was going. 'Jayarnagar,' I answered. 'Do you know where I can get a rickshaw?'

'They are by the bus stop, opposite the gate. I will take you.'

I was grateful for her offer because the road we had to cross was a minefield of obstacles and a runway for traffic flying into town. She questioned the first rickshaw-wallah intently to make sure he knew the way to Jayarnagar, dismissed him with contempt, and we moved on to the next. When she was satisfied that this one knew his way and had named his price, she took the extra precaution of insisting that he put on his meter and she took down his number. It was a wonder to me how the rickshaw-wallahs were cowed into submission by a young Indian girl telling them what to do, while I only ever provoked mutinous mayhem and unreasonable demands for money.

I was deposited by a gate and went through it to stumble over dozens of pairs of shoes at the bottom of some steep steps. I climbed up, directed by jabbering voices and the sound of people gathering and folding their belongings. Once in a large studio room it was clear that a class had just finished and that another was about to begin. More people were arriving and greeting one another. Mats flopped on to the floor and legs waved in the air as unsupervised warming-up exercises began. I stayed by the door hoping Mr Atuna would approach me. I studied the people spread around the room, stretching and bending their knees, legs, arms or backs, some silently folding, others creaking and groaning with uncooperative joints. Mr Atuna came up to me and said softly, 'Welcome.'

I delivered my prepared speech. 'I would like to join your class. I'm here for a few days and have done yoga before. I can't see, but I should be able to follow the instructions – that is, if we use the same names for the postures. Otherwise I might need some prompting.'

He did not ask any questions, just cleared me a space and began the class by asking everyone to extend into a standing forward bend. Throughout he demonstrated the *asanas*, named them and described them. Perhaps the careful verbal instructions were for my benefit, but unfortunately I found his accent too thick to understand a word. While some were unsuccessfully getting their limbs tangled and others were successfully holding a posture, Mr Atuna came over and wrapped me neatly into the right position.

Here was a quick, light and supple man, full of energy, swooping like a hawk to twist, turn or bend a pupil a little more into each *asana*, and our teacher gave all his pupils individual attention, coaxing the reticent and tired bodies of retired people and office workers alike. Mr Atuna worked like a physiotherapist, but treated twenty people at once. Impressively alert to every difficulty, he floated round with an inaudible step, stretching this woman's shoulders or loosening that man's lower back to counteract the negative influence of a day spent at a desk or the stiffness of old age.

There were some young children in the class who could bend effortlessly into every conceivable shape and some inconceivable ones. Towards the close, there was a series of balancing *asanas*, which demanded the strength and concentration to stand on one leg for several minutes. The children buckled in a heap on the floor, dismayed that they were no longer the stars of the show. Within seconds I had joined them but, I hasten to add, not because I was a complete weakling: these postures are best arrived at by focusing on something straight ahead. I knew that a yogic master could focus internally and therefore balance, but my third eye was not so highly developed. Anyway, isn't balance supposed to be to do with the ears? Perhaps I need a third ear instead.

When I left, I found the rickshaw-wallah waiting to take me back to the club. I was surprised because he had forfeited an evening's work and the rickshaw fraternity did not normally have the means to be altruistic.

Once underway I touched his shoulder and asked, 'Can we stop at a fruit stall? I want to buy a pawpaw.'

'I no understanding.'

'A pawpaw. You know, fruit. A pawpaw.'

It was silly of me to expect him to understand. Nevertheless, I persisted with some frantic signing, gobbling and sucking noises until the baffled driver pulled over. For a moment I thought he was going to evict me for demented behaviour but instead he asked some passers-by to translate. At first they did not understand, struggling with my accent more than with the English, but before long everyone was nodding and singing, 'Pawpaw, pawpaw,' as if it was the latest catchy pop hit. The poor rickshaw-wallah was none the wiser as no one remembered to translate.

When the celebration had quieted a little someone finally spoke with the driver who swung the rickshaw a hundred and eighty degrees, narrowly avoiding a goring from a cow's horn, which grazed my arm, and zoomed into a maze of narrow market streets. He stopped abruptly and I got down, hoping we were parked in front of a fruit stand. There was such a wall of people blocking my way that I could not judge where to go. The rickshaw-wallah called out from his seat. A pawpaw, wrapped in newspaper, was passed from person to person and finally pushed into my hands. 'Ten rupees,' the driver instructed. I handed the money to the closest person and it disappeared in the direction from which the ripe-smelling fruit had come. We sped away out of the market and through the quiet streets to the club. I sat in bed that night eating the most delicious pawpaw I had ever tasted.

After an early-morning swim, I left by rickshaw for Chamarajapet where the Vivekananda Kendra Bangalore had their offices. I joined the people on their way to stay at the ashram itself, some twenty miles south of Bangalore towards the Tamil Nadu border. When I arrived, I found a group sitting in a line of chairs backed against a wall, while two administrators sifted through files and completed detailed paperwork to register each newcomer.

When I was called I made for the seat opposite the desk and took an early opportunity to point out that I was blind. As I expected, the official was taken aback. He had no knowledge of my letter, which had explained my circumstances while requesting a short stay with an introduction to the in-patient treatments used in their 'Yoga Research Health Home'. There was also no record of my previous day's telephone call in which I had confirmed the arrangements. Due to the chaos the minibus, which made the twice-daily trip to the ashram, was heavily over-subscribed: telephone bookings and written applications must have been buried in the mounds of duplicate forms.

I had my letter from the director inviting me to see how yoga practices and community living were used to promote positive health in their centre. This put an end to the head-shaking and the obstructive pedantry, and I promptly received a bus pass.

On the bus I was introduced to Dr Nagaratna, who reeled off a list of illnesses that her patients wanted to have treated through the yoga practices, starting with bronchial asthma, nasal allergy, chronic bronchitis, diabetes, thyrotoxicosis, obesity, high and low blood pressure, epilepsy, tension headache, migraine, anxiety, neurosis, depression, low back pain, arthritis, rheumatism, irritable bowel syndrome, gastritis and peptic ulcer, mental retardation, cerebral palsy and finishing with cancer. It might have been quicker to ask her what the centre did not treat.

Although the list was breathtaking, I noticed that the concentration was on the sort of 'modern-society' health problems that I also treated, and not the diseases and hygiene-related conditions like polio and dysentery with which the ayurvedic hospital staff mainly dealt.

We were dropped off in the ashram's large reception area and waited while rooms were allocated and passes were examined. The whole morning had been consumed by officialdom and I was hot and bothered by the disregard for time and comfort that this had involved. Anyone with high blood pressure, or arriving to convalesce after an illness or operation, would have been made worse by the rigmarole surrounding his or her arrival.

By the time I reached my room I was wondering whether this visit was going to be worth the discomfort. In the gathering gloom of a depression I hobbled about lamely in a cheerless room. It had a dusty concrete floor, two single beds with one torn sheet each, bare walls and a wooden table. A door at the end led to a squat loo with a tap at ankle height and a jug to wash my hand and swill the enamel bowl. Another door led to a concrete cell with a single showerhead. I knew that the ashram philosophy would have me rise above inconveniences and not allow my spirit to be trapped by material needs, but when I thought of how pampering the treatments are that I give to my patients, I could not believe that a health-recovery programme had to be quite so austere.

The in-patient bedrooms were built around a square of grass lined by a low wall and some dry shrubs. I joined some patients who were sitting on the wall waiting to go into the dining hall for lunch. At lunch we sat in long lines. There was a table at the top of the room for people who found it too difficult to sit on the floor. Food was spooned on to a plate in front of each person and *rasam* – a thin vegetarian broth made from the juice of cooked dal – poured into metal beakers. During the chant at the start of the meal, flies buzzed like planes, zooming in to land on the flat surface of trays of tightly packed rice. They circled and dive-bombed when I disrupted their flight path with a wave of my hand. Everyone else was too busy chanting to notice the air attack. I drank some water and left my food for the flies.

During the early afternoon, I met Dr Raghuram, Dr Nagaratna's husband. There were three students in the room with him and he appointed one of them, Gita, to be 'my eyes'. I was to go with her to their teacher-training sessions, yoga practices and the patient programmes, which the students ran under supervision.

I observed with the students while Dr Raghuram conducted a series of consultations with the new arrivals. He prescribed a diet, medication, physical yoga exercises and a meditation for each one according to their complaint. A woman suffering from obesity and high blood pressure was given three daily meditations starting at four thirty in the morning, two yoga practice sessions including relaxation techniques and inverted poses, and a diet of *rasam* and raw vegetables only for five days. Given people's propensity to believe in the maxim 'no pain, no gain' I was not surprised to learn that most of the in-patients admitted themselves for regular treatment.

Gita and I made friends easily. She was from Assam and hoped to return as a qualified teacher to set up educational and health programmes in her state's rural villages. She was tall and skeletal but, as I saw when we were in yoga practice sessions together, strong and flexible like steel wire. In the lectures we attended I learnt how the yoga movements and practices were designed to improve both mental and physical health. For example the students would study the physiology and anatomy of the respiratory system in the same way as physiotherapy students, but then the subject would be the benefits of *pranayama*, yogic breathing, to an asthmatic patient rather than the soft-tissue techniques that a practitioner like myself would use.

On my first evening Gita and I walked in the thirty-five-acre campus at sunset. It was sandy scrub with a few low desert shrubs whose spindly, sharp branches spiked my legs. Dust and stones gathered under my feet in my open sandals. After the evening meal there was communal chanting, followed by *tratak*, candle-flame gazing. Each of the hundred or so people in the campus gathered to gaze at a candle flame to help them meditate. Lights were out by ten in the evening and chanting began again at four thirty in the morning.

Later each morning, after communal chores, the students took the patients through their assigned *asana* programmes. Two students worked with one patient while Gita and I circulated among the trios spread around the huge lecture theatre. One woman who had arthritis was working on spinal twists, another with depression was moving through a series of standing postures including the triangle sequence to strengthen the base *chakras*, or energy centres. A man was performing a routine of eye exercises to correct his squint and short-sightedness, opening and shutting his eyes alternately. Several people with chest and sinus problems were on the floor, working with back postures and movements to open the chest. Gita said that for these last patients the morning *pranayama* and *kriya*, breathing and cleansing exercises, which were held while the students did their own *asanas*, were essential. I was familiar with *neti*, the *kriya* practice of snorting salt water up the nose and spitting it out of the mouth because I

235

use the same method to treat people with sinusitis.

After lunch one day I met Sukumar, an attractive, charismatic Indian in his thirties. He was responsible for the yoga research and structure of the ashram's life, and held the mystique of a guru for most of the students. He listened stoically while Georg, a German student who had befriended me, introduced me enthusiastically with a lengthy monologue about my 'extraordinary powers of visual perception' despite my blindness. I tried to pass it off as a natural and necessary compensation. People often elevate to supernatural heights my ability to piece together my surroundings and I generally try to temper such enthusiasm before powers I do not possess are attributed to me. This metaphysical approach can be a little tiresome but is preferable to the other response I often encounter: total disbelief in my blindness. I hoped on this occasion that they were simply interested to explore other forms of awareness without venerating them to superhuman heights. Sukumar invited me to try an experiment with him in the late afternoon.

We met again, as arranged, and sat opposite one another on the matted floor of a large room. Sukumar placed a glass of water between us. He asked me to move my hand, palm down, from right to left and back again over the water in front of me. I was to stop when I thought my hand was directly over the glass. He moved the glass each time I stopped, and each time I brought my hand to a halt above it. For most of the experiment I kept my eyes shut to improve my concentration. It was very easy. Sukumar tried to put the glass down very quietly, but I could hear every time where it was.

'My students have to wear a blindfold.' Sukumar indicated Georg and Gita. 'We experiment with this in one of our lessons. They do not find the water.'

'Maybe they don't get enough practice,' I said, thinking about the endless amount I got at every mealtime. I like salt on my food and I'd never find it unless I listened.

Next, Sukumar sat closer to me, but not touching me. 'I will feel myself into an emotion. Happy, sad, fierce. You tell me what I am feeling.'

The only noise he made was a deep breath before he assumed each humour. At first, the intensity of his emotional pose was overwhelming and confusing, like music too deafening to identify. Gradually I was able to distinguish happiness from sadness and shyness from boldness. Apart from sensing his body grow and shrink, I was not sure what clues led me to each correct assessment. Every accurate answer from me brought about a series of glances and nods between him and Georg. At the time I felt pleased and surprised with myself but, once again, for me it was easy. I make assessments about people using clues of deportment and demeanour as a matter of course in my professional and personal life. It is hardly surprising that I will be better at this than a sighted person.

Finally Sukumar asked me to visualise the numbers and then the letters he was picturing in his head. I tried this. Some were right and some were wrong. It was random and, I felt, rather silly and contrived. I could no more guess what letter he was thinking about than I could guess the name of his grandmother. My original scepticism took over and I started to feel ridiculous. Here I was, sitting cross-legged on the floor opposite an intense, attractive young man who, with awe-inspiring seriousness and solemnity, was asking me to play 'I spy with my mind's eye'. I started to feel the corners of my mouth misbehaving and suggested that we stop.

After group chanting in the evening, I went and sat with Georg and Gita on the roof of the other dormitory building where some of the students and others I did not know were grouped and listening to a story from the *Vedas*. At first I thought the storyteller, some distance away, was Sukumar. I listened with great concentration while simultaneously recollecting my strange afternoon with him. I pictured his mouth and jaws moving as he unfurled his story to the silent and respectful gathering. Then he stood and was instantly too old. Sukumar was not round. Sukumar was not stooped. And, of course, Sukumar's story would have been far subtler. I remonstrated with my own foolishness. Let that be a lesson to teach me not to be too quick, too certain, I thought. While sitting I had been aware that a man had arrived behind me and leant against the low parapet wall. The charisma was unmistakable this time, his grace and litheness. When I turned to face the storyteller again, I was sure I could feel a gaze upon me from behind. I remained entranced by the attraction and heard little more of the sage's wisdom.

When we came downstairs again Sukumar came in from outside, which suggested he could not have been on the roof. I felt confused and stupid, evidently seeing a world of little Sukumars. There was undoubtedly something captivating and sexy about this mysterious young man.

In the dawn hours I said goodbye to the friends I had made and waited with a visiting researcher, Seema, for the minibus to return to Bangalore. This, of course, was an act of faith since half the officials informed us that the bus trip was confirmed, and the other half insisted it was against the rules and too expensive to order the bus on a Monday for just two people. We waited in suspense until 8.30 a.m. when we were duly picked up, along with others who had arrived and acted as though this was a regular Monday-morning routine and never in doubt. Once we were back in Bangalore, Seema had a long onward journey to make, but announced, 'I am coming with you,' and climbed into my rickshaw. 'These people cannot be trusted,' she said, glaring at our surly driver. As she rushed away, leaving me safely at the club, I knew her kindness had probably jeopardised her chance of catching her train.

With a free day ahead, I decided to devote it to well-deserved pleasure after the abstemious long weekend at the yoga centre. A day by the club swimming-pool would be perfect, I thought, and it would also be the ideal moment to explore the type of massage that was given in Indian health and beauty settings rather than the more medicated ayurvedic treatments I had sampled thus far. There is a type of aromatherapy in England given in health clubs and fitness centres for general relaxation which does not deal with physical health problems but is a wonderful way to relieve stress. I wondered whether the ayurvedic massages given in beauty salons were a similar indulgence and was looking forward to finding out.

I stopped at the fitness centre opposite the beauty salon to ask about massage. A beautician at the counter said, 'Very welcome. No massage, Monday no massage.'

I wondered why she was there and asked for a manicure so as not to miss out on the treat I had promised myself.

'No beauty, Monday, no beauty,' she said.

I walked away disappointed and stopped at the hair salon a little further along. One of the hairdressers was sharpening his scissors. From what I had been told, Indian head massage is at its best in the hair salons and I had been meaning to try one. I asked if anyone was free.

'Salon closed, ma'am. It is Monday.'

I was beginning to dislike Mondays. I continued to the swimming-pool where a waiter approached and said, 'No swimming, Monday, no swimming.' I could hardly believe they would close the pool as well and proceeded to the changing rooms. The attendant was carrying such a tall pile of towels that her voice was muffled but nevertheless I understood the dreaded 'Monday closed, ma'am.'

I gave up.

Rather than waste the day, I confirmed my arrangements by telephone to visit Jindal, a health spa outside Bangalore. I was put through to Reception but could hardly hear what was said because of an extraordinary cacophony of hammering, sawing and drilling blasting down the line. I suspected that my request to arrive that afternoon would have been either not heard or not understood, and was greatly discouraged when the polite receptionist was just a bit too quick to say, 'Yes, madam, very good, as you like.' That benign Indian 'Yes, very good' had become progressively unreassuring. I had gleaned from the directions that Jindal was further out of town than I had first imagined, and did not want to struggle to get there to find no one expecting or having the time to see me.

I could have got a taxi, but still preferred, even after weeks of being in India, the excitement and interest of travelling with ordinary Indians on local buses. I asked the club receptionist to write down the name of the main city bus stand, Shivigeenager, for I knew no one would understand my pronunciation when I asked my way, but in such a big city someone would certainly be able to read. The receptionist also confirmed that a bus from the stop outside the club went to the bus stand.

I used my cane and was surprised by the degree of recognition that it received. Bangalore's business and higher-education opportunities had attracted and developed a more cosmopolitan population than elsewhere. As I got off the first bus at the station, I asked the conductor to put me on the bus for Jindal. He climbed down and stood with me. Some of his colleagues joined us to satisfy their curiosity as to why he had me on his arm. Once he had explained, we moved through tangles, knots and strands of loitering people, stopped again to wait and after a while I was surrounded by a group of admirers. They questioned my travels to date, my circumstances, and kept telling me I was very brave. 'How are you not seeing? Where is your mummy and daddy? Where is your father's house? Why are you being here alone?' The group was all male, searching and staring, fascinated like cack-handed surgeons poking around to examine a vital organ they had never seen before. I smelt sugary ripe bananas on a stall behind me and, despite the men pressing, tried not to step back any more for fear of squashing them.

When I was finally on the bus, the conductor led me to a seat and the driver appointed the woman next to me to make sure I changed buses and got the right one for Jindal. People were standing and leaning against one another. Bags and babies were dropped into stranger's laps for secure keeping. The woman who agreed to look out for me got up to go, but before I could worry about her untimely desertion, she volunteered two women sitting in front to take over.

The two women got off at the same stop and walked with me a long way down a dusty main road. They were loaded with bags and children, but seemed concerned only to get me to the next bus stop. A man crossing the road towards us called out, the women greeted him and handed me into his care, turning and laughing goodbye. They went back with their heavy loads the way we had come. I could not work out who the man was but felt as if I should know him. I continued by his side as he beckoned me, desperately trying to make connections. He must have sensed my confusion because he announced suddenly, 'I am the driver. I finishing my shift now. I coming to take you to the bus stop. It is a little far.'

He waited with me for twenty minutes on a small stretch of pavement by the side of a highway thundering with speeding vehicles. A few other people paced or stood, scouting for the bus. Behind us there was the throaty rattling of a sugar-cane grinder, crushing canes, coughing and splurging out the sticky juice. I smelt the paraffin rag used to oil the wheels and looked towards the contraption.

The driver followed my gaze and asked, 'You like to be trying some?'

The thought of the health risks dissuaded me from sampling the sugar-cane juice, but it was hard to resist because it is a nourishing and thirst-quenching drink. Also, I had no water with me and I had not eaten that day.

When the bus came the two drivers conferred and I relaxed, knowing I would be dropped outside the gates to Jindal. Once we arrived I persuaded a post boy to walk some of the way down the drive with me. Then I followed the whining of drills and the sawing of wood to find my way to Reception. The receptionist could hardly hear, let alone understand, me, but made encouraging affirmations as he had on the telephone earlier.

Mrs Sangham, the public relations officer, was summoned and she took me to her office, closing the door to dull the noise from the workmen. She was interested in aromatherapy and the possibility of introducing it to Jindal's list of treatments. Jindal is a naturopathic hospital, the closest thing India has to a health farm. It is known to attract dignitaries, film stars and foreigners who want to repair a variety of health problems arising out of the excesses of their lifestyles. Although the guests received a daily massage and other body and hydrotherapy treatments, there was no aromatherapy. Mrs Sangham became more and more enthusiastic about aromatherapy as I described how it was used in health spas in the West to promote relaxation, and in other settings as an alternative medical treatment.

She ordered some fruit juice and telephoned Dr Ramesh, the director of Jindal. He was not immediately willing to see me, but she told him forcefully yet diplomatically that it was in his interest to do so. When she hung up, she said apologetically, 'He is a very busy man but he will be seeing you in one hour. I can be showing you around now.'

I nodded and sipped the freshly squeezed tomato and pawpaw juice a girl had put down in front of me. It was delicious. A two-week fruit fast at Jindal would not be an endurance test with drinks like that, and Jindal had its own orchards and farm to grow all the grain and vegetables it needed to provide its guests with fresh, wholesome food. I was keen to look around these facilities and had no need to talk to Dr Ramesh, especially since he seemed not to want to meet me, but it was hard to see how to extricate myself from the meeting now that Mrs Sangham had set it up.

We started our tour with the yoga *asana* practice rooms where in-house yoga teachers tailored a programme for each visitor. Although yoga exercise was the therapeutic mainstay of the physical-fitness programmes at Jindal, there was also some western style fitness apparatus. There was a large aerobic and dance hall with a gymnasium at each end, one for women and one for men. The sophisticated hydraulic equipment ran smoothly, puffing at each exertion like bellows. The gentle hum and purr of machinery was eclipsed by the whiz and pant of people pedalling furiously on stationary bikes and pounding relentlessly on treadmills. One machine throbbed as it pummelled its occupant's thighs. A woman's voice juddered a greeting to Dr Sangham.

Outside the main building, the grounds descended through orchards to an artificial lake. Duplex accommodation was designed like a mini housing estate with a network of paved paths joining the dwellings. Three standards of room were available. The most expensive, a complete house, was only around ten pounds a night, including all the treatments and use of the facilities. Even the higher rate expected from foreign guests made the two hundred pounds a night charged by British health spas seem ludicrous.

A sign hanging on a mango tree amused me. Mrs Sangham read aloud, 'Please do not pick the fruit,' and I imagined starved residents, unable to tolerate the prescribed fast or diet a moment longer, sneaking out at night to go scrumping.

When Mrs Sangham finally took me to Dr Ramesh's office he was on the telephone talking about the purchase of some land. He was neither discreet nor hurried in his dealings, despite my presence. Eventually, he hung up and we talked, but our conversation was stilted because he was reluctant to reveal his ignorance of aromatherapy. We were interrupted by a knock, and the doctor invited a man to come and sit down. The two men puffed and preened like peacocks, fluffing up pages in their diaries to fix a date for a round of golf. When the man left I said, 'You are clearly very busy. Thank you for allowing me to take a look around, but I think I will make my way back to Bangalore now.'

My departure was delayed by the receptionist buzzing him to take a call from someone whose name I recognised as that of a state minister. After putting down the telephone again Dr Ramesh seemed pleased with himself and said pompously, 'You can come back the day after tomorrow to show us your aromatherapy.'

I bristled and said, 'If you want to find out more maybe you should come to England. I took the time and trouble to come to India, which has proved most informative. Perhaps you could do likewise.' With that I smiled sweetly and left.

When I reached town I decided to take a bus to Mr Atuna's evening yoga class rather than go back to the club. After another vigorous class, Mr Atuna said to a class member, 'Arun, please be taking our guest to the bus stop.' There was no sense in which a favour was being granted, or that I was causing an inconvenience, and I felt comfortable with my need for help.

I was so inspired by Mr Atuna's presence and the physical demands of his classes that I returned for the six-thirty class the next morning. This time he appointed another young woman to accompany me to the bus stop. Before I left, I offered to pay him for the classes I had attended. Until then he had always deferred payment with a casual 'Next time.' Knowing I was not going to return, he still refused to accept anything from me. I shook his hand warmly and left with Nirmala.

The next touch of kindness came from Nirmala herself, who invited me to a south Indian breakfast with her parents.

I loved the spontaneous kindness and generosity with which I was showered by so many people, regardless of how little or how much they knew of me. However, I was uncomfortable with the way people questioned or stared at me when there was hardly any connection. I remember a boy from the yoga class coming up to me while I was in the club grocery shop with Sagarie.

'What are you doing here?' he asked.

'I am shopping with my friend.' I tried to keep my answer short in an attempt to avoid the inevitable torrent of questions.

'Are you staying here?'

'Yes.'

'Why are you coming here?'

'For work.'

'Are you blind?'

'Yes.'

'For what reason are you blind?'

'Congenital.'

'What is this meaning?'

'I was born with a weakness.'

'Are you always being blind?'

'No.'

'You are doing yoga for a long time?'

'Yes.'

He had dissected me with his persistent probing, squeezing out information like one of the roadside fruit extractors. I was left feeling flaccid.

Sagarie finished her shopping and motioned for us to leave. On the way out, she said, 'How rude these people can be.' I had always excused such interrogations as a cultural difference but Sagarie's remark made me realise it was more symptomatic of an educational divide. The unsubtle stares and questions came from adults who had never learnt not to behave like children.

That day Sagarie was triumphant because she had procured a certificate of blindness for me from a friendly doctor. We returned to the Indian Airlines office and handed it over to the duty manager, who gave us a disabled passenger authorisation. Then I had only to decide whether I was going to fly to Bombay and home, or Calcutta and embark on the second half of my trip, to north India. Although travel weariness and the struggle of managing without sight had sometimes been intimidating during the past weeks, I was pleased that I had seen and done so much. However, I was worried that I had left my clients for too long and that on my return I would have no work. On the other hand, there was the allure of more adventure and more discoveries, both personal and professional.

We spent the rest of the day visiting Sagarie's relatives. Her mother had prepared us a tasty dish of *uptma*, made with semolina and rice, before she went for her rest.

Our next visit took us to the military hospital within the Army barracks just outside Bangalore. Field Marshal Cariappa, Nalini's father, was in a bungalow in a compound surrounded by guards. He was attended by two captains and two orderlies. At ninety-four, he was thin and weak, with rasping, whistling breath. It was hard to imagine that this tiny, bedridden man had been one of the most powerful men in India. The young soldiers were attentive to his every gasping breath, full of reverential concern for his ebbing life.

Sagarie asked the captain what sort of night the Field Marshal had passed. The reply was detailed and loving, from a man who could not have been more than a boy when the Field Marshal was in his prime.

'Uncle, you have a visitor,' Sagarie told him. 'This is Nalini's friend all the way from England. You remember? Nalini has written to you about her.'

He murmured and moved his hand towards mine. It cost him a chesty, rattling cough. The orderlies jumped forward and waited, leaning over him, while the spasm shuddered through his bones like an earthquake. He settled and, with an Olympian effort, took my hand and kissed it gallantly. He tried to speak but his words were lost in his chest.

We continued to sit by the bed and gradually his breathing became slower and quieter. After a while Sagarie said, 'Uncle, our visitor is leaving tomorrow.'

There was no reply not even a flicker to indicate that he had heard Sagarie speak. I thought he might have drifted into sleep or into the semiconscious world that the dying inhabit for increasing periods of time before they finally leave this one.

Sagarie turned to me and asked, 'Have you decided yet where you are going next?'

I shook my head. 'It is so difficult. I keep thinking how tiring some of my visits have been over these past months, but I have learnt a lot, not just professionally but about myself too. I don't know of many massage or ayurvedic centres to visit in the north. Maybe I have done enough.' I paused and thought a little before continuing, 'There will always be people, places and opportunities if I am prepared to journey on. I would like to see the rest of India, even if I have less research to do. I want to travel in every state, even through the restricted areas. I have always wanted to, and I know now that things will somehow work themselves out. So far some wonderful people have turned up to help me just when I thought I knew no one.' As an aside I added, almost wistfully, 'I have started writing again. There has been so much I want to remember and tell to my friends and I do that best in words. There could be so much more. But I don't...'

Before I could continue or Sagarie could question me further, she was called outside by the captain. I shuffled my feet, looking down at them, thinking about what I had said. I heard a murmur from the bed, so faint that I thought the Field Marshal was just trying to moisten his lips and swallow. I looked at him intently, as did the orderlies, who had advanced at the sound. It came again, only this time it was a definite whisper. One of the orderlies bent to place his ear close to the Field Marshal's lips.

'What did he say?'

'He say, Missahib, he say, 'Not to finish is to rue the start.''

I spent my last night in Bangalore with Sagarie and her family. News arrived in that evening that Field Marshal Cariappa was weakening fast. He survived the night and in the morning a tired, worried Sagarie drove me to Bangalore airport. When we arrived, a message had been left that the Field Marshal had died.

An airline representative took charge of me.

'I will take you to check in for Bombay.'

We wove our way through the packs of travellers. So the Field Marshal had completed his long journey. The sound of his whispered voice came to me: 'Not to finish is to rue the start.'

'Please can you take me to Airline Reception?'

'We go to check in for Bombay.'

'No, no. I want to change my ticket to... Calcutta.'

'Very good, Madam.'

I continued to travel in north India for several months, making my way from Calcutta across to Delhi, up to the western Himalayas, around Rajasthan and into the desert before returning to Bombay. On this part of the journey, I had a private audience with the Dalai Lama and stayed with the British High Commissioner, Sir Nicholas Fenn. My travels became more varied and adventurous, with less of a focus on the discovery of massage techniques and oils. They included an arduous trek in the mountains and a white-knuckle white-water raft down the Ganges. The ways and lives of the people I encountered absorbed me, and I returned with the desire to write about these experiences.

Although the insight into Indian natural medicine was fascinating, I found it difficult to introduce the techniques into my work in England. The large quantity of oil used requires a more barren setting, without towels, padded electric couch, carpets and blankets. Ayurveda is a complex healing art and it takes many years to qualify as an ayurvedic doctor. However, I now use some of the techniques such as the herbal waxes and some of the oils I discovered. Apart from the interesting foot massage, I believe our

Swedish massage and soft-tissue manipulation are more effective and prefer these methods.

The trip rekindled my desire to write and to travel, two things I thought I would never do again after losing my sight. On my return I wrote a feature for the *Daily Telegraph,* my first article in years, and I began *Jasmine and Arnica*, encouraged by my friend, the novelist Elizabeth Buchan. Seven years of dispiriting treks around various publishers, of bright hopes and dark disappointments, and *Jasmine and Arnica* was consigned to the recycle bin of an old computer that reluctantly whirred back into life when interest in this book was resurrected. In the final months of a pregnancy complicated by my liver condition and in the first weeks of my daughter's life, I found myself furiously rewriting and editing the manuscript in between treating my clients.

I have revisited India several times in the intervening years with the intention of exploring every state. Entry into the north-eastern ones was difficult to arrange as they are normally out of bounds to foreign visitors. The tea gardens of Assam, the hills of Meghalaya and the remote parts of Mizoram bordering Myanmar delighted me, as they are areas largely unaffected by present-day travellers and western society. I cannot deny that the perilous nature of these forays into places where insurgency and rebel activity are commonplace appealed to the frustrated war correspondent in me. However, armed with a recorder and a microphone, I made a travel feature and documentary series for Radio 4.

I have now travelled alone, with guides and with friends, with relatives and with lovers. My companions often added and occasionally subtracted from each experience, and the developing relationship formed part of each journey. One of the next tales I want to tell is about cycling on a tandem for two thousand miles from Bangkok to Hanoi, through northern Thailand, across Laos, one of the least developed countries in the world, and into Vietnam with a man who was so wonderful that we are now journeying through the rest of our lives together. But each experience has been born of this first magical trip to India that opened my eyes onto the world and into myself. The world is full of doors ajar whose light tantalises and torments.

To step through a few is vital for me because in my daily life, I struggle with the frustrations of who I can go shopping with, how I can get to a friend's house, how I will get my child to school. So I take my moment, reach out and step.

Nicola Naylor has run a complementary health practice in London for the past twelve years. She utilises a combination of soft tissue manipulation and massage techniques with essential and herbal oils to treat a variety of health problems.

Much of her work is concerned with the management of a range of chronic conditions from work-related back problems to asthma. Clients with other serious conditions such as rheumatiod arthritis, oedema, lupus, epilepsy,etc., also benefit from prophylactic treatment to ease their pain and/or increase their mobility. Some clients seek help with anxiety and stress states, including the associated physical consequences such as migranes or insomnia. Nicola also treats many pregnant women who come for help with back pain, nausea and other problems.

It is not recommended that the oils and techniques mentioned in this book are used without first seeking the advice of a qualified practicioner. There are many books on the subject of medicinal herbs and essential oils, which are good informational guides, including *Healing with Essential Oils* by Nicola Naylor.

TravellersEye Club Membership

Each month we receive hundreds of enquiries from people who've read our books or entered our competitions. All of these people have one thing in common: an aching to achieve something extraordinary, outside the bounds of our everyday lives. Not everyone can undertake the more extreme challenges, but we all value learning about other people's experiences.

Membership is free because we want to unite people of similar interests. Via our website, members will be able to liase with each other about everything from the kit they've taken, to the places they've been to and the things they've done. Our authors will also be available to answer any of your questions if you're planning a trip or if you simply have a question about their books.

As well as regularly up-dating members with news about our forthcoming titles, we will also offer you the following benefits:

Free entry to author talks / signings
Direct author correspondence
Discounts off new and past titles
Free entry to TravellersEye events
Discounts on a variety of travel products and services

To register your membership, simply write or email us telling us your name and address (postal and email). See address at the front of this book.

About TravellersEye

I believe the more you put into life, the more you get out of it. However, at times I have been disillusioned and felt like giving up on a goal because I have been made to feel that an ordinary person like me could never achieve my dreams.

The world is absolutely huge and out there for the taking. There has never been more opportunity for people like you and me to have dreams and fulfil them.

I have met many people who have achieved extraordinary things and these people have helped inspire and motivate me to try and live my life to the fullest.

TravellersEye publishes books about people who have done just this and we hope that their stories will encourage other people to live their dream.

When setting up TravellersEye I was given two pieces of advice. The first was that there are only two things I ever need to know: You are never going to know everything and neither is anyone else. The second was that there are only two things I ever need to do in life: Never give up and don't forget rule one.

Nelson Mandela said in his presidential acceptance speech: "Our deepest fear is not that we are inadequate. Our deepest fear is that we are powerful beyond our measure... as we let our own light shine, we unconsciously give other people permission to do the same."

We want people to shine their light and share it with others in the hope that it may encourage them to do the same.

Dan Hiscocks
Managing Director of TravellersEye

New For 2001

Jungle Janes   **Peter Burden**
12 middle aged women take on the Borneo Jungle: Seen on Channel 4
ISBN: 1903070058   Price: £7.99 $14.95

Travels with my Daughter   **Niema Ash**
Forget convention, follow your instincts.
ISBN: 190307004X   Price: £7.99 $14.95

Grey Paes And Bacon   **Bob Bibby**
A hillarious romp through the bowels and vowels of the Black Country.
ISBN: 1903070066   Price: £7.99 $14.95

What For Chop Today?   **Gail Haddock**
Experiences of VSO in Sierra Leone.
ISBN: 1903070074   Price: £7.99 $14.95

Riding With Ghosts: South Of The Border   **Gwen Maka**
Second part of Gwen's epic cycle trip accross the Americas.
ISBN: 1903070090   Price: £7.99 $14.95

Triumph Around The World   **Robbie Marshall**
He gave up his world for the freedom of the road.
ISBN: 1903070082   Price: £7.99

Travellers Tales From Heaven And Hell...Part 3
Winners of this year's competition
ISBN: 190307112   Price: £6.99 $14.95

Cry From The Highest Mountain   **Tess Burrows**
A tale of the struggle to free Tibet.
ISBN: 1903070120   Price: £7.99 $14.95

Already Available

Desert Governess   Phyllis Ellis
An inside view of the Soudi Royal Family
ISBN: 1903070015   Price: £7.99 $14,95

Fever Trees Of Borneo   Mark Eveleigh
A daring expedition through uncharted jungle
ISBN: 0953057569   Price: £7.99 $14,95

Discovery Road   Tim Garrett & Andy Brown
Their mission was to mountain bike around the world.
ISBN: 0953057534   Price: £7.99 $14.95

Frigid Women   Sue & Victoria Riches
The first all female expeditin to The North Pole
ISBN: 0953057526   Price: £7.99 $14.95

The Jungle Beat   Roy Follows
Fighting Terrorists in Malaya
ISBN: 1953057577   Price: £7.99 $14.95

Slow Winter   Alex Hickman
A personal quest against the back drop of the war torn Balkans
ISBN: 0953057585   Price: £7.99 $14.95

Riding With Ghosts   Gwen Maka
One woman's solo cycle ride from Seattle to Mexico
ISBN: 1903070007   Price: £7.99 $14.95

Tea For Two   Polly Benge
She cycled around India to test her love.
ISBN: 0953057593   Price: £7.99 $14.95

Touching Tibet   Niema Ash
One of the first westerners to enter Tibet
ISBN: 0953057550   Price: £7.99 $14.95

Travellers Tales From Heaven and Hell
More Travellers Tales From Heaven and Hell
Past winners of our competition
ISBN: 0953057518/1903070023   Price: £6.99 $14.95

A Trail Of Visions: Route 1: India Sri Lanka, Thailand, Sumatra
A Trail Of Visions: Route 2: Peru, Bolivia, Columbia, Ecuador
Vicki Couchman
A stunning photographic essay.
ISBN: 1871349338/095305750X   Price: £14.99/16.99